Greens Glorious Greens!

Greens Glorious Greens!

MORE THAN 140 WAYS TO PREPARE
ALL THOSE GREAT-TASTING, SUPER-HEALTHY,
BEAUTIFUL LEAFY GREENS

JOHNNA ALBI AND CATHERINE WALTHERS

ILLUSTRATIONS BY PAUL HOFFMAN

 ST. MARTIN'S PRESS ✹ NEW YORK

Greens Glorious Greens!: More Than 140 Ways to Prepare All Those Great-Tasting, Super-Healthy, Beautiful Leafy Greens
Copyright © 1996 by Johnna Albi and Catherine Walthers.
Illustrations copyright © 1996 by Paul Hoffman

All rights reserved. Printed in the United States of America. For information, address St. Martin's Press, 175 Fifth Avenue, New York, N.Y. 10010.

Book design by Gretchen Achilles

Library of Congress Cataloging-in-Publication Data
Albi, Johnna.
    Greens glorious greens!: more than 140 ways to prepare all those great-tasting, super-healthy, beautiful leafy greens/ Johnna Albi and Catherine Walthers.
       p. cm.
    Includes index
    ISBN 0-312-14108-4
    1. Cookery (Greens) I. Walthers, Catherine. II Title.
TX803.G74A43 1996   95-43940
641.6'54–dc20   CIP

20 19 18 17 16

Contents

Acknowledgments

For the two of us, working on a book that combined our passion for cooking and eating as well as our love of greens was more pleasure than work. The ease and creativity within our collaboration, the great meals and companionship, made our partnership and this project seem like a gift. After a typical morning of testing recipes, we would often sit back on Johnna's porch talking about food and feasting on our morning's work—two or three delicious and healthy greens dishes. If this was work, we'd found the secret.

Our partnership, however, extended beyond the two of us to our friends and family, who offered suggestions, tested recipes, and couldn't help but be caught up in a project that dominated our waking thoughts for an entire year.

We would like to thank all of them, especially those who tested our recipes, which meant taking the time to buy ingredients, cook the dish, and write down their comments. Our gratitude to Kathy Ball-Toncic, Eileen Cherry, Kathy D'Amico, Cate Conniff Dobrich, Nancy Elliott, Rene Faraca, Tim Fichter, Rachel Gibson, Ann Grosz, Stephanie Hanks, Rena Howell, Barbara Harris, Nancy Hamm, Jody James, Jay and Peigi Jolliffe, Ruby Machnaigh, Laura Martin, Jenet Miller, Meg Moncy, Teddi Parsons, Rachel Reid, Marjie Rome, Lorna Sass, and Dan Seamens. We especially appreciate Elizabeth Germain and Kristen Kinser for their great suggestions and support as well as recipe testing and recipe contributions.

We are grateful to Russell Cohen, Lindsey Lee, Ruth Dreier, and Rosemary Gladstar for sharing their expertise on collecting and cooking wild greens.

A special thanks to our agent, Doe Coover, whose support and expertise helped us make this book a reality, and to St. Martin's Press.

And finally, where would we be without Louis, Ariana, and Gabe Vanrenen (Johnna's husband and children), Zizza Vanrenen, and David Kelliher—the people who have tried most of these recipes with us.

—*Johnna Albi*
—*Cathy Walthers*

Introduction

As a shopper, you may pass by them many times, looking but not buying, noticing the dazzling array of fresh, crisp, and nutritious greens—curly kale, red and green chard, collards, bok choy, mustard greens, arugula, frisée, mesclun, and other exotic-looking lettuces. A little uncertain, a little confused, you tuck these impressions into a corner of your mind. Then, at a favorite restaurant, an exotic-looking salad is served, or perhaps tender beet greens with garlic and olive oil. The next trip to the market once again serves to conjure up these tasty dishes. This time, you buy some beet greens, some arugula, even frisée, and take them home. Now what?

We hope *Greens Glorious Greens!* will serve as a resource for help in preparing any green you buy—whether it is a bunch of spicy mustard greens or a pound of broccoli rabe. It's a guide to more than thirty different leafy green vegetables, from arugula to watercress, with specific cooking and preparation tips for each green, as well as recipes. We wanted to offer a book full of our best recipes for greens as well as a cooking lesson to help you become familiar and excited about preparing greens on a regular basis.

The recipes capitalize on the many virtues of greens: They are low in fat, high in nutrients, quick cooking, and delicious.

There is little question of the health benefits of eating a variety of vegetables, including leafy greens. "Diets that are rich in vegetables and fruits are protective against many cancers—there is an enormous amount of work on this," says Lee Wattenberg, a professor at the University of Minnesota who has been studying cancer prevention for thirty years. "Over the last decade a fairly large number of prevention compounds have been found in fruits and vegetables. When you look at the totality, it's quite impressive."

Dark leafy green vegetables supply minerals such as calcium and iron, along with vitamins, folic acid, and fiber. Their combination of vitamins A, C, and E make them antioxidant cancer fighters in the body. Greens are also rich sources of carotenoids, a huge family of substances (including beta-carotene) researchers are studying for their antioxidant properties, their effect on the immune system, and their role in cancer prevention. Leafy greens contain dozens of other phytochemicals or micronutrients such as indoles and sulforaphane, which have only begun to be studied for their disease-prevention properties.

As impressive as the health benefits of greens may be, you should not picture a pile of tasteless, hard-to-chew greens on your plate. You don't have to eat them just because they are healthy for you. We are here to say that leafy greens are not only beautiful to behold, but also tasty and capable of transporting us (through recipes) to far corners of the earth where greens have been a way of life for centuries. The knowledge that you can transform greens into a variety of delicious dishes is what we hope to pass along.

With the exception of spinach and lettuce, and some use of collards and turnips greens in the South, leafy greens have generally not been part of the American diet. We have found that most people are generally unfamiliar with the leafy vegetables, but are curious about them, because we're often asked how to use them. When we began researching leafy greens for a magazine article, we were surprised at how little information really existed. We checked dozens of cookbooks. There were recipes for broccoli, cabbage, and carrots, but few or none for cooking mustard greens, bok choy, or collards. At the same time, we were seeing an abundance of newer greens turn up in markets—from beet greens to mesclun to rabe.

So we started working on a book dedicated to this one subject. We spent a year perfecting our favorite recipes, developing new ones, and testing greens side by side to learn which cooking techniques produced the best tasting greens. The result is before you—from our kitchens to yours.

Greens Glorious Greens!

Getting Started

General Cooking Guidelines for Greens

Specific tips and recipes fill the book. But we have found a few general guidelines or rules to help you get started.

❖ Greens served plain are often not very appetizing. Just as a leaf of lettuce in a bowl would be dull and tasteless without some dressing, the same applies to greens. We have tried plain collard greens and broccoli rabe and would not have looked forward to eating them again had this been our only option.

  Most greens need a little help, a little company, to taste good. A little olive oil with garlic or leeks, a squirt of lemon juice, or a sprinkling of sesame seeds, olives, or raisins may be all it takes. Greens are often enhanced with strong flavors that may be hot, spicy, or sour. Some greens, especially spicy ones such as broccoli rabe and mustard greens, can be tempered with the mild flavors of potatoes, pasta, beans, or rice.

❖ When cooking and presenting greens, think color. Again, picture your bowl of plain-dressed Bibb lettuce or side plate mounded with kale. Now mix the pale green Bibb lettuce with some dark green watercress and cranberry-hued radicchio with thin strips of yellow peppers. Add diced chunks of carrots and fresh corn to the rich green kale, as we do in Basic No-Fat, No-Fuss Colorful Kale (page 158), and picture the difference. Many times vegetables such as corn, carrots, yellow squash, red pepper, and tomatoes add sweetness and flavor to greens while making them more visually appealing. Certain fruits produce the same dual effect of great taste and presentation, as in Shredded Beets and Greens with Sliced Oranges (page 26) or Apple-Cinnamon Beet Greens (page 22).

❖ Even pairing a dark green such as beet tops with a lighter green like cabbage gives a beautiful contrast. Spinach with mustard greens. Parsley and dill with cabbage. Kale and celery. Watercress and corn chowder. Mustard greens and red lentils. When you buy a green or make a salad, just look around the produce section for inspiration.

Nuts and seeds, while not wildly colorful, also make a great match for greens. Sunflower seeds, pine nuts, and sesame seeds are some examples that taste and look good with greens. We love the crunchy addition to the soft greens.

❖ Take a global view of cooking methods with greens. It's best to get out of the habit of automatically steaming greens. The steam treatment may work for broccoli, but not for greens. After a variety of tests using different cooking methods, we found that steaming greens produces a concentrated bitterness and grayish-green color in most of them (see The Science of Cooking Greens, page 208). There is a wide range of preferred ways, including sautéing, stir-frying, quick-boiling, and grilling. The results produce softer, tastier greens.

It's also best to tailor the method to the particular green. Tender greens such as spinach, chard, and beet greens can be directly sautéed with garlic and olive oil or with just the water clinging to their leaves. Strong-flavored greens such as kale, collards, and turnip and mustard greens need a different cooking method. These assertive greens are generally too tough to be wilted in a skillet. They are best cooked briefly in shallow boiling water to reduce bitterness and increase tenderness. They can then be drained and sautéed.

❖ When you cook greens in a small amount of water, drink the cooking water, also called "pot likker." Any non-water-soluble vitamins or minerals that leach from the green while cooking will be found in cooking water. In some Italian communities, the broth made from blanching assorted greens is thought of as very medicinal. In the South, where greens are cooked in water flavored with ham hocks or smoked turkey bones, the pot likker is served alongside the green, usually with corn bread for dipping.

   When our recipes call for greens to be precooked in water, the amount of water is usually only 1 or 2 cups. When the cooking is complete, drain the small amount of leftover water into mugs or cups. Let cool slightly before drinking. In cooking classes when we serve this "green cocktail," students are surprised at how good it tastes.

❖ You don't have to make radical alterations in your eating lifestyle to include lots of greens in your diet. With the exception of possibly tomatoes, greens are virtually unmatched in their cooking possibilities. Think about what you normally eat, and then ask, "can I add a green?" If you enjoy broiled or baked fish, consider serving it atop a bed of simple sautéed greens and garlic. If you make pizza, add greens as one of the toppings. Likewise in pasta or lasagne dishes. In the fall or winter, soups or stews will benefit from the addition of any number of greens, such as kale, cabbage, chard, and spinach.

❖ Celebrate the healthfulness of greens. These light, crisp leafy greens do not have to swim in oil, butter, or cheese to be delicious. A little oil goes a long way. A sprinkling of Parmesan cheese may do the trick. A teaspoon or two of cold-pressed sesame oil with its abundance of flavor works just as well as 3 tablespoons of a blander variety.

Cooking Utensils: The Basics for Cooking Greens

In a *New York Times* article about kitchen equipment, one chef was quoted as saying that a skilled home cook could perform most kitchen tasks with just "two knives and two pots and pans." It's quite possible to add greens into your daily menu with a minimum of equipment, but your results may be more successful if you have a few additional items on hand. These are the kitchen tools we find helpful.

❖ *A large skillet with a lid.* We find this the most useful pot for cooking greens. It can be referred to as a sauté pan or by quantity size—3-quart or 6-quart pans. The wide, open pan makes it easier to spread the greens, cooking them quickly to preserve nutrients and taste.

The larger the skillet, the easier it is to cook greens, which take up a lot of space uncooked. A pound of kale equals 7 or 8 cups of chopped raw greens, but cooks down to less than 2 cups. Our 10-inch (3-quart) and 13-inch (6-quart) sauté pans with lids were all we needed to test hundreds of greens recipes.

Our favorite brand of pots is All Clad, a top choice among many chefs as well. All Clad pots are constructed of three bonded layers of metal, including a stainless steel cooking surface and an aluminum core for great heat conduction. These pans have a thick bottom for long sautéing, clean very easily, and last a lifetime. They are expensive, but worth it in our opinion.

❖ *A stockpot.* This is our second pot of choice. We use it for cooking soups, stews, pasta, and beans, and for precooking greens, because it is wider than most saucepans and can accommodate a large amount of uncooked greens. Plus it has a lid. We prefer a heavy-bottomed stockpot that allows you to sauté onions, leeks, or garlic easily without burning them.

❖ *A chef's knife.* One good chef's knife is generally more useful than a set of kitchen knives. For working with greens we recommend a blade length of 8 inches—long enough to cut through a pile of greens, yet small enough for easy handling. A sharp, heavy chef's knife makes cutting greens and other vegetables like garlic, onions, and carrots a joy rather than a chore.

We prefer the 8-inch Wustof chef's knife. This is also a popular brand among home cooks and chefs.

❖ *A small paring knife.* This is handy for jobs like cutting sections of an orange.

❖ *Metal tongs.* We reach for tongs when cooking a large amount of greens. They work to lift and stir at the same time, moving uncooked greens from the top of a cooking heap to the bottom and vice versa.

❖ *A large bowl and colander.* These inexpensive kitchen staples are indispensable for cleaning the grit from greens. Dunking greens in a bowl filled with cool water is the single best way to rid them of sand or dirt. Rinsing under the faucet doesn't usually dislodge the dirt and can damage leaves. You want to purchase a stainless steel bowl and strainer large enough to accommodate 10 to 12 cups of chopped greens.

❖ *A salad dryer or spinner.* A salad spinner saves you the time of drying salad greens by hand after you wash them to remove dirt or sand. And drying by hand won't usually remove enough water unless you waste a handful of paper towels. Salad dressing won't cling as well and becomes diluted mixed with wet greens. We also use a salad spinner to dry other greens and herbs—such as watercress, arugula, parsley, and basil—before chopping and adding them to dishes.

❖ *A wok.* Not necessary, but handy. The high water content of some Asian greens, such as bok choy and tatsoi, makes them a natural for a quick-cooking wok. You can also stir-fry in a heavy skillet, such as cast iron.

Arugula

BECAUSE OF ITS FLAVOR-ENHANCING QUALITY, ARUGULA can be used to perk up a number of dishes. It has been used primarily as a salad green, either with other lettuces or by itself, but it can become just the right addition to make potato salad or pasta salad stand out. Even the mildest or blandest salads perk up just by adding a bunch of peppery arugula leaves. "Putting these wonderful spicy leaves in your salad is like adding a $20 bill," says one gardener in the Shepherd's Garden Seeds catalog.

One of the reasons for arugula's rising popularity is its distinctive taste and character. It becomes addictive once you've tried it. Descriptions range from "spicy," "tender and mustard-flavored," and "a nutty and warm pungent green" to "peppery with a sweet tang."

Arugula belongs to the mustard family, but its flavor resembles the mildly spicy watercress more than the stronger, more bitter mustard or turnip greens. It looks like a cross between dandelion greens and oak leaf lettuce and comes in one large bunch consisting of smaller bunches of 5 to 6 small flat leaves with long stems.

Native to the Mediterranean region, arugula is also called roquette, rugula, rucola, rocket salad, and Mediterranean rocket. When it was first sold in specialty markets in the United States and featured in restaurant salads, it acquired—possibly because of its exotic name—a rather trendy or snobby image. But it started out as a peasant food in countries such as Italy, where it is picked wild.

Arugula is one of the most nutritious of the salad greens. It tops lettuce, chicory, romaine, and watercress in beta-carotene, vitamin C, and calcium. A cruciferous, cancer-fighting vegetable as well, arugula contains more calcium than kale and collards, two greens noted for their high calcium content.

This nutritious green has versatility beyond the salad bowl and is easy to introduce into your meals. After the tender leaves are washed and separated from the stems, they can be torn or cut and are ready for use.

Arugula makes a great substitute for lettuce in sandwiches, adding a nice sharp and nutty dimension. Try it with grilled vegetable, turkey, cheese, or any other sandwich.

Arugula can also be used as a fresh herb (which is sometimes how it is classed). Just as parsley or watercress add flavor and visual appeal to dishes, arugula can be added to pastas, soups, and vegetable and grain dishes like potato salad, tabouli, coleslaw, or carrot salad. It provides a green sparkle and that unmistakable light spiciness that subtly elevates these everyday salads.

This leafy green combines well with citrus fruits, berries, avocado, and mild lettuces like butterhead and Bibb. It is delicious when served with dressings made with balsamic vinegar or citrus.

SHOPPING TIPS

Select bunches with fresh, crisp, emerald green leaves. Avoid bunches with wilted or yellowed leaves. Arugula is susceptible to flea beetle attacks, which mar the leaves with tiny holes. It is otherwise fine to eat.

As arugula matures, it can get unpleasantly sharp or peppery. Taste a leaf in the market before you make the purchase.

STORAGE

Arugula is highly perishable, and is best used immediately. It will keep for 1 or 2 days, however, with the roots submerged in a glass of water and with a plastic bag over the leaves. You can also wrap a wet paper towel around the roots and place them in a plastic bag not tightly closed. Do not store greens in the same drawer as fruits because fruits release ethylene gas, which triggers deterioration in vegetables.

PREPARATION

Arugula can be quite sandy and needs a thorough washing. While the arugula is still bunched, cut off as much of the stem as possible to the base of the leaves. Fill a large bowl with cold water, plunge in the leaves to rinse, lift greens out of water to a colander, and check bottom of bowl. If there is any sand, discard the water and repeat the process.

Pinch off any long, thin stems not previously cut off. You can either tear the leaves or gently cut them with a knife. Leave whole if small enough.

Arugula Walnut Salad

*This wonderful salad is excellent fare for dinner parties. The sharp
yet nutty taste of the arugula and the crisp bitterness of the radicchio
are enhanced by the warm, sweet orange balsamic vinaigrette.
What's more, it's lovely to look at!*

ARUGULA FLOWERS

*If you have ever grown
arugula, you may have
noticed that it tends to
grow rapidly. The leaves
become quite sharp and
bitter, but then it
blossoms to offer you a
special visual and
culinary treat. The
pretty cream-colored
flowers with tiny reddish
brown veins on the
elongated, rounded
petals can be eaten, and
make an attractive
accent in tossed salads or
on sliced tomatoes.*

SERVES 4 TO 6

3 TABLESPOONS LIGHTLY TOASTED WALNUT HALVES

2 BUNCHES ARUGULA LEAVES (ABOUT 4 CUPS)

1½ CUPS SHREDDED RADICCHIO

1 YELLOW PEPPER, SLICED INTO THIN STRIPS

3 TABLESPOONS EXTRA VIRGIN OLIVE OIL

2 TABLESPOONS FINELY MINCED RED ONION

⅛ TEASPOON SEA SALT

1 TABLESPOON MINCED FRESH PARSLEY

1 TABLESPOON BALSAMIC VINEGAR

¼ CUP FRESHLY SQUEEZED ORANGE JUICE (USE BLOOD
ORANGES IF AVAILABLE)

1. To toast walnuts, preheat oven to 325° F. Place walnuts on a
cookie sheet and toast for 5 to 7 minutes. Check after 5 minutes
to avoid burning. Set aside.

2. Wash arugula well (see page 9) and trim stems if necessary.
Use whole leaves or tear into bite-size pieces if leaves are too
large. Place in a medium-size bowl.

3. Add shredded radicchio, yellow pepper, and cooled walnuts to
arugula and toss gently. Set aside while you prepare the dressing.

4. In small skillet, heat 1 tablespoon of the olive oil. Add red
onion and sauté until soft, about 5 minutes. Sprinkle salt over red
onion and add parsley. Stir.

5. Just before serving, add remaining olive oil and balsamic
vinegar and heat through. Remove from heat and add orange
juice. Pour over salad, toss very gently, and serve immediately on
individual salad plates.

Potato Salad with Arugula

In this recipe, arugula is used more as an herb than a lettuce. The pungent flavor is distinct, but nicely balanced by the smoothness of the potatoes, the lushness of the olive oil, and the tang of the tomatoes. Great for picnics and barbecues.

SERVES 6 TO 8

2 POUNDS SMALL (APPROXIMATELY 2½ INCHES IN DIAMETER) RED POTATOES

½ CUP VERY THINLY SLICED RED ONION

2 LARGE TOMATOES, CUT INTO ½-INCH WIDE WEDGES

1 CUP CHOPPED ARUGULA LEAVES, WASHED AND TOUGH STEMS TRIMMED (SEE PAGE 9)

DRESSING:

3 TABLESPOONS WHITE WINE VINEGAR

6 TABLESPOONS EXTRA VIRGIN OLIVE OIL

½ TEASPOON DRY MUSTARD

SALT AND FRESHLY GROUND BLACK PEPPER TO TASTE

GROWING ARUGULA

Arugula is foolproof to grow. A cool-weather vegetable, it is best sown in succession in the spring or late summer for fall harvest. Pick before the plants begin to bloom to avoid bitterness.

1. Scrub potatoes well. Steam over boiling water until tender when pierced with the tip of a sharp knife, 15 to 20 minutes.

2. Cool potatoes slightly under running water to allow easy handling. Peel potatoes and cut in half lengthwise. Cut each half into 3 pieces. You should have about 5 cups of 1-inch chunks. Place in a large mixing bowl.

3. When potatoes have cooled to room temperature, add the red onion, tomatoes, and arugula. Toss gently to combine.

4. In a small jar, combine the vinegar, olive oil, mustard powder, and salt and pepper. Pour over the vegetables and toss gently to incorporate dressing. Taste and adjust seasonings.

Arugula, Cheese, and Tomato Quesadilla

Serve as a quick lunchtime treat or as a party appetizer. This is adapted from a basic quesadilla recipe made by Katie Le Lievre, a Boston caterer.

MAKES 36 WEDGES

2 CUPS WASHED AND ROUGHLY CHOPPED ARUGULA LEAVES, TOUGH STEMS TRIMMED (SEE PAGE 9)

2 CUPS SHREDDED CHEESE (CHEDDAR, FONTINA, OR A COMBINATION)

1 CUP CHOPPED TOMATOES

½ CUP CHOPPED SCALLIONS

1 CAN MILD GREEN CHILIES, CHOPPED

1 TEASPOON CHILI POWDER

1 TEASPOON CUMIN

12 FRESH FLOUR TORTILLAS

CANOLA OIL

NOTE

Instead of frying, you can bake quesadillas in a preheated 375°F oven until crisp, which allows you to cook several at a time.

1. In a large bowl, combine arugula, cheese, tomatoes, scallions, chilies, chili powder, and cumin. Place ½ cup of the filling between 2 tortillas.

2. In a large frying pan, heat 1 teaspoon canola oil over high heat. Cook quesadilla until the cheese is melted and both sides are crisp. Repeat procedure, keeping cooked quesadillas in a warm oven, until all quesadillas are cooked. Slice each into 6 wedges and serve immediately.

Pasta with Summer Squash, Arugula, and Fresh Herbs

Arugula is used more as a fresh herb in this quick and easy recipe. It's one of our favorites— great for summer evenings when you want to spend less time in the kitchen and more time on the patio. Serve with succulent, ripe garden tomatoes.

SERVES 3 TO 4

8 TO 12 OUNCES PASTA

3 TABLESPOONS EXTRA VIRGIN OLIVE OIL

½ CUP SLICED RED ONION

1 TO 2 YELLOW SUMMER SQUASH, QUARTERED LENGTHWISE AND CUT INTO ½-INCH CHUNKS TO EQUAL 2 CUPS

2 GARLIC CLOVES, CRUSHED OR MINCED

1 CUP WASHED AND ROUGHLY CHOPPED ARUGULA LEAVES, TOUGH STEMS TRIMMED (SEE PAGE 9)

1 TABLESPOON FINELY MINCED CHIVES

¼ CUP FINELY CHOPPED ITALIAN PARSLEY

¼ CUP FINELY CHOPPED FRESH BASIL

SALT AND PEPPER TO TASTE

FRESHLY GRATED PARMESAN CHEESE TO TASTE (OPTIONAL)

WHICH PASTA?

Try a tubular-shaped pasta such as penne or rotelle to pick up and hold the chopped herbs in this summer sauce.

1. In a large stockpot, bring 4 quarts of water to a boil with 1 tablespoon salt.

2. Meanwhile, in a medium skillet heat 1 tablespoon of the olive oil. Add onion and sauté for 3 minutes. Add squash and continue to cook for 5 more minutes. Add garlic and cook another 2 minutes. Turn off heat and set aside.

3. Cook pasta until *al dente*. Drain, place in a large, shallow serving bowl, and toss with the remaining 2 tablespoons olive oil, sautéed vegetables, arugula, and fresh herbs.

4. Season to taste with salt and pepper and serve immediately. Pass the Parmesan cheese, if desired.

Pasta with Eggplant and Arugula

A simple tomato sauce jazzed up with chunks of eggplant and summer squash and fresh arugula, basil, and parsley. In the summer, if you have an abundance of garden-ripe tomatoes, feel free to substitute fresh for canned.

WHICH PASTA?

We've found that this sauce works best with spaghetti, fusilli, rotelle, and penne.

SERVES 4 TO 6

1 POUND PASTA

2 TABLESPOONS EXTRA VIRGIN OLIVE OIL

2 MEDIUM EGGPLANTS, CUT INTO ¾-INCH CUBES, UNPEELED (8 TO 9 CUPS)

1 TABLESPOON MINCED GARLIC

1 RED PEPPER, CORED AND CUT INTO STRIPS

2 28-OUNCE CANS WHOLE TOMATOES WITH JUICE (ABOUT 8 CUPS)

1 YELLOW SQUASH, QUARTERED LENGTHWISE AND CUT INTO ¼-INCH PIECES

¼ CUP MINCED FRESH PARSLEY

¼ CUP CHOPPED FRESH BASIL

2 CUPS WASHED AND ROUGHLY CHOPPED ARUGULA LEAVES, TOUGH STEMS TRIMMED (SEE PAGE 9)

SALT AND PEPPER TO TASTE

⅓ CUP GRATED PARMESAN CHEESE

1. Bring a large pot of water to a boil for pasta.

2. In a large skillet, heat olive oil over medium heat. Stir in eggplant and cook over medium heat, covered, for 10 minutes. Stir often to prevent burning. Add garlic and red pepper and sauté for 2 minutes.

3. Break apart whole tomatoes and stir in with yellow squash. Cover and cook for 15 minutes, until eggplant and squash pieces are tender. Season with salt.

4. While squash is cooking, cook the pasta in salted water.

5. Add the parsley, basil, and arugula to eggplant. The arugula will wilt slightly. Taste and season with salt, pepper, and Parmesan cheese.

6. Stir in hot pasta and serve immediately.

BEST CANNED TOMATOES

The best canned tomatoes we have found are Muir Glen organic. They have a fresh tomato flavor and are packed in lead-free, enamel-lined cans so there is no "tinny" taste. Give them a try if your grocery store carries them.

Sautéed Arugula with Raisins and Hot Pepper

Sautéing arugula will mellow its peppery taste. This makes a nice side dish or base on which to place baked fish or chicken.

SERVES 2

2 BUNCHES ARUGULA LEAVES (ABOUT 5 CUPS)

2 TEASPOONS EXTRA VIRGIN OLIVE OIL

1 TEASPOON MINCED GARLIC

⅛ TEASPOON HOT RED PEPPER FLAKES

3 TABLESPOONS RAISINS OR CHOPPED DRIED APRICOTS

SALT TO TASTE

1. Separate arugula leaves from long stems and roots, if attached. If leaves are more than several inches long, slice them in half. Wash leaves well (see page 9) and drain.

2. In a skillet, heat oil over low heat. Add garlic and red pepper flakes and cook for 1 minute. Add raisins and sauté for 2 minutes.

3. Stir in the arugula, cover, and cook over medium heat for 4 to 5 minutes, until tender. Greens will be soft, rather glossy, and deliciously succulent. Add a pinch of salt and serve hot or at room temperature.

Arugula Roll-ups

A simple, tasty, and colorful appetizer. You can substitute sliced beef, smoked salmon, or any spreadable cheese for the Boursin; arugula enhances the flavor of any of these ingredients.

SERVES 8 TO 10 AS AN APPETIZER

1 ½ (1 BUNCH) ARUGULA LEAVES

1 LARGE ROASTED RED PEPPER (SEE PAGE 46)

4 PIECES OF VERY FRESH FLATBREAD (ABOUT 8 INCHES IN DIAMETER)

1 4- TO 6-OUNCE PACKAGE OF BOURSIN CHEESE

1. Wash arugula well (see page 9) and remove any tough stems. No need to cut. Set aside. Roast the red pepper. Peel off blackened exterior, halve, and remove stem and seeds. Cut into strips. Set aside.

2. Lay flat one piece of flatbread. Using a knife, spread a thin layer of cheese on half of the flatbread. Lay two lines of arugula leaves and one line of red pepper strips on top of the cheese.

3. From the cheese-filled end, roll up like a jelly roll. Insert a row of toothpicks about 1 inch apart. Cut between each toothpick on a diagonal. (The toothpicks will hold each individual piece together.) Place on a serving dish garnished with a few arugula leaves.

Beet Greens

BEET GREENS ARE EASY TO PREPARE AND QUICK COOKING, as well as being nutritious. The edible and delicious tops are better sources of vitamins and minerals than the beets themselves, with more vitamin C, calcium, and iron. But despite these attributes, some people still discard them. To us, buying a bunch of beets with the handsome green tops intact is like getting a bonus of two vegetables for the price of one.

Beet greens have a beautiful dark wine-green color and a wonderfully complex flavor that is earthy yet mild with overtones of the sweet beetroot. Generally speaking, if you like fresh, sweet beets you'll enjoy the edible beet leaves. Even if you don't like beets but enjoy spinach or chard, you might want to give beet greens a try. All three are mild and nonbitter cooking greens of the goosefoot (*Chenopodium*) family. Beet greens offer a slightly more robust flavor and a denser leaf than either spinach or chard, but cook down just as tenderly and delicately.

Cooking beet greens is easily and best accomplished by wilting them in a skillet with a little water. In a classic and delicious preparation, the beet greens are sautéed in olive oil (1 tablespoon or less does the trick) with several cloves of minced garlic, then covered and cooked for 8 to 10 minutes. Add a squeeze of lemon juice just before serving. Besides just a little oil, add a few tablespoons of water to prevent sticking. Beet greens can also be steamed and dressed up afterward.

Some of the flavors that complement the beetroot also highlight the greens: dill, lemon, apples, balsamic vinegar, oranges, and orange juice. Other seasonings to use include cinnamon, nutmeg, cloves, and ginger. Different cheeses also balance the deep taste of the greens.

Beet greens taste absolutely delicious in soups that also contain beets, such as the Quick and Delicious Borscht (page 25) and Fall Root Soup with Turnip and Beet Greens (page 243). Try the recipes and see for yourself.

SHOPPING TIPS

The most tender greens are those atop small- to medium-size beets. Choose greens that are crisp. Avoid bunches with yellow or wilted leaves.

STORAGE

Store beet greens in the refrigerator in a plastic bag not tightly closed, either separate from or together with the fresh beets. Beet greens are more perishable than fresh beets and keep only for 3 to 4 days.

PREPARATION

Before washing, cut off the beets and then separate the leaves from the stalks at the base of the leaf. Either discard the stalks or cook them for a few minutes longer than the beet greens. The French consider beet stalks a treat.

Wash well; beet greens can be very sandy. Fill a large bowl with cool water, plunge in the leaves to rinse, lift greens out of water to a colander, and check bottom of bowl. If there is any sand, discard the water and repeat the process.

To cut, stack greens on top of each other and cut into ½-inch strips. Depending on the recipe, you can leave the greens in strips or chop into bite-size pieces.

Basic Beet Greens

Beet greens cook rather quickly, unlike the beet itself. Most of the time we use only the leaves, but beet stalks (and beetroot, of course) are edible and can be quite tasty. Either add the stalks to the skillet before the greens or braise them as a separate dish. Be careful when adding salt to beet greens, which are already high in sodium. You may not need more than a pinch, if that. Try this basic beet recipe to begin with. But we urge you to try one of the other recipes with herbs, spices, or fruit to get a true picture of this delectable green.

SERVES 2

1 POUND BEET GREENS (2 TO 3 BUNCHES, DEPENDING ON SIZE)

1 TABLESPOON EXTRA VIRGIN OLIVE OIL

2 SMALL GARLIC CLOVES, THINLY SLICED

2 TO 3 TABLESPOONS WATER

SALT TO TASTE

FRESH LEMON JUICE, TO TASTE

1. Separate the greens from the stalks by pinching off the leaves where the stalk meets the leaf. Wash the leaves well (see page 20).

2. Heat oil in a large skillet with a tight-fitting lid over medium-low heat. Add garlic and sauté for 15 to 30 seconds. Add greens and water and toss to coat with oil and garlic. Cover and cook for 8 to 10 minutes, until greens are tender. While greens are cooking, lift cover once or twice to stir and add additional water if necessary. Season with salt and serve hot, with a squeeze of lemon juice.

Apple-Cinnamon
Beet Greens

*The sweet taste of Golden Delicious apples marries nicely
with the earthy flavor of beet greens.*

SERVES 3 TO 4

1 POUND BEET GREENS (2 TO 3 BUNCHES,
DEPENDING ON SIZE)

3 TABLESPOONS TOASTED, CHOPPED WALNUTS

1 TABLESPOON EXTRA VIRGIN OLIVE OIL

1 ONION, SLICED INTO THIN HALF-MOONS

1 GOLDEN DELICIOUS APPLE, PEELED, CORED AND
SLICED ¼ INCH THICK

¼ TEASPOON CINNAMON

SCANT ¼ TEASPOON FRESHLY GRATED NUTMEG

SALT TO TASTE

2 TO 3 TABLESPOONS WATER

1. Separate the greens from the stalks by chopping off the leaves
and discarding the long stems. Wash greens well (see page 20)
and cut into strips about ½ inch wide. Set aside.

2. Toast walnuts by spreading them in a baking dish and placing
them in a 375°F oven or toaster oven for 5 to 7 minutes. Set aside.

3. In a large skillet with lid, heat the oil over medium heat. Add
onion and sauté until soft and golden, 7 to 10 minutes, adjusting
heat as necessary to avoid burning.

4. Add beet greens, apple slices, cinnamon, nutmeg, a pinch of
salt, and 2 to 3 tablespoons of water. Mix thoroughly, cover, and
cook over medium-low heat for 8 to 10 minutes, stirring occasionally. Serve hot, garnished with chopped walnuts.

Balsamic Beets and Beet Greens

Our cooking clients make requests for this side dish again and again.

SERVES 4

¼ CUP TOASTED WALNUTS

2 BUNCHES BEETS WITH GREENS (ABOUT 6 MEDIUM BEETS)

2 TABLESPOONS FRESH LEMON JUICE

1 TABLESPOON BALSAMIC VINEGAR

2 TABLESPOONS EXTRA VIRGIN OLIVE OIL

SEA SALT OR VEGETABLE SEASONING SALT TO TASTE

1 VIDALIA OR RED ONION, SLICED INTO THIN HALF-MOONS

1. Preheat oven to 375°F. Spread the walnuts in a baking dish and toast in the oven for 5 to 7 minutes. Coarsely chop and set aside.

2. Cut off the beets, then separate the leaves from the stems at the base of the leaf. Discard the stems. Wash greens (see page 20) and cut into strips about ½ inch wide. Set aside.

3. Scrub beets and place unpeeled in a steamer and cook until tender, approximately 30 minutes for small to medium beets and 40 for large beets. Alternatively, pressure-cook the beets. Peel beets by running them under cold water while slipping off skins.

4. Cut beets into quarters, and cut each quarter into ¼ inch-thick slices. Place in a medium-size bowl and toss with the lemon juice, balsamic vinegar, 1 tablespoon of olive oil, and salt. Set aside.

5. In a large skillet, heat 1 tablespoon olive oil over medium heat. Add onions and sauté for 3 minutes. Add sliced greens and cook, covered, for 5 to 7 minutes, until wilted.

6. Just before serving, add beets to the beet greens and heat through (1 to 2 minutes). Place greens and beets on a platter and garnish with toasted walnuts.

QUICK-COOKING
BEETS

To save time, you can cook the beets in a pressure cooker. Place scrubbed and unpeeled beets on steamer rack with manufacturer's indicated amount of water. Bring cooker to full pressure and cook for 12 minutes for small to medium beets and 20 to 25 minutes for large beets. Bring pressure down quickly.

Dill-Flavored
Beet Greens

Fresh dill is a great match for beets, and it works equally well as an accompaniment for beet greens. This easy side dish takes about 10 minutes to prepare.

BEET GREENS

To some, the leafy tops of beets are disposable. The earliest beets, however, dating to prehistoric times, were grown just for the leaves, according to food historian Waverley Root. The practice of eating the root of the beet for food started around the beginning of the Christian era.

SERVES 2 TO 3

1 POUND BEET GREENS (2 TO 3 BUNCHES, DEPENDING ON SIZE)

2 CARROTS, PEELED

1 TABLESPOON EXTRA VIRGIN OLIVE OIL

2 TEASPOONS MINCED FRESH GARLIC

¼ CUP FINELY CHOPPED SCALLIONS

1 TABLESPOON CHOPPED FRESH DILL

SALT TO TASTE

FRESH LEMON JUICE TO TASTE

1. Separate the beet greens from the stems at the base of the leaf. Discard the stems. Wash greens well (see page 20) and cut into strips about ½ inch wide. Set aside.

2. Cut carrots into matchsticks by first slicing the carrot on the diagonal into ¼ inch-wide ovals. Stack 2 to 3 ovals, then cut them lengthwise into ⅛-inch strips. Set aside.

3. In a large skillet with a lid, heat olive oil over medium heat. Add garlic, carrots, and scallions and sauté over medium heat for about 2 minutes, stirring constantly.

4. Stir in beet greens and 1 to 2 tablespoons water to keep the greens from sticking to the pan. Cover and cook over medium heat for 8 to 10 minutes, stirring occasionally. Greens should be tender.

5. Stir in the chopped dill and season to taste with salt. Squeeze lemon juice on greens immediately before serving, or serve greens with a wedge of lemon.

Quick and Delicious Borscht

This soup utilizes the beetroot, stems, and leafy green tops. It can be ready in 25 minutes if you have precooked the beans. Avoid overcooking the grated beets; they can lose their color.

1 BUNCH BEETS WITH GREENS (ABOUT 3 MEDIUM BEETS)

1 TABLESPOON EXTRA VIRGIN OLIVE OIL, OR UNSALTED BUTTER

1 LARGE ONION, FINELY CHOPPED

1 LARGE CARROT, FINELY CHOPPED

1 PARSNIP, FINELY CHOPPED

2 CUPS FINELY SHREDDED CABBAGE

1½ TO 2 CUPS COOKED WHITE BEANS WITH 1 CUP COOKING LIQUID

5 CUPS VEGETABLE STOCK OR WATER

2 TO 4 TABLESPOONS MIRIN OR SHERRY

2 TABLESPOONS FRESH LEMON JUICE

SEA SALT OR VEGETABLE SEASONING SALT TO TASTE

FRESHLY GROUND BLACK PEPPER

DRAINED YOGURT OR SOUR CREAM (OPTIONAL)

1. Cut off the beets, then separate the leaves from the stems at the base of the leaf. Save the stems. Scrub beets well with a vegetable brush and wash greens and stems well (see page 20). Peel beets and grate coarsely. Chop stems and set aside. Coarsely chop greens and set aside.

2. In a large soup pot, heat the olive oil over medium heat. Add the onion, carrot, parsnip, and beet stems and sauté for 10 minutes.

3. Add the cabbage and cook for 5 minutes. Add the beans and their liquid, the vegetable stock or water, and the grated beets and cook for 5 minutes.

4. Add beet greens and cook for about 5 minutes. Season to taste with mirin or sherry, lemon juice, salt, and pepper. Serve with a dollop of drained yogurt or sour cream, if desired.

BEAN BASICS

Beans are a near-perfect food: cheap, low in fat, extremely healthful, and great tasting. We do prefer the taste of home-cooked beans to canned, however. There are many books that give you the basics of cooking beans, including ways to reduce gas. Romancing the Bean: Essentials for Creating Vegetarian Bean Dishes, *by Joanne Saltzman (Tiburon, CA: H.J. Kramer, Inc., 1993) and* Boutique Bean Pot: Exciting Bean Varities in Superb New Recipes!, *by Kathleen Mayes and Sandra Gottfried (Santa Barbara, CA: Woodbridge Press Publishing Co., 1992) are two good books.*

Shredded Beets and Greens
with Sliced Oranges

Shredding the beets in this pretty side dish cuts down the cooking time considerably. Slices of orange top the jewel-tone beets and dark greens. The finished dish, one tester reported, "tastes as good as it looks."

SERVES 3 TO 4

1 POUND BEET GREENS (2 TO 3 BUNCHES, DEPENDING ON SIZE)

1 TABLESPOON EXTRA VIRGIN OLIVE OIL

1 MEDIUM ONION, SLICED INTO THIN HALF-MOONS

1 CUP COARSLEY GRATED BEETS

1 ORANGE, PEEL AND PITH REMOVED

DRESSING:

¼ CUP FRESHLY SQUEEZED ORANGE JUICE (1 ORANGE)

1 TEASPOON PREPARED MUSTARD

1 TABLESPOON OLIVE OIL

PINCH OF SALT

NOTE

Either Dijon or whole-grain mustard will work for this recipe.

1. Cut off the beets, then separate the leaves from the stems at the base of the leaf. Discard the stems. Wash the leaves well (see page 20) and cut into strips about ½ inch wide. Set aside.

2. Heat oil in a large skillet. Add onions and sauté for 5 to 8 minutes, until soft and translucent.

3. Meanwhile, peel and coarsely grate the beets with a hand grater or in a food processor. Add the beets to the onions and sauté for about 2 minutes.

4. Add the greens and stir well. Cover and cook on medium-low heat for 8 to 10 minutes, until greens are tender.

5. Cut between membranes of the orange to section. Set aside.

Mix together the orange juice, mustard, olive oil, and salt. Drizzle over cooked beets and beet greens just before serving. Top with orange sections. Serve hot.

BEET GREENS AND VITAMIN C

When we added fresh oranges and juice to these beet greens we didn't realize the nutritional benefit of the combination. Beet greens, along with spinach and Swiss chard, are very good sources of iron. According to medical sources, if you include a source of vitamin C (oranges) with your iron-rich food (beet greens) you will increase the amount of iron your body can absorb.

Very Veggie Beet Soup

*Both beet and beet greens are used in this delicious soup. Loaded with
lots of other vegetables, this soup packs a nutritional punch.
The juice of fresh lemon squeezed right into the soup gives
this soup its tang—don't go without it.*

SERVES 6

1 BUNCH BEETS WITH GREENS (ABOUT 3 MEDIUM BEETS)

1 TABLESPOON EXTRA VIRGIN OLIVE OIL

1 CUP SLICED LEEKS, WHITE PART ONLY

2 ONIONS, DICED

2 CARROTS, DICED

2 CELERY STALKS, DICED

1 PARSNIP, DICED

8 CUPS WATER OR VEGETABLE OR CHICKEN STOCK

2 BAY LEAVES

2 TEASPOONS SEA SALT OR HERBAMARE OR TO TASTE

4 TABLESPOONS CHOPPED FRESH DILL

2 CUPS SHREDDED SAVOY CABBAGE

FRESHLY GROUND BLACK PEPPER

2 TO 3 TABLESPOONS FRESHLY SQUEEZED LEMON JUICE.

1½ CUPS YOGURT, DRAINED FOR 1 HOUR, TO EQUAL 1
   CUP THICK YOGURT (OR SUBSTITUTE 1 CUP LOW-FAT
   SOUR CREAM) (BOTH ARE OPTIONAL)

1. Cut off the beet roots, then separate the leaves from the stems at
the base of the leaf. Discard the stems. Peel and dice the beet roots.
Wash the leaves well (see page 20) and chop into bite-size pieces.

2. In a large 7- to 8-quart soup pot, heat the oil over medium heat.
Add the leeks and onions. Sauté for 15 minutes, stirring frequently
until golden and soft.

3. Add the carrots, celery, parsnip, diced beets, water or stock, bay
leaves, salt, and 2 tablespoons of the dill. Bring to a boil, reduce
heat, and cook covered for 25 minutes.

4. Add cabbage, beet greens, and the remaining 2 tablespoons fresh dill. Cook for another 20 minutes, until cabbage is tender.

5. Add freshly ground black pepper and lemon juice. Taste and adjust seasonings. Serve hot, garnished with a dollop of drained yogurt or sour cream, if desired.

HERBAMARE

Herbamare is a delicious seasoning salt made in Switzerland by Bioforce, a company dedicated to sustainable agricultural practices. More than a dozen kinds of ground fresh herbs and vegetables are combined with sea salt and "steeped" for 1 year before the moisture is removed. The result is a tasty mix to use instead of salt. It's available in health food stores.

Bok Choy

HAVE YOU EVER WONDERED WHAT THOSE SUCCULENT, 1½- TO 2-inch pieces of white vegetable are in Buddha's Delight from your favorite Chinese take-out? It's the white leaf stalk of bok choy, also known as pac choi.

Although found in supermarkets across the United States, bok choy is not a vegetable that most American cooks use on a regular basis. But once you become familiar with this delicately flavored and quick-cooking Asian green, you may just find yourself purchasing it every week.

Bok choy is a tall plant, ranging from 12 to 18 inches from the base of the plant to the leaf top. The long leaf stalks are crisp, thick, and white and all emerge from the base of the plant. The leaves are a very dark green and slightly thick. Both the leaves and leaf stalks are edible. The leaves are loaded with vitamins A and C, and, as a member of the cruciferous vegetable family, contain sulforaphane, which can help stimulate enzymes that protect against cancer.

Since bok choy has a high water content, especially in the white leaf stalks, it lends itself to quick-cooking techniques, such as stir-frying. The white remains crisp yet succulent and the leaves become tender but retain their bright green color.

Baby bok choy is more tender and, as the name implies, smaller. Baby bok choy is 6 to 8 inches tall and can be found in most Chinese markets and in a few large farmer's markets. Because of the smaller size, baby bok choy can be cut from top to bottom in sections, leaving the root end intact.

Both bok choy and baby bok choy can be stir-fried, added to soups or one-pot Asian dishes, or very finely cut for salads. The taste and texture of either type of bok choy go well with Asian seasonings such as tamari or shoyu (naturally brewed soy sauce), toasted sesame oil, and hot red peppers.

Shanghai pac choi is a related vegetable that looks very similar to bok choy. The difference is that the leaf stalks are a pale green instead of white and the leaves are just a shade or two darker than the stalks. It is very tender, has a mild cabbage taste, and is delicious in many dishes.

SHOPPING TIPS

Choose vegetables that are intact at the bottom, with white stalks, and leaves that are crisp looking and upright. As with other members of the cabbage family, any wilting or yellowing in the leaves indicates old age or improper handling by the produce department.

In Chinese markets, the baby bok choy often comes in a large box, with all the heads thrown together. Just take the time to look through to pick out the best heads. You will be rewarded with tenderness and great taste.

STORAGE

Store bok choy in the refrigerator in a plastic bag that is large enough to hold the vegetable, covering the leaves, but not tightly closed. Bok choy keeps quite well; for best results, use within 4 to 5 days.

PREPARATION

Chop off the base of the plant to separate the stalks for washing. Rinse each stalk and leaf under water, gently rubbing the stalk to remove grit. Use a vegetable brush if they are particularly dirty.

Both the leaf stalk and leaf of bok choy are edible, but the stalk usually takes a minute or two longer to cook. With a knife, cut the leaves away from the stalks.

Double Sesame Bok Choy or Shanghai Pac Choi

THE BEST
SESAME OIL

*Omega Nutrition USA,
a Washington state
mail-order company,
makes a luscious,
unrefined sesame oil
with a flavor you realize
is missing from most
sesame oils. Because of
the rich natural taste, a
little oil goes a long
way. Omega uses
organic seeds and
presses them the old-
fashioned way, without
any heat, chemicals, or
preservatives. They also
make other flavored oils,
including sunflower and
hazelnut. Call (800)
661-3529.*

Bok choy has very white leaf stalks and dark green leaves, rich in minerals and vitamin A. Shanghai pac choi, equally rich in nutrients, has greenish leaf stalks and pale green leaves. Both are suitable for this recipe. Since a head of pac choi is usually shorter than a head of bok choy, you may need 2 heads. If you are feeling indulgent, splurge and use an ample amount of the toasted sesame oil as one of the final seasonings. The combination of the tamari and toasted oil is unctuously delicious and complements rice and steamed fish or grilled chicken very nicely.

SERVES 3 TO 4

1 LARGE HEAD BOK CHOY, OR 2 SMALLER HEADS PAC CHOI

2 TEASPOONS LIGHT SESAME, CANOLA, OR CORN OIL

2 TEASPOONS TOASTED (DARK) SESAME OIL, OR TO TASTE

2 TEASPOONS TAMARI (NATURALLY BREWED SOY SAUCE)

1 TEASPOON RICE VINEGAR (OPTIONAL)

1 TABLESPOON TOASTED SESAME SEEDS

1. Wash bok choy (see page 33) and cut the leaves away from the stalks. Cut stalks into ⅓- to ½-inch pieces and set aside.

Place leaves one on top of the other, roll up, and slice into ½-inch strips. Cut in half if they are too long. Set aside.

2. Heat a large wok over high heat. Add the oil and swirl in wok to coat sides. Do not burn the oil. Add the sliced leaf stalks and leaves and stir-fry over high heat to coat with the oil. Cover for about 30 seconds to create some steam. Check greens and stir-fry until bright green and crisp-tender, 2 to 3 minutes. Add 1 table-spoon water, if necessary, to prevent sticking.

3. When greens are done, season with the toasted sesame oil, tamari, and rice vinegar, if using. Garnish with toasted seeds.

Chinese Bok Choy, Shiitake, and Tofu

If this recipe is too big for your wok, cook in batches.

SERVES 4 TO 6

6 TO 7 DRIED OR FRESH SHIITAKE MUSHROOMS

1 MEDIUM HEAD LARGE BOK CHOY, OR 3 TO 4 HEADS BABY
BOK CHOY

1 POUND SOFT TOFU, CUT INTO ¾-INCH CUBES

1 TO 2 TABLESPOONS SHOYU OR TAMARI (NATURALLY
BREWED SOY SAUCE)

2 CARROTS, PEELED AND JULIENNED

1 TABLESPOON CANOLA OIL

1 TO 2 TABLESPOONS MINCED FRESH GINGER

1 TEASPOON TOASTED (DARK) SESAME OIL

1. If using dried shiitake mushrooms, bring 2 cups water to a boil. Place the dried mushrooms in a medium-size bowl. Pour enough boiling water over the mushrooms to cover. Soak for 20 to 30 minutes. Cut off and discard the stems, which are very tough. Slice caps into thin strips. Set aside.

2. While mushrooms are soaking, wash bok choy (see page 33) and cut the leaves away from the stalks. Cut stalks into 1-inch squares. Cut leaves into strips. Set aside.

3. Put cubed tofu in a bowl and sprinkle with 1 tablespoon shoyu or tamari. Have carrots and all other ingredients ready to go. Heat a large wok over high heat. Add the canola oil, and swirl in wok to coat sides, then add ginger. Stir-fry for 15 seconds. Add shiitake and stir-fry over high heat for 1 minute. Add carrots and tofu and continue to stir-fry over high heat for 2 minutes.

4. Add the bok choy stalks and continue to cook over high heat for 30 seconds. Add the leaves and stir-fry for 2 minutes. Cover occasionally to develop a bit of steam, and add a small amount of water if necessary to avoid sticking. Season to taste with additional shoyu or tamari and the sesame oil.

Oriental Cabbage Salad

Terrific summer slaw alternative!

SERVES 6

6 INNER STALKS BOK CHOY, WASHED AND VERY THINLY
SLICED (SEE PAGE 33)

2 CUPS VERY THINLY SLICED CHINESE CABBAGE

1 CUP VERY FINELY SHREDDED RED CABBAGE

1 MEDIUM CARROT, JULIENNED OR COARSELY GRATED

3 SCALLIONS, GREENS INCLUDED, THINLY SLICED

¼ CUP MINCED PARSLEY OR CILANTRO

DRESSING:

3 TABLESPOONS CANOLA OIL

2 TABLESPOONS RICE VINEGAR

1 TABLESPOON MIRIN OR SHERRY

2 TEASPOONS TOASTED (DARK) SESAME OIL

½ TEASPOON TAMARI OR PINCH OF SEA SALT

½ TEASPOON DRY MUSTARD OR PINCH OF CHINESE
HOT MUSTARD

1 TABLESPOON TOASTED BROWN OR BLACK SESAME SEEDS

1. Place the bok choy, Chinese cabbage, red cabbage, carrot, scallions, and parsley or cilantro in a large mixing bowl.

2. In a small bowl, whisk together the oil, vinegar, mirin, sesame oil, tamari, and dry mustard. Pour over the vegetables and toss gently to combine.

3. Serve garnished with the toasted sesame seeds.

Stir-Fried Bok Choy

Bok choy lends itself to the Chinese technique of stir-frying. The white ribs are at their best when deliciously juicy and not overcooked, and the dark green leaves are quickly tenderized by the high heat. Plus, this dish is ready in minutes.

SERVES 3 TO 4

1 HEAD BOK CHOY

1 RED PEPPER

2 TEASPOONS CANOLA OIL

3 GARLIC CLOVES, MINCED

1 TABLESPOON MINCED FRESH GINGER

PINCH OF SEA SALT (OPTIONAL)

3 TABLESPOONS WATER, OR VEGETABLE OR CHICKEN BROTH

1. Wash bok choy (see page 33) and cut the leaves away from the stalks. Thinly slice the stalks and set aside. Slice or chop the leaves and set aside.

2. Seed the red pepper. Cut into thin strips and set aside.

3. Heat a large wok over high heat. Add the oil and swirl in wok to coat sides. Add the garlic and ginger and stir-fry for 15 seconds; add the bok choy stalks, red pepper, and salt and stir-fry over high heat for 1 minute.

4. Add the greens and stir-fry to mix with the other vegetables. Add 2 to 3 tablespoons water or broth to create a little steam, cover, and cook for 2 minutes, or until greens have wilted. Stalks should be crisp-tender and greens still bright green. Serve immediately.

VARIATIONS

❖ *For a less spicy taste, substitute olive oil for the canola oil and omit the ginger.*

❖ *When dish is finished, stir in ½ teaspoon toasted (dark) sesame oil and sprinkle with 1 tablespoon toasted sesame seeds.*

❖ *Substitute 1 cup julienned carrots for the red pepper.*

Baby Bok Choy with Celery and Ginger

Cutting baby bok choy into lengthwise pieces makes for a nice presentation in this quick and easy recipe. The paler green celery blends nicely with the green and white of the baby bok choy. Mmmmm, delicious! Substitute regular bok choy if baby bok choy is unavailable.

SERVES 4

4 HEADS OF BABY BOK CHOY

3 ⅛-INCH SLICES PEELED FRESH GINGER

3 LARGE CELERY STALKS, SLICED INTO ¼-INCH DIAGONAL PIECES

1 TEASPOON EXTRA VIRGIN OLIVE OIL OR CANOLA OIL

1 TABLESPOON WATER

SALT TO TASTE

2 TABLESPOONS COARSELY CHOPPED TOASTED WALNUTS (OPTIONAL)

1. Plunge the whole heads of baby bok choy into a large bowl of cool water. Do not separate the leaf stalks from the base of each bunch. Check to see if there is dirt lodged at the base of the stalks, and, if so, separate any dirt-laden leaf stalks from the head and wash them well. Drain.

2. Cut each head lengthwise from the top of the green leaves to the base of the bunch into pieces about ⅓ inch thick. If the leaves are particularly wide, slice them in half. Set aside.

3. Julienne the ginger by stacking the slices one on top of one another. With a sharp chef's knife, cut the slices into thin strips. While you prepare celery and ginger, preheat a large wok over high heat.

4. When all ingredients are ready, put the oil in the wok and swirl to coat the bottom and sides. Add the ginger and stir-fry for 10 seconds. Add celery and stir-fry for 1 minute, until color brightens.

5. Add all the baby bok choy and stir to combine with celery and ginger. Cook, stirring frequently, until leaves begin to wilt, about 2 minutes. Add 1 tablespoon of water, sprinkle with salt, and cover. Cook for another minute, until stalks are crisp-tender and leaves are wilted but still bright green.

6. Remove to a white platter and serve hot, garnished with the toasted walnuts, if desired.

NOTE

To toast walnuts, place on a cookie sheet and bake in a 325°F oven for 5 to 7 minutes, until nuts are lightly toasted and fragrant. Take care to avoid burning.

Broccoli Rabe

PEOPLE OFTEN ASK, "WHAT PART OF THE PLANT DO YOU eat?" The answer is: all of it. Rabe is a mix of long thin broccoli-like stalks, leafy greens, and small florets. Chop them all together and cook them at the same time. Because of this nice mix of textures, broccoli rabe is visually more interesting than other leafy greens.

But it's the taste of broccoli rabe that makes it one of our favorite cooking greens. "Nothing else has quite the presence of this aggressive green—it packs a wonderful wallop," says food writer Elizabeth Schneider. And we agree. Traditionally found in small Italian and Asian markets, broccoli rabe now frequently appears on restaurant menus and in supermarkets nationwide.

Broccoli rabe is a relative of broccoli, but don't expect many similarities—in taste or cooking. In our experience, pungent, somewhat bitter rabe does not fare well steamed like broccoli, or served plain. On an impulse one day, Cathy's sister and her husband bought broccoli rabe, steamed it, and served it plain. "It was horrible, really horrible," her sister repeated several times. At Cathy's urging, they reluctantly tried it again. But this time it was precooked to mellow some of its assertive flavor, and served with currants, pecans, garlic, and olive oil. The results met with approval.

Italians serve broccoli rabe most commonly as a side dish, cooked with garlic and olive oil. They also serve it with potatoes, white beans, and pasta (along with garlic and olive oil, of course). Flavorful rabe adds zest to these blander foods.

Those who do not have Italian roots may never have come across broccoli rabe, much less learned ways to cook this delicious green. We use two methods for preparing rabe: cooking it in water, and wilting it in a skillet. By using one of the two, you can easily tailor or control the pungency or bitterness of the green to your own liking.

If you are new to broccoli rabe, you might want to start by cooking it in water. The question is how much water? Some Italian cooks recommend blanching the rabe for 3 to 4 minutes in a large pot of boiling water. Using a large quantity of water allows more of the bitter compounds to be dispersed, but we feel that too much water allows too much of the characteristic flavor of broccoli rabe to be lost.

We find that 1 or 2 cups of water to one bunch of rabe is enough to disperse some of the bitter compounds, making it palatable to most people while still preserving flavor.

Even with a small quantity of water, it takes only 3 to 4 minutes to cook broccoli rabe. Left longer, it can become rather mushy and unappealing.

Another method is to wilt broccoli rabe in a skillet. This method is ideal for those who enjoy a pungent green. First, cook garlic, onions or other aromatics in a little oil, then add the rabe. Cooking time will be 8 to 10 minutes, or until the green stalks and leaves become tender but are still bright green. You can add a few tablespoons of water to prevent sticking.

Sometimes you may get an especially bitter crop of rabe— too bitter to sauté. In this case, cooking in water is the best bet.

Regardless of the cooking method, rabe needs accompaniment for balance and eating enjoyment. Vinegar, oil, garlic, sausage, sweet red peppers, anchovies, and capers all work well, as does a mix of rabe with beans, pasta, or potatoes.

SELECTION

Choose heads of rabe that are bright green, not yellowed or limp. Florets should be closed and green, with as few yellow flowers as possible.

STORAGE

Store the rabe in a plastic bag, not tightly closed, in the refrigerator for a few days.

PREPARATION

Before washing, while the rabe is still bunched, chop off about 1 inch of the base of the stalks and discard. Using a chef's knife, chop the bunch into ½ inch or bite-size pieces— stems, leaves, and florets. You can also cut into longer pieces or leave whole, depending on the dish. Some people suggest peeling the stems, but we find this unnecessary and too tedious. Wash well by plunging into a bowl of cool water. Swish pieces around, then place them in a colander to drain.

Broccoli Rabe with Toasted Pecans and Currants

Broccoli raab or rabe, often called simply rabe or rapini, is a very assertive green with a slightly bitter flavor. In this recipe the bitterness is deliciously offset by the sweetness of both the pecans and currants. Expand your horizons—try rabe!

PICKING PECANS

When buying the mild, sweet-flavored pecan, look for nuts that have the whitest flesh. Pecans have a shorter shelf life than other nuts because of their high fat content. To keep fresh, store in a plastic bag in the refrigerator or freezer. For optimal freshness, buy pecans in the shell.

SERVES 3 TO 4

⅓ CUP LIGHTLY TOASTED PECANS, COARSELY CHOPPED

1 POUND BROCCOLI RABE (ABOUT 6 CUPS CHOPPED)

2 CUPS WATER

1 TABLESPOON EXTRA VIRGIN OLIVE OIL

2 LARGE GARLIC CLOVES, MINCED

⅓ CUP CURRANTS

SALT TO TASTE

1. To toast pecans, place them on a pie tin or cookie sheet and bake at 325°F for 5 minutes, or until lightly toasted. Take care not to burn the nuts. Set aside.

2. Chop off about 1 inch of the base of the stalks of the broccoli rabe and discard. Slice the stalks into ½ inch pieces and coarsely chop the leaves and florets. Wash well (see page 43). Place 2 cups water in a 10- to 12-inch skillet with a tight-fitting lid. Bring to a boil and add the cleaned and cut rabe. Cover and cook over high heat, stirring occasionally, until tender, 3 to 4 minutes. Remove to a colander to drain.

3. Rinse the skillet and dry it. Heat the olive oil over medium-low heat, lifting and tilting the pan to coat. Add garlic and currants and sauté for 30 to 60 seconds. Stir constantly to prevent garlic from burning. Currants should be glossy and slightly puffed.

4. Add precooked rabe and stir to combine. Season with salt and cover for a minute until greens are heated through. Serve hot, garnished with the toasted pecans.

Rabe with Roasted Red Peppers and Garlic

Although we often precook rabe to tame some of its bitterness, it is also delectable if cooked quickly in an adequate amount of oil. Serve with steamed fish or white beans, which are high in protein but low in fat. Rabe aficionados will love this recipe. Just roast the red pepper before you start.

SERVES 4

1 POUND BROCCOLI RABE (6 TO 7 CUPS CHOPPED)

2 TABLESPOONS EXTRA VIRGIN OLIVE OIL

1 TABLESPOON MINCED GARLIC

1 ROASTED RED PEPPER, DICED (SEE PAGE 46)

WATER AS NEEDED

SALT TO TASTE

1. Chop off about 1 inch of the base of the stalks of the broccoli rabe and discard. Slice the stems into 1-inch pieces and coarsely chop the leaves and florets. Wash well (see page 43).

2. Heat a skillet over medium-high heat. Add oil and swirl to coat pan. Add garlic and cook for 15 to 20 seconds. Do not burn.

3. Add rabe and toss to combine well with the oil and garlic. Stir in roasted red pepper.

4. Cook over medium-high heat, stirring constantly, for 1 to 2 minutes. Add 3 tablespoons water, cover, and continue to cook until the rabe is tender but still bright green, 8 to 10 minutes. Adjust heat if necessary to avoid burning.

5. Season to taste with salt and serve hot.

Broccoli Rabe with Roasted Red Peppers, Onions, and Capers

We like to precook the rabe to rid it of excess bitterness. In this dish the flavor is perked up by the sweet and smoky roasted red peppers and the salty capers. What a combo! Serve over pasta or as a bed for grilled fish.

See page 43.

ROASTING RED PEPPERS

To roast a red pepper, place pepper directly over a gas burner with the flame turned to high. Char the outside of the pepper, turning as needed with kitchen tongs. Try not to pierce the pepper. When the entire pepper is charred, place in a brown paper bag, and allow it to "sweat" for 10 minutes. Remove from the bag, peel off charred exterior, seed pepper, and rinse if necessary. Pat dry with a paper towel. If you don't have a gas stove, char under the broiler.

SERVES 4

1 POUND BROCCOLI RABE (ABOUT 6 CUPS, CHOPPED)

2 TEASPOONS EXTRA VIRGIN OLIVE OIL

1 CUP CHOPPED ONIONS

1 TEASPOON MINCED GARLIC

2 RED PEPPERS, ROASTED, PEELED, SEEDED, AND CUT INTO ½-INCH DICE

2 TABLESPOONS CAPERS, DRAINED AND CHOPPED

2 TO 3 TEASPOONS BALSAMIC VINEGAR OR FRESH LEMON JUICE

SALT TO TASTE

WEDGES OF LEMON FOR GARNISH

1. Chop off about 1 inch of the base of the stalks of the broccoli rabe and discard. Slice the stalks into 1-inch pieces and coarsely chop the leaves and florets. Wash well (see page 43).

2. Bring 2 cups of water to a boil in a 10- to 12-inch skillet that has a tight-fitting lid. Add the rabe, cover, and cook over high heat, stirring occasionally, until tender, 3 to 4 minutes. Remove to a colander to drain. Set aside.

3. Heat a large skillet over medium heat. Add the olive oil, and swirl to coat pan. Add onions and cook over medium heat until soft and golden, 5 to 7 minutes.

4. Add garlic to onions and cook for another 2 minutes.

5. Add diced roasted red peppers, capers, balsamic vinegar or lemon, and salt to taste. Mix in rabe and heat through for 1 to 2 minutes. Serve with lemon wedges.

Broccoli Rabe
Vegetable Pasta

This recipe is a great way to introduce broccoli rabe to your family and friends. It is quick, easy, and satisfying. The slightly bitter taste of the rabe is mellowed by the sweet onions and summer squash, and the final sprinkle of cheese brings all the flavors together.

SERVES 4

1 POUND BROCCOLI RABE (ABOUT 6 CUPS, CHOPPED)

3 TABLESPOONS EXTRA VIRGIN OLIVE OIL

1 LARGE ONION, SLICED INTO THIN HALF-MOONS

1 TABLESPOON MINCED FRESH GARLIC

2 SMALL OR 1 LARGE YELLOW SUMMER SQUASH, QUARTERED LENGTHWISE AND CUT INTO ¼-INCH SLICES

SALT TO TASTE

12 OUNCES PASTA

FRESHLY GRATED PARMESAN OR ROMANO CHEESE, TO TASTE

1. Bring a pot of water to boil for the pasta.

2. Chop off about 1 inch of the base of the stalks of the broccoli rabe and discard. Slice the stalks into 1-inch pieces and coarsely chop the leaves and florets. Wash well (see page 43).

3. In a large skillet, heat 2 tablespoons of the olive oil over medium heat. Add the onions and cook for 10 minutes, or until soft and translucent. Add the garlic and cook for another minute.

4. Stir the broccoli rabe, squash, and a pinch of salt into the onion mixture. Cover and cook over medium heat for 8 to 10 minutes, stirring often. If the broccoli rabe starts to stick, add 2 to 3 tablespoons water.

5. Cook the pasta. Toss the vegetables with the cooked pasta and the remaining tablespoon of olive oil. Serve hot, topped with a sprinkle of freshly grated Parmesan or Romano cheese.

RABE AND SAUSAGE

Greens served with sausages are common in a number of cuisines. The Portuguese soup caldo verde *pairs sausages, kale, and potatoes. Italians often serve broccoli rabe alongside sausage. If pork sausage isn't your thing, try the spiced chicken or turkey variations. Any of them is delicious in combination with rabe and pasta, and it becomes a whole meal.*

Lemon-Rosemary Grilled Swordfish and Greens

The swordfish, grilled or broiled, is served on a platter atop a beautiful bed of sautéed broccoli rabe and escarole, drizzled with a rosemary-lemon vinaigrette. Serve with a crusty loaf of bread.

SERVES 3 TO 4

DRESSING/MARINADE:

2 TABLESPOONS LEMON JUICE

¼ CUP EXTRA VIRGIN OLIVE OIL

1½ TEASPOONS MINCED FRESH ROSEMARY

¼ TEASPOON SALT

⅛ TO ¼ TEASPOON FRESHLY GROUND BLACK PEPPER

FISH AND GREENS:

1 TABLESPOON, PLUS 1 TEASPOON MINCED GARLIC

1 TO 2 POUNDS SWORDFISH

1 HEAD ESCAROLE (4 TO 6 CUPS CHOPPED)

1 POUND BROCCOLI RABE (ABOUT 6 CUPS CHOPPED)

1 TABLESPOON EXTRA VIRGIN OLIVE OIL

⅛ TEASPOON RED PEPPER FLAKES

10 TO 15 OIL-CURED OLIVES, PITTED AND
     SLICED (OPTIONAL)

LEMON WEDGES, TO GARNISH

1. In a small bowl or blender, whisk together lemon juice, olive oil, and minced rosemary. Season with salt and pepper. Separate the dressing into two equal portions, and add 1 teaspoon of the minced garlic to one of the portions. Use this portion to marinate the swordfish. Let sit for 15 to 20 minutes. Reserve the other half of the dressing to drizzle on greens and swordfish later.

2. While the swordfish is marinating, prepare the greens. Chop the escarole into 1-inch pieces. Wash well in a basin of cold

water. Lift to drain. Set aside. Do the same with the rabe, using all the leaves and stalks, but first cut off and discard about 1 inch of the base of the stalks (see page 43).

3. In a large skillet with a lid, heat oil over medium heat. Add the remaining tablespoon of minced garlic and red pepper flakes and sauté for 1 minute. Stir in chopped escarole and rabe, and 3 to 4 tablespoons water and cook, covered, over medium-high heat for 8 to 10 minutes until wilted and tender. Stir occasionally to distribute greens evenly in pan. They will cook down considerably. Drain any excess water. Stir in olives at the end.

4. While the greens are cooking, grill or broil the swordfish for about 5 minutes on each side.

5. Arrange the hot greens on a large platter. Drizzle with 2 to 3 teaspoons of the dressing. Place the swordfish on top. Drizzle another 1 to 2 teaspoons of dressing on the fish. Any remaining dressing could be placed on the table; it's great for dipping bread. Garnish the platter with lemon wedges.

Sicilian Pasta with Italian Greens

This recipe is from our friend and cook, Cate Conniff Dobrich.
Sicilians add raisins and pine nuts to many of their pasta sauces,
especially to those made with slightly bitter greens such as
broccoli rabe, escarole, chicory, or even cooked radicchio.

SERVES 4

2 TABLESPOONS EXTRA VIRGIN OLIVE OIL

1 TABLESPOON BUTTER

1 MEDIUM RED ONION, THINLY SLICED

1 28-OUNCE CAN PEELED, WHOLE TOMATOES

1 TEASPOON HONEY OR NATURAL CANE SUGAR

¼ TO ½ CUP RAISINS

2 GARLIC CLOVES, MINCED

⅛ TEASPOON RED PEPPER FLAKES

1 POUND BROCCOLI RABE, WASHED AND ROUGHLY CHOPPED
(INCLUDE STEMS, LEAVES, AND SMALL FLORETS)
(SEE PAGE 43)

1 BUNCH (12 TO 14 OUNCES) ESCAROLE, WASHED AND
ROUGHLY CHOPPED (SEE PAGE 143)

SALT AND FRESHLY GROUND PEPPER TO TASTE

1 POUND PENNE OR OTHER PASTA

¼ TO ½ CUP GRATED PARMESAN OR ASIAGO CHEESE

¼ CUP TOASTED PINE NUTS

1. In a large skillet, warm 1 tablespoon of oil and the butter over
medium-low heat. Add red onion and cook over medium-low
heat for 15 to 20 minutes, until very soft and sweet. Bring a large
pot of water to boil for pasta.

2. Break apart tomatoes, and add along with sweetener and
raisins to onions. Bring to a boil, reduce heat, and simmer for
about 15 minutes.

3. While tomato sauce is cooking, warm remaining tablespoon of oil in another large skillet over medium heat. Add garlic and red pepper flakes and warm in oil for 30 seconds. Add greens and a pinch of salt, stir well to coat with oil, and cook, covered, until wilted, 8 to 10 minutes. Remove cover to prevent greens from overcooking.

4. While greens are cooking, add pasta and salt to boiling water and cook according to package directions.

5. When pasta is done, combine with greens, sauce, and Parmesan cheese. Season to taste with salt and pepper. Top with toasted pine nuts.

BROCCOLI RABE
ALSO KNOWN AS

There are several different names or spellings for this green, but it's all the same vegetable. You might also see broccoli rape or raab, rapini, broccoletti, cima di rapa, or brocoletti di rape. Broccoli rabe is a member of the Brassica *family, along with* broccoli, kale, and cauliflower. Rapa *is the Latin name for turnip.*

Italian-Style White Bean Soup with Broccoli Rabe

Garlicky broccoli rabe adds zest to creamy white beans and potatoes to make a memorable and colorful soup, perfect for lunch or dinner when served with some chewy bread.

MAKES 2½ QUARTS

1 CUP DRIED WHITE NAVY OR GREAT NORTHERN BEANS (SOAKED OVERNIGHT)

4 MEDIUM-SIZE RED POTATOES, PEELED AND DICED

1 BAY LEAF

2 WHOLE CELERY STALKS

8 CUPS COLD WATER

2 TABLESPOONS EXTRA VIRGIN OLIVE OIL

1 COARSELY CHOPPED LARGE ONION

1 LEEK, WASHED AND SLICED, WHITE PART ONLY

3 CARROTS, PEELED AND DICED

1 POUND BROCCOLI RABE (ABOUT 6 CUPS, CHOPPED)

4 GARLIC CLOVES, MINCED

1 HOT RED PEPPER, MINCED, OR ⅛ TEASPOON OF RED PEPPER FLAKES

1. Drain beans and discard soaking water. Place beans, potatoes, bay leaf, and whole celery stalks in a large soup pot with 8 cups water and bring to a boil. Reduce heat, cover, and simmer for 30 minutes. (Like the bay leaf, the whole celery adds flavor and is discarded when the soup is finished.)

2. In a large skillet, heat 1 tablespoon of the oil and sauté onion and leeks for 8 to 10 minutes. Add carrots and sauté for another 2 to 3 minutes. Add mixture to beans. Continue simmering for another 20 to 30 minutes, until beans are tender.

3. While the soup is cooking, prepare the rabe. Chop off about 1 inch of the base of the stalks and discard. Chop the stalks and leaves into ½-inch pieces. Wash well (see page 43). Heat remaining tablespoon of oil in skillet and add minced garlic and red pepper. Cook for about 1 minute, until garlic is fragrant but not burned. Add chopped rabe and 2 to 3 tablespoons water. Cover and cook for 5 to 8 minutes, until rabe is tender. Don't overcook or it will turn mushy.

4. When the beans are tender, add the rabe and cook for an additional 5 minutes to allow flavors to mingle. Remove the bay leaf and celery stalks. The entire cooking time should be just over 1 hour.

AN ITALIAN VEGETABLE

Broccoli rabe is a favorite in Tuscany, as well as in Rome and southern Italy. It is often blanched whole, then chopped and sautéed with olive oil, garlic, salt, black pepper, and lemon juice— the way many vegetables are served in Italy.

Lorna Sass's Pasta With Broccoli Rabe

"This is one of my favorite last-minute meals. When I'm especially hungry, I use a very quick-cooking pasta, such as Eden's brown rice udon, which cooks in 5 minutes!
"The recipe is especially delicious when you make the dressing with Consorzio infused oils, but if you don't have them on hand, a fruity olive oil also does the job nicely. You can also make endless variations by using flavored pastas, such as black pepper or parsley-garlic."
— LORNA SASS

SERVES 2

1 BUNCH BROCCOLI RABE

8 OUNCES PASTA

1 TABLESPOON BASIL OLIVE OIL

1 TABLESPOON ROASTED GARLIC OLIVE OIL

1 TO 2 TABLESPOONS TAMARI (NATURALLY BREWED SOY SAUCE)

GRATED PARMIGIANO-REGGIANO (OPTIONAL)

FRESHLY GRATED BLACK PEPPER (OPTIONAL)

1. Cut off about 1 inch of the base of the stalks of the broccoli rabe and discard. Slice the stalks into 1-inch pieces and set aside. Coarsely chop the leaves and florets. Wash well (see page 43).

2. Cook the pasta in boiling water for 3 minutes less than directed on the package. Add the broccoli rabe stems and cook for 2 minutes. Add the leaves and cook until the pasta is *al dente*, about 1 minute. Make sure that the leaves are submerged in the water during cooking.

3. Drain well. Toss immediately with oils, tamari, and Parmesan, if using. Grate a bit of black pepper on top, if desired. Serve hot or at room temperature.

Sass's Fast Food

Lorna J. Sass is the author of one of our favorite and most used cookbooks: Lorna Sass' Complete Vegetarian Kitchen *(New York: Hearst, 1992). Her recipes have style and flair with a delicious combination of flavors.*

Sass is also the person we turn to for information about pressure cooking. A New York City food writer and historian, she has pioneered cooking vegetarian meals in minutes using the new and safer second-generation pressure cookers. Her latest book is Great Vegetarian Cooking Under Pressure *(New York: William Morrow, 1994). Next up will be* The Short-Cut Vegetarian. *We look forward to it.*

Growing Great Greens:
Growers Share Their Secrets

Lisa Fisher weighs out a bunch of Red Russian kale for a customer at the West Tisbury Farmer's Market on Martha's Vineyard off Massachusetts. The buyer also stocks up on Italian kale, juicy kyona mizuna, and spicy Japanese red giant mustard.

This bonanza of greens can't be found in a supermarket—at least not today. But they can be grown in a commercial garden like Fisher's or in your own backyard garden.

Seed companies such as Johnny's Selected Seeds in Maine offer up to fifty cultivated greens from around the world, from nutty arugula to succulent baby bok choy. With the popularity of mesclun salad, a mix of baby lettuce and cooking greens, seed companies have competitively looked for newer, more interesting greens to differentiate mixes, according to Karen Siske, director of commercial sales for Johnny's. The resulting explosion of greens available for commercial growers has been a boon for home growers, who can now choose from such greens as purslane, vegetable amaranth, and miner's lettuce, in addition to favorites such as kale and Swiss chard.

"Greens are fairly easy to grow," says Lynda Simkins, president of the Northeast Organic Farmers Association and one of several expert growers contacted for tips on growing greens. "People should be encouraged to try new ones and explore some of the varieties that are grown in other parts of the world." Simkins says her farm is growing more Asian greens, including tatsoi, pac choi, and mizuna, deliciously mild-flavored Japanese greens that are great in salads and stir-fries.

With this diverse assortment available, choosing greens for the garden can be fun, as long as you try to learn basic requirements for different varieties. Some varieties of greens thrive and taste best during certain seasons, and it's best to read seed catalogs to figure out your growing strategy.

So-called winter greens or cold-resistant greens such as kale, radicchio, escarole, and collards can be harvested in late fall and actually taste better after a frost.

Wendy Krupnick, a trial manager at the California office of Shepherd's Garden Seeds who has been growing greens for twenty-five years, says that, during a frost, the starch in these plants turns to sugar to protect the plant from freeze damage. "The plant really is sweeter." It doesn't mean you can't grow these vegetables in the summer, Krupnick says. "But I don't think kale [for example] tastes very good in hot weather."

Some greens fall into a more heat-tolerant category: leaf amaranth, New Zealand spinach, mizuna, and chard. Others still are considered spring crops.

Before growing greens, Simkins suggests that urban growers first test their soil for lead, which accumulates in the leafy part of the vegetable. Those with a lead problem can bring in new soil and grow the greens in a raised bed, she suggests.

Greens are heavy feeders, and sensitive to heat stress. The root system is fairly shallow, spreading in the top six inches of soil. This presents a challenge to provide consistent moisture and nutrients closer to the top of the soil. Growers find that rich soil that can hold water, and soil fertilized regularly with compost, work best for growing greens.

"In general, we don't plant greens in light, sandy soils—they're not going to do well," reports Gordon Bemis of Hutchins Farm in Concord, Massachusetts. "Use a good loam to a heavier soil. You can grow some greens in light soil in the fall when you get enough rain."

Hutchins Farm uses organic farming methods to produce many beautiful leafy greens, including kale, arugula, collards, and broccoli rabe. Bemis says he applies composted chicken manure in the fall before planting and rotates crops each year.

Lisa Fisher, who specializes in organically grown greens on Martha's Vineyard, says she also applies composted chicken manure. "Leafy greens are heavy nitrogen feeders and chicken manure offers the highest nitrogen content."

Both growers say that one application of compost a year is enough food for the season. "In general, you want moderate fertility; you don't want too much compost or too much nitrogen," says Bemis.

"I think the main thing about growing greens is to pay attention to them," says Fisher. A healthy "unstressed" plant will taste best. That may be as easy as seeing they get an inch of water each week, and a constant level of nutrients. That's the benefit of growing organically, she says. The fertilizer in the form of compost provides a constant level for the plant. Chemical fertilizers shock the plant with an abundance of fertilizer all at once, and then starve them until the next treatment.

Pick the plant in the early morning or evening for best taste, Fisher adds. "Don't pick greens in the hot bright sunshine. If you pick a plant in the middle of a stressful time, it's not going to taste as good. I know it doesn't look as good."

Bemis says another technique he uses that produces high-quality greens is successive plantings throughout the season. "We plant [from seed] every week so we have a continuous supply of fresh young greens." In addition, another advantage of successive planting is that if you have a problem with insects damaging one crop, you have another crop on the way.

For home growers, successive planting works well with greens such as arugula and lettuces, which will flower quickly and then become bitter. "One of the common mistakes is that people sow lettuce once and expect it to grow for months and then complain lettuce is bitter. If you plant once a month, then you always have fresh new lettuce," says Wendy Krupnick of Shepherd's.

Cabbage

CABBAGE HAS BEEN CULTIVATED FOR 2500 YEARS AND IS ONE of the world's most widely grown vegetables. The Romans enjoyed cabbage, as have the Italians, English, Irish, Germans, and Eastern Europeans since that time. Green cabbage was introduced to China in the nineteenth century and is now a very popular vegetable there, where it is called *yeh choi* or coconut vegetable, which probably refers to both the shape and crisp texture of the vegetable.

European cabbages have a delicious, clean, sweet taste when prepared properly. They can be steamed, stir-fried, boiled, added to soups, and pickled. What an incredibly versatile vegetable! Wild cabbage, which is rather like kale and grows on coastal cliffs in Europe, is the "mother" of many varieties of cabbage: green and red cabbages, savoy cabbage, kale, broccoli, cauliflower, and kohlrabi. All members of this family have small mustardlike seeds and four-petaled flowers in the shape of a cross. Thus, the name cruciferous vegetables, *cruz* or *crucis* meaning cross in Latin. Scientists have found that a certain component of the cruciferous vegetable family, sulforaphane, helps stimulate enzymes that guard against the development of cancerous tumors.

Green Cabbage

Green cabbage has a compact, round, or rather conical shape, with smooth-textured light green leaves that form a firm head. This cabbage is crisp when fresh and raw, and mildly cabbagy in taste. Its sweetness is highlighted by quick-cooking methods such as stir-frying or light steaming, but it can also be cooked longer in soups and stews to lend a depth and richness to the broth. Sometimes people avoid cabbage because they have only tasted and smelled the sulfurous odor of the overcooked vegetable. Green cabbage keeps very well in the refrigerator or root cellar, and is a vegetable that gardeners often store and use all winter.

Red Cabbage

Red cabbage has a compact, dense head, and is purple or reddish purple. The taste is less sweet than that of green cabbage, and the texture is often a bit tougher. We find the reddish purple or magenta heads to be more tender and less biting in taste than the deeply colored variety. In preparation, raw red cabbage can benefit from a bit of soaking in a vinegary dressing to help tenderize the leaves. Cut very thin, red cabbage makes a nice addition to any salad.

The color of red cabbage is caused by anthocyanin pigments. If red cabbage remains in alkaline water, however, it can turn blue! Therefore, in cooking and in salads, the bright color of red cabbage is enhanced and preserved by the addition of an acid, such as vinegar or lemon juice. Simple chemistry!

Although similar in color, radicchio is not to be confused with red cabbage at the supermarket. Red cabbage will always be located near the green cabbages. Radicchio is usually found near the endives and lettuces.

Savoy Cabbage

Savoy cabbage is a delicious though little known vegetable. Like green cabbage, savoy is also a head cabbage but less compact. The leaves are curled, "savoyed," and more crumpled than the smooth leaves of green cabbage. Savoy leaves range from a rich dark green on the outside to a pale yellowish green on the inside of the head. The flavor is more delicate and sweet than that of regular green cabbage; and it's sweetness is highlighted by quick cooking. The leaves are often stuffed, since they are more loosely layered than those of green cabbage. Although savoy cabbage is usually cooked, the paler, softly textured inside leaves are wonderful served raw in a salad.

In Italy there is a variety of nonheading cabbage that has the coloration and crumpled look of savoy in its elongated leaves. Called *cavolo nero* or black cabbage, it is rarely eaten outside Tuscany but is much enjoyed there. Its flavor is similar to that of kale mixed with savoy cabbage—sweetly cabbagy—and it takes well to olive oil and a sprinkle of salt.

SHOPPING TIPS

Choose green and red cabbage heads that are firm and feel heavy for their size. The outer leaves should not be discolored or shriveled; if they are, peel away a bit to see that the leaves that lie underneath are smooth and fresh looking. The stems should be healthy looking and not split. Choose savoy cabbage heads that are nicely colored and rather firm. The outer leaves should look fresh and not shriveled. Avoid purchasing precut cabbage heads; the loss of vitamin C is significant.

STORAGE

Store all cabbages in plastic bags in the refrigerator. Green cabbage and red cabbage keep the best, even up to 4 weeks or more in the refrigerator if uncut. Savoy should be used within 1 week.

PREPARATION

To use, remove outer leaves. The inner leaves rarely hold grit and do not need to be washed. We find that the best way to slice cabbage is to cut the head into four quarters. Using a chef's knife, cut the cabbage in half by slicing through the stem. Cut each half in half (to make four quarters) and remove core by slicing a wedged-shaped section.

To use cabbage in salads, use a chef's knife to shred it as thin as possible. With a sharp, heavy chef's knife, slicing a whole head takes only a few minutes. Alternatively, use a hand grater or food processor to cut a large quantity. For side dishes or stir-fries, cut cabbage into ¼- to ½-inch ribbons.

Dazzling Red Cabbage Salad

This crunchy and colorful salad is best when the vegetables are sliced or shredded as thin as possible.

SERVES 4 TO 6

3 CUPS VERY FINELY SHREDDED RED CABBAGE

1 RED PEPPER, VERY FINELY SLICED INTO 2-INCH LENGTHS

1 LARGE CARROT, PEELED AND JULIENNED OR SHREDDED

½ CUP FINELY MINCED FRESH PARSLEY

3 SCALLIONS, WHITE AND GREEN PARTS FINELY SLICED ON THE DIAGONAL

DRESSING:

2 TABLESPOONS BROWN RICE VINEGAR OR OTHER MILD VINEGAR

1 TABLESPOON BALSAMIC VINEGAR

1 TEASPOON FRESH GINGER JUICE

1 TABLESPOON FRESH LEMON JUICE

1 TEASPOON MAPLE SYRUP

4 TABLESPOONS LIGHT SESAME OR CANOLA OIL

1 TEASPOON TAMARI SOY SAUCE OR SEA SALT TO TASTE

GARNISH:

2 TABLESPOONS TOASTED BLACK OR BROWN SESAME SEEDS

1. Place finely shredded red cabbage in a medium-size bowl, with red pepper, carrot, parsley, and scallions.

2. In a small jar, shake together the dressing ingredients. Toss with the vegetable mixture and set aside.

3. To toast the sesame seeds, place the seeds in a small, dry skillet. Toast over medium heat until the seeds start popping and emit a deliciously nutty aroma. Remove from skillet to a bowl to cool. When ready to serve salad, garnish with the toasted seeds.

VARIATION

For a more exotic taste, substitute 1 tablespoon toasted (dark) sesame oil for the light sesame oil or canola oil.

GINGER JUICE

Ginger juice imparts a light, gingery taste to this salad. To make the juice, grate a chunk of gingerroot with a hand grater using the smallest holes. Gather the grated ginger in one hand and simply squeeze. One tablespoon of grated ginger is enough to produce a teaspoon of juice.

Chunked Salmon with Shredded Savoy Salad

Sometimes tasty recipes happen because you are trying to be creative with leftovers. In this recipe, leftover poached or grilled salmon is combined with light and tender savoy cabbage leaves for a coleslaw that is a nice change from the usual. Since both the mustard and the oil-cured olives are salty, no additional salt is needed. Makes a nice luncheon salad.

VARIATIONS

❖ *If you prefer, 2 teaspoons small capers may be substituted for the oil-cured olives.*

❖ *Add ¾ cup seedless red grapes, sliced in half.*

SERVES 2 TO 3

1 CUP FINELY SHREDDED SAVOY CABBAGE

½ CUP SHREDDED RADDICCHIO, WATERCRESS, OR ARUGULA

8 OIL-CURED OLIVES, PITTED AND FINELY CHOPPED

¼ CUP MINCED SCALLIONS, WHITE AND GREEN PARTS

1 CELERY STALK, FINELY DICED

1 CUP (LEFTOVER) CHUNKED POACHED OR GRILLED SALMON

DRESSING:

2 TABLESPOONS MAYONNAISE

1 TEASPOON DIJON MUSTARD

2 TABLESPOONS FRESHLY SQUEEZED LEMON JUICE

½ TEASPOON PURE MAPLE SYRUP OR HONEY

¼ TEASPOON CELERY SEED

FRESHLY GROUND BLACK PEPPER TO TASTE

1. Combine savoy cabbage, raddicchio, olives, scallions, and celery in a medium-size mixing bowl.

2. In a separate small bowl, mix together mayonnaise, mustard, lemon juice, maple syrup or honey, and celery seed.

3. Combine dressing with salad and toss. Add salmon and mix gently.

4. Taste and add lots of black pepper for an extra kick. Squeeze on additional lemon juice to taste.

Colcannon

Colcannon is a traditional Irish dish of potatoes, milk, and kale. Our version packs in nutrition with kale and savoy cabbage and eliminates fat by omitting milk. Serve with Turkey Loaf with Greens (see page 89), or any meal calling for mashed potatoes. It's great for breakfast and leftovers, too. In this recipe, we chose Yellow Finn or Yukon Gold potatoes for their rich flavor.

SERVES 6 TO 8

2 POUNDS YELLOW FINN OR YUKON GOLD POTATOES, PEELED AND QUARTERED

1 TABLESPOON PLUS ½ TEASPOON BUTTER

2 ONIONS, DICED

4 CUPS SHREDDED SAVOY CABBAGE

2½ CUPS OF WATER

3 TO 4 CUPS WASHED AND CHOPPED KALE (SEE PAGE 155)

1. Bring a large pot of water to a boil. Add potatoes and boil until fork tender, 20 to 30 minutes. Remove from water, saving water. Mash potatoes with up to 1 cup of cooking liquid. Season with salt and pepper and set aside.

2. While potatoes are cooking, heat the 1 tablespoon of butter in a large skillet over medium heat. Add diced onions and sauté over medium heat until soft and translucent, about 10 minutes. Do not burn. Add savoy cabbage and ½ cup of water. Cover and cook over medium-low heat until cabbage is just tender. Set aside.

3. Preheat oven to 350° F.

4. In a separate skillet, bring 2 cups of water to a boil. Add chopped kale and cook for 4 to 5 minutes, until just tender. Sprinkle with a pinch of salt. Remove kale from liquid and drain well. Set aside.

5. After the potatoes have been mashed, stir in cooked kale, onions, and savoy cabbage. Season well with salt and pepper. Place mixture in an ovenproof casserole dish and top with ½ teaspoon butter. Bake for 15 to 20 minutes, just to reheat.

VARIATIONS

❖ *Form colcannon mixture into patties and sauté in a small amount of oil. Serve for breakfast.*

❖ *Take 2 to 3 eggs, crack open, and beat with fork. Pour uncooked eggs over colcannon mixture in casserole dish, cover, and bake until eggs cook, 20 to 30 minutes.*

Quick Savoy and Celery

Savoy cabbage is lighter in texture and flavor than regular green cabbage. It shines alongside celery in this easy and delicious recipe.

SERVES 3 TO 4

2 TEASPOONS EXTRA VIRGIN OLIVE OIL

3 SMALL GARLIC CLOVES, SMASHED AND PEELED

2 CELERY STALKS, THINLY SLICED ON THE DIAGONAL

6 CUPS SHREDDED SAVOY CABBAGE

PINCH OF SALT

UMEBOSHI VINEGAR (SEE PAGE 67)

1. In a 13-inch wok or large skillet, heat the oil over high heat. Swirl to coat pan. Add garlic and cook for 5 seconds. Add celery and stir-fry vigorously for 30 seconds.

2. Add cabbage, stir-frying to mix well with celery and garlic, for about 1 minute. Sprinkle on a small pinch of salt, cover, and continue to cook for about 2 minutes. Stir after 1 minute to make sure cabbage is not burning. Lower heat slightly if necessary.

3. Test cabbage. It should be light, bright green, and slightly crunchy. Serve hot with a splash of umeboshi vinegar.

Sautéed Green Cabbage with Carrots and Thyme

Simple to make, this dish plays up the sweetness and crunch of lightly cooked green cabbage. Overcooking can destroy that sweet taste. The umeboshi vinegar splashed on after cooking adds a tart and tangy dimension.

SERVES 4

1 TABLESPOON EXTRA VIRGIN OLIVE OIL

2 CARROTS, JULIENNED

4 INCHES DAIKON, QUARTERED LENGTHWISE AND CUT INTO ⅓-INCH SLICES

4 SCALLIONS, WHITE AND GREEN PARTS, THINLY SLICED ON THE DIAGONAL

6 CUPS FINELY SHREDDED GREEN CABBAGE

SALT TO TASTE

LARGE PINCH OF DRIED THYME

2 TABLESPOONS WATER

1 TEASPOON UMEBOSHI VINEGAR, OR TO TASTE

1. In a large skillet, heat the oil over medium high heat. Add carrots, daikon, and scallions and cook for 1 minute, stirring constantly.

2. Add cabbage and toss to coat with oil. Stir-fry for 2 minutes. Sprinkle with a pinch of salt, and add thyme and the water. Cover and cook for 6-8 minutes, stirring occasionally, until cabbage is tender but not overcooked. Reduce heat slightly, if necessary, to avoid burning.

3. Season to taste with umeboshi vinegar and serve hot.

UMEBOSHI VINEGAR

Umeboshi vinegar is the salty brine resulting from the pickling of unripe ume plums with shiso leaves. Shiso leaves, from the perilla or beefsteak plant, are purple, thus the beautiful pink, almost magenta color of the umeboshi vinegar. It is really not a vinegar in the true sense of the word. It is called that because of its tart and tangy taste, so it can often be substituted in small quantities for lemon juice or vinegar. Pay attention to quantities, because it is salty. A few drops of umeboshi taste good on greens of all kinds. It also enhances the flavor of bean soups and dishes with corn.

Savoy Cabbage and Kale Sauté

This is an easy side dish to accompany any meal.

SERVES 4

1 TABLESPOON BUTTER

2 ONIONS, DICED

2½ CUPS WATER

6 CUPS WASHED AND COARSELY CHOPPED KALE, WITH
STEMS REMOVED (SEE PAGE 155)

4 CUPS SHREDDED SAVOY CABBAGE, ABOUT ¼-INCH
THICK

SALT TO TASTE

UMEBOSHI VINEGAR OR LEMON JUICE TO TASTE (OPTIONAL)

VARIATIONS

❖ *Add 1 cup fresh
corn kernels with
savoy cabbage and
continue with
recipe.*

❖ *Try "sea seasonings"
such as nori-ginger
in place of salt.*

1. In a large skillet, heat butter over medium heat. Add onions and sauté for 10 to 15 minutes, until soft and translucent. Do not burn.

2. While onions are cooking, bring 2 cups of the water to a boil in another skillet that has a tight-fitting lid. Add kale, cover, and cook for 4 to 5 minutes, until tender. Drain and set aside. (Save liquid for drinking, if desired.)

3. When onions are tender, stir in savoy cabbage and remaining ½ cup water. Cover and cook for 6 to 8 minutes, stirring occasionally, until cabbage is tender but still bright in color.

4. Stir in the cooked kale and heat through. Season to taste with salt and umeboshi or lemon juice, if desired.

Sweet-and-Sour Cabbage with Beet Greens, Apples, and Raisins

This side dish of light-colored cabbage and dark green beet greens with a backdrop of apples and raisins looks as good as it tastes. If beet greens are unavailable, substitute Swiss chard leaves.

SERVES 4

1 TABLESPOON BUTTER

1 ONION, SLICED INTO THIN HALF-MOONS

5 CUPS SHREDDED GREEN CABBAGE

1 CUP WATER

⅓ CUP RAISINS

1 BUNCH BEET GREENS (2 TO 3 CUPS, CHOPPED) WASHED AND SLICED (SEE PAGE 20)

½ GOLDEN DELICIOUS APPLE, PEELED, CORED, AND THINLY SLICED

2 TEASPOONS APPLE CIDER VINEGAR

1½ TEASPOONS MAPLE SYRUP OR HONEY

SALT TO TASTE

1. In a large skillet with a lid, heat butter over medium heat. Add onion and sauté until soft and translucent, 8 to 10 minutes.

2. Add cabbage, water, raisins, and apple slices. Cover and cook for 5 minutes. Stir in beet greens and cook for another 6 to 7 minutes.

3. When the greens are tender, stir in vinegar, maple syrup or honey, and salt to taste. Serve hot.

HIGH STATUS OF CABBAGE

Cabbage has a rather lowly status today, but that hasn't always been the case. At the time of the Romans, cabbage was in such demand that its high price could be afforded only by the wealthy, according to food historian Waverley Root. But in the Middle Ages, Root reports, vegetables were not very popular until the fourteenth century, when the chef to Charles VI of France dared to serve one during the first course of a banquet. The vegetable he chose was the cabbage.

Cabbage Potato Soup

A satisfying and quick-cooking winter greens soup.

SERVES 4 TO 6

1 TEASPOON OLIVE OR CANOLA OIL

½ TEASPOON CUMIN SEEDS

1 TEASPOON BROWN MUSTARD SEEDS

2 CUPS DICED ONIONS

6 CUPS WATER

4 CARROTS, DICED

½ TEASPOON TURMERIC

4 MEDIUM-SIZE POTATOES, CUT INTO ¾-INCH CUBES

1 TEASPOON SALT

2 CUPS FINELY SHREDDED SAVOY CABBAGE

2 CUPS FINELY SHREDDED COLLARDS

SALT AND BLACK PEPPER TO TASTE

⅛ TO ¼ TEASPOON CAYENNE (OPTIONAL)

VARIATION

For additional texture and protein, stir in 2 cups cooked chick-peas along with the savoy cabbage.

1. Heat oil in a stockpot. Cook cumin and mustard seeds for 1 to 2 minutes, until fragrant. Add diced onions and sauté until golden and soft, 10 to 15 minutes.

2. Add water, carrots, turmeric, potatoes, and salt. Bring to a boil. Reduce heat and simmer, covered, for about 20 minutes, until potatoes are tender. Add cabbage and cook, covered, for 10 minutes. Add shredded collards and cook for another 10 minutes.

3. Stir enough to break up some of the potatoes. Season with salt, pepper, and cayenne, if desired.

Spicy Coleslaw

A light but spicy dressing takes the place of the traditional calorie-filled, mayonnaise-based coleslaw.

SERVES 6 TO 8

1 SMALL HEAD SHREDDED GREEN CABBAGE (4 TO 5 CUPS)

3 PEELED AND SHREDDED CARROTS

6 TO 10 RADISHES, SLICED OR SHREDDED

¼ CUP FINELY CHOPPED FRESH PARSLEY

2 TABLESPOONS FINELY CHOPPED FRESH DILL

DRESSING:

¾ CUP FRESHLY SQUEEZED ORANGE JUICE

2 TABLESPOONS DIJON OR WHOLE-GRAIN MUSTARD

1 TABLESPOON FRESHLY GRATED HORSERADISH ROOT

2 TABLESPOONS MINCED RED ONION

1 TABLESPOON FRESH LEMON JUICE

1 TEASPOON PURE MAPLE SYRUP OR OTHER SWEETENER

2 TABLESPOONS OLIVE OR CANOLA OIL

½ TEASPOON SALT, OR TO TASTE

1. In a medium-size bowl, combine cabbage, carrots, radishes, parsley, and dill. Mix gently.

2. Combine all the ingredients for the dressing in a blender or food processor and blend thoroughly. Pour over salad and stir to combine. Before serving each time, mix to incorporate dressing.

ANTICANCER
CRUCIFER

Indoles, one of the many compounds found in cabbage (and other cruciferous vegetables), are being studied for their effect in reducing breast cancer. Researchers have found that indoles stimulate enzyme systems in the body that break down estrogen into less potent or harmful forms.

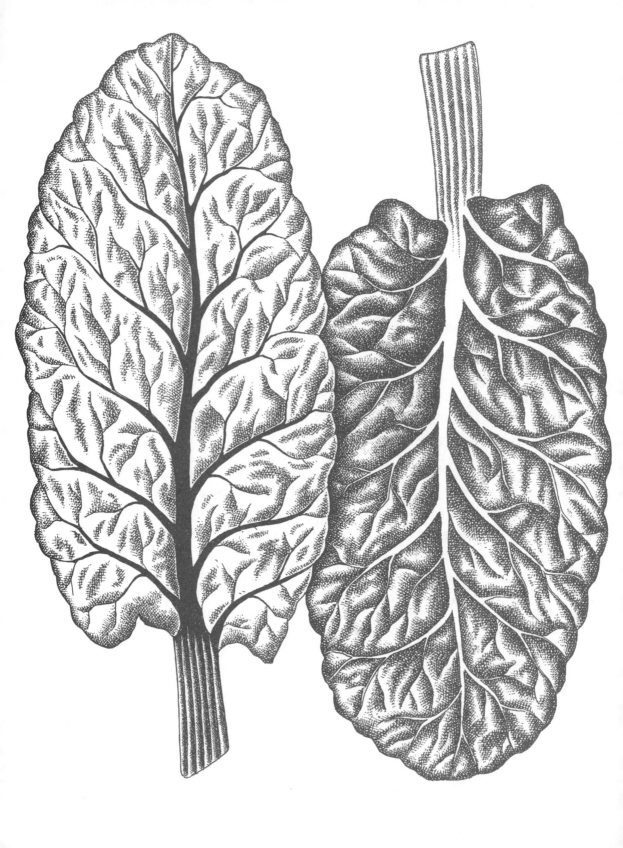

Chard

CHARD, LIKE SPINACH, IS ONE OF THE MOST MILD-TASTING cooking greens: sweet, slightly earthy, and succulent. It is also one of the most versatile. It can be used, leaf and stalk, as a vegetable in its own right; the leaves or stalks can be used in soups; and the leaves make a light wrap for fish and grains. This green is quite easy to prepare and is loaded with vitamins A and C. In the garden, long after spinach has bolted or gone to seed, chard hangs in there, offering us delicious flavor and abundance all summer and fall.

The two most common forms of chard are Swiss chard and red or rhubarb chard. The two types of chard can be used interchangeably (unless you want to avoid a red tinge left behind by the red chard) or together, for a stunning effect. Swiss chard has rather glossy dark green leaves with white, celerylike ribs or leaf stalks. The edges are slightly curled and the plants can range from 10 to 18 inches from bottom of stalk to top of leaf. Red or rhubarb chard is similar in size but has a rhubarb-red leaf stalk and red veining in the leaf.

Chard takes well to olive oil and lemon juice. One of our favorite ways to prepare it is to cook the leaves, without the stalks. Either steam the chard over bubbling water or place it in a skillet with just the water clinging to the washed leaves. The chard is ready when it wilts and has no raw taste, about 5 minutes. It can be served with a drizzle of olive oil, a squirt of fresh lemon juice, and a pinch of salt. Equally delicious is chard sautéed with olive oil and slices of garlic. Cooked properly, chard has a soft velvety texture. It has minimal acidity when thoroughly cooked. There is a slight tang from the oxalic acid present in the vegetable and this taste can come through if chard is undercooked. Chard can also have a rich, satisfying flavor when cooked with strong seasonings.

When we use the stalks as well as the leaves, we cut the stalks crosswise into ½-inch pieces, or lengthwise into 3-inch-long julienne. They are placed in the skillet with 1 cup boiling water and cooked, covered, for 3 to 4 minutes to tenderize before adding the coarsely chopped leaves. The French, who eat chard as regularly as we eat spinach and have been doing so since the fifteenth century, rarely serve the stalks and leaves together and cultivate separate subvarieties of each, according to food historian Waverley Root.

Baby chard leaves are extra tender, sweet tasting, and often found in mesclun mixes. If you have your own garden, you can nip off some of those baby leaves for any salad of mixed greens. Chard is one of those cut-and-come-again vegetables that gardeners just love. And it looks so pretty in the garden with its tall green leaves and stalks like soldiers standing erect all in a line.

Choose bunches that have fresh, lively-looking leaves. Wilting or yellowing in leaves can indicate old age or improper handling. Chard should look as if it has just been picked from the garden.

STORAGE

Store chard in a clear plastic bag in the refrigerator. The bag should be large enough to cover the entire bunch; otherwise, the leaves sticking out of the bag may wilt. Use within 2 to 3 days for best results.

PREPARATION AND CUTTING

First chop off the base of the plant to separate the stalks for washing. Fill a large bowl with cool water, plunge in the leaves to rinse, lift greens out of water to a colander, and check bottom of bowl. If there is any sand, discard the water and repeat the process.

We have found two methods for removing the stalks from the leaves. One is to run a knife along the rib where it meets the leaf. The other is to strip the leaf from the stalk with the thumb and fingers. To master the hand-stripping method, use one hand to hold the chard by the stalk, rib side up. Use the other hand to grasp the leaf just where it meets the rib and draw the hand toward the top of the leaf. This works with most chard, but sometimes the knife method works best if the rib is very wide. Experiment to see what works best for you. Either method is fairly easy.

To prepare leaves, tear them into bite-size pieces or coarsely chop them. If you want thin shreds, pile several leaves on top of one another, roll into a cigar shape, and thinly slice with a chef's knife.

Braised Red Chard and Shiitake Mushrooms

This dish has only a modicum of oil. The flavor of the dried shiitake lends a richness without lots of fat. For a fat-free recipe, try sautéing the shiitake with 1 to 2 tablespoons of the shiitake soaking water instead of the oil. This dish has a deep, dark color.

SERVES 2 TO 3

10 TO 12 DRIED SHIITAKE MUSHROOMS

1 POUND RED CHARD

1 TEASPOON EXTRA VIRGIN OLIVE OIL

1 ONION, CUT INTO ½-INCH DICE

1 LARGE GARLIC CLOVE, MINCED

1 CUP WATER

SALT TO TASTE

1. Place the dried shiitake in a medium-size bowl. Pour enough boiling water over mushrooms to cover them by ½ inch. Set aside to soak for 20 minutes.

2. Meanwhile, wash the chard and strip the stalks from the leaves (see page 75). Cut the stalks into ½-inch pieces and set aside in a bowl. Coarsely chop the leaves and measure to equal 6 cups. Set aside in another bowl.

3. Heat a 10- to 12-inch skillet that has a tight-fitting lid over medium heat. Add the oil and swirl to coat pan. Add diced onion and garlic and sauté for 5 to 10 minutes, or until softened and translucent.

4. Remove mushrooms from the soaking liquid, saving the liquid. Cut away the tough stems of the mushrooms and discard. Quarter the caps and set aside.

5. Add the mushrooms to the onions and cook for about 2 minutes to brown lightly.

6. Stir in the chard stalks and enough mushroom-soaking liquid and water to equal 1 cup. Cook, covered, over medium heat for 5 minutes, until stalks are almost tender.

7. Stir in the chard leaves, cover, and simmer for 4 to 5 minutes, until the leaves are tender and wilted, but not dull in color. Drain any excess cooking water and save.

8. Season with salt and serve hot. Place the cooking liquid in a small bowl and pass some crusty bread for dipping. Great flavor.

SHIITAKE MUSHROOMS

Shiitake mushrooms are available fresh or dried in Asian or natural foods markets. We found them a little cheaper in Asian markets. Shiitake mushrooms are prized in Asian countries, where they are said to have many medicinal qualities, including as an immune system stimulator and high blood pressure regulator.

Lovely Chard Leaves and Stalks

SERVES 4

1 POUND RED CHARD

1 CUP WATER

2 TEASPOONS EXTRA VIRGIN OLIVE OIL

SALT AND FRESHLY GROUND BLACK PEPPER TO TASTE

1 LEMON, CUT INTO WEDGES

SWISS CHARD

Swiss Chard originated in the Mediterranean region (not Switzerland) and is related to spinach and beets. Its stalks and leaves (instead of the root) were developed from prehistoric times, giving chard its original name of leaf beet, according to historian Waverley Root. As for the name, food historians trying to track how chard acquired its "Swiss" prefix have been unable to find any satisfactory answers.

1. Wash chard well and cut or strip the stalks from the leaves (see page 75). Cut the stalks into 3-inch lengths and cut these into thin strips. Set aside.

2. Roll the leaves into a cigar shape and slice lengthwise into 1-inch strips. Cut the strips crosswise once or twice to reduce length. Set aside.

3. In a skillet, bring the water to a boil. Add the stalks, reduce heat slightly, cover, and cook rather vigorously for 3 to 4 minutes, until tender. There will be a small amount of water left in the pan.

4. Add the leaves with any water clinging to them to the stalks. Cover and continue to cook until wilted and tender, 3 to 4 minutes. Taste to make sure there is no raw edge to the taste and add a bit of water, if necessary, to prevent sticking.

5. Remove from the skillet with a slotted spoon to a serving platter. Drizzle with the olive oil and season with salt and pepper. Arrange the lemon wedges around the edge of the plate in an attractive fashion. Serve immediately, each guest squeezing a bit of lemon onto his or her serving.

Pasta e Ceci with Chard

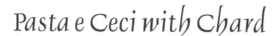

One of Johnna's relatives, Ione Aiello, used to make a satisfying and delicious soup with pasta and chick-peas (ceci). We have eliminated some of the fat and added chard to make a truly delectable soup. Betcha won't have leftovers! Great served with crusty bread and salad.

SERVES 4 TO 6

10 CUPS CHICKEN STOCK

2 ONIONS, DICED

2 LARGE GARLIC CLOVES, MINCED

1½ CUPS CHARD STALKS, SLICED ½ INCH THICK

4 MEATY BACON SLICES, CUT INTO ½-INCH CROSSWISE PIECES (OPTIONAL)

4 CUPS COOKED CHICK-PEAS WITH 1 CUP COOKING LIQUID

1 TEASPOON SALT, OR TO TASTE

1½ CUPS TUBE-SHAPED PASTA (TUBETTI)

¼ CUP CHOPPED FRESH PARSLEY

¼ CUP CHOPPED FRESH BASIL

3 CUPS COARSELY CHOPPED CHARD LEAVES

GRATED PECORINO ROMANO OR PARMIGIANO-REGGIANO TO TASTE

1. In a 7- to 8-quart soup pot, heat ¼ cup of the chicken stock. When stock is bubbling, add the onions and sauté until soft and translucent, about 10 minutes. Add more stock if mixture gets dry.

2. Add garlic and cook 1 more minute. Add all remaining stock and chard stalks. Bring to a boil.

3. Meanwhile, fry bacon (if using) in a medium-size skillet until browned and crispy. Drain on paper towels. Add to the stock along with the chick-peas and their cooking liquid. After the soup has come to a boil, reduce heat and simmer for 10 minutes.

4. Add salt and pasta and cook for 5 minutes. Add parsley, basil, and chard leaves and cook for 5 to 7 minutes, or just until the pasta is *al dente* and the chard is tender.

5. Taste and adjust seasonings. Serve hot with gratings of pecorino romano or Parmigiano-Reggiano.

Authentic Parmesan cheese, Parmigiano-Reggiano, comes from the Emilia-Romagna region of central Italy, around the towns of Parma and Reggio. It is a salty, hard cheese that is excellent for grating but can also be eaten as a table cheese. The flavor is full but not overly pungent or salty. There is no comparison between authentic Parmesan and the commercial cheese found in shakers in American supermarkets.

PECORINO ROMANO

Pecorino romano, from the region of Lazio in south-central Italy, is saltier and more strongly flavored than Pargiano-Reggiano. It is an aged cheese made from sheep's milk. A little goes a long way, offering the diner great flavor for not too many calories.

Pasta with Leeks and Greens

If you are lucky enough to find a farmer's market that sells baby greens such as kale, collards, mizuna, and arugula, these work well. Regular-size kale and collards are too tough for this recipe.

SERVES 4

3 TO 4 TABLESPOONS EXTRA VIRGIN OLIVE OIL

3 LEEKS, WHITE AND LIGHT GREEN PART, WASHED AND THINLY SLICED

3 GARLIC CLOVES, PEELED AND MINCED

2 POUNDS MIXED GREENS (CHARD, ARUGULA, SPINACH, OR BEET GREENS), WASHED, STEMMED, AND COARSELY CHOPPED

1 POUND PASTA

SALT AND PEPPER TO TASTE

GRATED PARMIGIANO-REGGIANO CHEESE TO TASTE

1. In a large skillet or stockpot, heat 3 tablespoons of the oil over medium heat. Add leeks and sauté until very soft, about 10 minutes. Add minced garlic and sauté for 1 more minute. Do not brown the garlic.

2. Add chopped greens and continue cooking for 5 to 8 minutes, until greens are soft and tender. Set aside.

3. Cook pasta with salt according to package instructions. Drain and toss with greens. Moisten mixture with the additional tablespoon of olive oil (or substitute stock). Season to taste with salt, pepper, and Parmesan cheese if desired.

Red and Green Chard with Sweet and Savory Spices

A side dish with an intriguing flavor. It goes well with grilled chicken or fish kabobs and basmati rice.

SERVES 4

- 1 BUNCH SWISS CHARD, STALKS AND GREENS (½ TO ¾ POUND)
- 1 BUNCH RED CHARD, STALKS AND GREENS
- 1 TABLESPOON CANOLA OIL
- 2 MEDIUM ONIONS, SLICED INTO THIN HALF-MOONS
- ⅛ TEASPOON EACH OF GROUND BLACK PEPPER, CINNAMON, CLOVES, AND FRESHLY GRATED NUTMEG
- ½ TEASPOON CORIANDER
- 1 TEASPOON PAPRIKA
- ½ CUP WATER
- SALT TO TASTE

1. Wash each bunch of chard well in a basin of cold water, drain and strip or cut the leaves from the stalks (see page 75). Slice stems crosswise into ½-inch pieces. Set aside. Slice the leaves into ½-inch ribbons and cut again crosswise. Set aside.

2. In a large skillet, heat canola oil over medium-high heat. Add onions and sauté, stirring frequently, until soft and golden, 10 to 15 minutes.

3. When onions are tender, add the spices and stir for 1 minute. Add chard stalks and water. Cover and cook for 5 to 7 minutes, until stalks are just tender.

4. Stir in chard leaves, cover, and cook until wilted, about 8 minutes.

Risotto with Crimini Mushrooms, Sun-dried Tomatoes, and Chard

Risotto is an Italian-style comfort food, creamy and delicious. It's made with arborio rice, a highly glutinous rice imported from Italy. This savory risotto is from Boston caterer Katie Le Lievre.

SERVES 4 AS A MAIN COURSE
OR 6 AS AN APPETIZER

½ CUP SUN-DRIED TOMATOES (NOT PACKED IN OIL)

6 TO 7 CUPS HOT CHICKEN OR VEGETABLE BROTH

3 TABLESPOONS EXTRA VIRGIN OLIVE OIL

2 MEDIUM LEEKS, WHITE AND LIGHT GREEN PART,
WASHED AND SLICED

½ POUND CRIMINI MUSHROOMS, BRUSHED
CLEAN AND SLICED

3 OR 4 FRESH THYME SPRIGS

2 CUPS ARBORIO RICE

½ CUP DRY WHITE WINE

2 CUPS LOOSELY PACKED SWISS CHARD LEAVES THAT
HAVE BEEN WASHED, STRIPPED FROM THEIR STALKS
(SEE PAGE 75), AND SLICED INTO 1/2-INCH STRIPS

½ TEASPOON SALT, OR TO TASTE

⅓ CUP GRATED PARMESAN CHEESE

FRESHLY GROUND BLACK PEPPER TO TASTE

2 TABLESPOONS MINCED FLAT-LEAF PARSLEY

1. Pour boiling water over the sun-dried tomatoes and soak for about 15 minutes, until the tomatoes are soft. Drain, saving liquid, and cut into thin strips.

2. Heat the stock in a saucepan.

3. In a separate 6-quart saucepan, heat the oil over medium heat. Sauté the leeks and mushrooms with the thyme for about 7 minutes.

4. Add the rice and wine and cook until the liquid is absorbed. Continue to cook over medium heat, adding the broth 1 cup at a time. Stir constantly after adding each cup and stir until the liquid is absorbed before adding more broth.

5. Before adding the second-to-last cup of broth, add the tomatoes and chard. Then add the last 2 cups of hot broth, 1 cup at a time. The risotto is done when the rice is tender but still firm to the bite, 25 to 30 minutes altogether. You may need to use more broth or water. Chard should be tender. Taste and add salt to taste; remove thyme stems.

6. Stir in the cheese and black pepper and garnish with the chopped parsley. Serve immediately.

Note: You can substitute part of tomato soaking liquid for part of the broth, if desired.

RISOTTO AND GREENS

You can make endless variations on risotto, using seafood, different vegetables, and different greens. Quick-cooking tender greens such as spinach, chard, arugula, and watercress work best. Kale can also be used if you finely chop the leaves. As in the recipe on this page, greens should be added in the final stages, giving them about 10 minutes to cook. Arugula and watercress wilt very quickly so should be added at the very end.

Spicy Indian Wilted Greens

This deliciously spicy side dish is from our friend Cate Conniff Dobrich at the Culinary Institute of America Greystone in Napa Valley.

SERVES 4

2 TABLESPOONS CANOLA OIL, BUTTER, OR GHEE (CLARIFIED BUTTER)

2 TABLESPOONS MINCED SHALLOTS

1 TABLESPOON GRATED FRESH GINGER

1 TEASPOON GROUND CUMIN

1 TEASPOON GROUND TURMERIC

1 TEASPOON GROUND CORIANDER

1 JALAPEÑO PEPPER, STEMMED, SEEDED, AND MINCED

½ TEASPOON SALT (OPTIONAL)

2 TABLESPOONS WATER

⅓ TO ½ CUP SCALLIONS, WHITE AND GREEN PARTS TRIMMED AND ROUGHLY CHOPPED

1½ POUNDS RED OR GREEN SWISS CHARD LEAVES (ABOUT 12 CUPS), THAT HAVE BEEN WASHED, STRIPPED FROM THEIR STALKS, AND VERY THINLY SLICED (SEE PAGE 75)

VARIATION

Use 1 to 2 tablespoons curry paste in place of the cumin, turmeric, and coriander. The curry paste is convenient to use and adds a rich flavor.

1. In a large skillet or wok, warm oil or butter over low heat. Add shallots, ginger, cumin, turmeric, coriander, jalapeño, and salt and sauté for 3 minutes, stirring occasionally. Do not allow ingredients to burn.

2. Add water and mix with spices in case they stick to pan and to get steaming started. Add scallions and chard and toss with spice mixture. Cover and cook over medium-high heat, allowing greens to wilt. Remove cover periodically to stir. Cook until chard is tender, 6 to 8 minutes. If there is too much liquid, remove cover, turn heat to high, and cook it off, while stirring greens. Serve immediately.

GREENS GLORIOUS GREENS!

Super Simple
Savory Chard

Sometimes the simplest recipes are the best. Of utmost importance is the quality of food used, from the greens to the olive oil. Look for organically grown chard for this recipe and top-quality extra virgin olive oil and you won't be disappointed. If you cannot get organically grown chard, purchase the freshest, liveliest looking bunch of chard possible. The leaf stalks are reserved for another use in this recipe.

SERVES 4

1 ½ POUNDS RED OR SWISS CHARD

1 TABLESPOON EXTRA VIRGIN OLIVE OIL

2 GARLIC CLOVES, THINLY SLICED

2 TABLESPOONS WATER

SALT AND FRESHLY GROUND BLACK PEPPER TO TASTE

1 LEMON, CUT INTO WEDGES

1. Wash the chard leaves and strip the leaves from the stalks (see page 75). Save the stalks for another use.

2. Coarsely chop the greens. In a large skillet or stockpot with a lid, heat oil over medium heat. Add garlic and sauté for about 2 minutes, until golden.

3. Turn heat to medium high. Add greens and stir to coat with oil. Add 2 tablespoons water, cover, and cook until greens are wilted and soft, about 5 minutes.

4. Taste the greens to make sure there is no raw edge to the flavor. Turn off the heat. Season with salt and freshly ground black pepper. Serve hot with fresh lemon wedges for squeezing.

NOTE

After washing well, the leaf stalks can be sliced and added to vegetable soups or they can be cooked on their own— whole or sliced—in a small amount of water. Cook until very tender, season with a dab of olive oil or unsalted butter, and serve.

Vegetable Soup with Swiss Chard

The U.S. Department of Agriculture has issued guidelines calling for a diet that includes at least three ½-cup servings of vegetables daily. That's no problem with soup. When you look at this lengthy list of ingredients, just think of all the vegetables you'll be eating in each bowl. Makes enough for several days.

MAKES 4 1/2 QUARTS, SERVING 8

1 TABLESPOON EXTRA VIRGIN OLIVE OIL

2 MEDIUM-SIZE ONIONS, SLICED

1 LEEK, WHITE AND LIGHT GREEN PART, THINLY SLICED

12 CUPS WATER OR VEGETABLE STOCK

2 CELERY STALKS, SLICED LENGTHWISE AND CUT INTO DIAGONAL SLICES

3 CARROTS, PEELED, CUT LENGTHWISE, AND CUT INTO DIAGONAL SLICES

1 TABLESPOON DRIED OREGANO

1 TABLESPOON DRIED BASIL

½ TEASPOON DRIED THYME

2 BAY LEAVES

4 TABLESPOONS CHOPPED FRESH PARSLEY

2 TEASPOONS SALT, OR TO TASTE

2 EARS OF CORN, KERNELS SCRAPED OFF

1 BUNCH SWISS CHARD STALKS (ABOUT 2 CUPS), SLICED DIAGONALLY

1 YELLOW SQUASH, QUARTERED AND SLICED ON A DIAGONAL

1 CUP GREEN BEANS, CUT INTO 1-INCH PIECES

1 14-OUNCE CAN CRUSHED TOMATOES

1 CUP UNCOOKED PASTA SHELLS OR TUBETTI

3 CUPS SWISS CHARD LEAVES THAT HAVE BEEN WASHED, STRIPPED FROM THEIR STALKS (SEE PAGE 75), AND SLICED INTO STRIPS

1 CUP COOKED CHICK-PEAS, OR KIDNEY OR WHITE BEANS

PARMESAN CHEESE TO TASTE

1. In a large stockpot, heat oil and sauté onions and leek for 10 to 15 minutes, until golden and sweet.

2. Add water or stock, celery, carrots, herbs, 2 tablespoons of the fresh parsley, and salt. Bring to a boil and simmer, partially covered, for about 15 minutes.

3. Add corn, chard stalks, squash, green beans, and tomatoes and simmer for another 10 minutes. Turn up heat. Add pasta and cook for 5 minutes. Add Swiss chard leaves and simmer for 5 minutes longer, or until pasta is just cooked and chard is tender. Add the cooked beans and last 2 tablespoons of parsley.

4. Taste and adjust seasonings. Serve each bowl with a sprinkling of Parmesan cheese.

Ghee, a nutty-tasting Indian-style clarified butter, is easily made at home, although it can be purchased in Indian markets and some well-stocked natural foods stores. To make ghee at home, place 2 sticks (½ pound) unsalted butter in a heavy 1-quart saucepan. Melt slowly over medium-low heat. Reduce heat to low and continue to cook the ghee for 30 to 40 minutes, until the milk solids start to brown very slightly on the bottom of the pan. Remove immediately from heat and strain through a small, fine-mesh strainer into a clean heatproof glass or ceramic jar. The milk solids will be caught in the strainer.

Ghee has a much longer shelf life than fresh butter because it is pure fat. It will keep indefinitely, even at room temperature. What makes fresh butter turn rancid rather quickly are the milk residues that remain in the butter.

The taste of ghee is absolutely delicious, fragrant and nutty.

Swiss Chard with Ghee

Ghee is rich in calories—like all other fats—but the flavor is so distinctive that a small amount is sufficient.

SERVES 4

1 POUND GREEN SWISS CHARD OR RED CHARD OR
    A COMBINATION
½ MEDIUM RED OR YELLOW ONION
1 TO 2 TEASPOONS GHEE
½ CUP WATER
HERBAMARE (SEE PAGE 29) OR SEA SALT TO TASTE

1. Wash the chard leaves and strip the leaves form the stalks (see page 75). Slice stalks crosswise into ½-inch pieces. Set aside. Cut leaves into thin pieces and set aside, separate from the cut stems. Slice the onion into thin crescents.

2. Heat a large stainless steel skillet over medium-high heat. Add the ghee and swirl to coat bottom of pan. Add the onions and sauté over medium heat for 5 minutes. Take care to avoid burning.

3. Add chard stalks and the water. Cook for 3 minutes. Add the leaves and steam for 4 to 5 minutes, until leaves have wilted but are still bright green.

4. Sprinkle with salt if desired, toss gently, and serve hot or at room temperature.

Turkey Loaf with Greens

This recipe is chock-full of vegetables and great flavor. It is low in fat and delicious. Because only the chard leaves are used, reserve the stalks for soup or for braised chard stalks. Although the recipe calls for a pie pan, you can also make this in a loaf pan, which makes it especially good for slicing for sandwiches.

SERVES 4 TO 6

1 ⅓ POUNDS GROUND NATURAL TURKEY BREAST

½ CUP MINCED ONION

¾ CUP FRESH WHOLE WHEAT BREAD CRUMBS

1 EGG OR 2 EGG WHITES

⅓ CUP MINCED CELERY

3 TABLESPOONS CHOPPED FRESH PARSLEY

1 CUP FINELY CHOPPED SWISS CHARD LEAVES THAT HAVE BEEN WASHED AND STRIPPED FROM THEIR STALKS (SEE PAGE 75)

½ TEASPOON MINCED FRESH GARLIC

¼ CUP LOW-FAT MILK OR NONDAIRY BEVERAGE

½ TEASPOON SALT

FRESHLY GROUND WHITE OR BLACK PEPPER TO TASTE

½ TEASPOON DRIED THYME

½ TEASPOON DRIED OREGANO

½ TEASPOON DRIED BASIL

DIJON MUSTARD AS NEEDED FOR TOP

1. Preheat oven to 350°F. Oil a 9-inch pie plate and set aside.

2. In a medium-size bowl, mix all ingredients except mustard. Pat mixture into the prepared pie plate.

3. Spread top with a thin layer of Dijon mustard and bake for 45 minutes, or until meat begins to pull away from sides of pan. Allow to stand for 10 minutes before cutting into wedges. Serve with additional mustard, if desired.

FRESH BREAD CRUMBS

To make fresh bread crumbs, place 3 pieces whole wheat sandwich bread in a food processor fitted with the metal blade. Process for about 1 minute, until bread crumbs are formed.

GROUND TURKEY

Turkey breast is the leanest of all meats, with just 1 gram of fat per 3½-ounce serving. If preground turkey is unavailable, have your butcher grind skinned turkey breast meat. Most ground turkey on the market includes dark meat and skin, so check with your butcher or read the label.

Sautéed Chard and Salmon

A quick, easy, and very tasty dinner featuring greens.

SKINNING THE SALMON

Have the fishmonger skin the salmon for you or do it yourself. It's easy. Using a very sharp slicing or boning knife, cut and lift one edge of the skin off the flesh of the salmon. Carefully pull back the skin by grasping the edge with the fingers of the left hand and holding down the pink flesh with the other hand. The skin should strip off quite easily without tearing the flesh.

SERVES 3 TO 4

1 POUND SALMON FILLET, SKINNED

FRESHLY GROUND BLACK OR WHITE PEPPER TO TASTE

JUICE OF ½ LEMON

1 TEASPOON TAMARI

1 TEASPOON TOASTED (DARK) SESAME OIL

1 POUND ORGANIC SWISS CHARD

4 TEASPOONS EXTRA VIRGIN OLIVE OIL OR CANOLA OIL

1 MEDIUM ONION, SLICED INTO THIN CRESCENTS

3 GARLIC CLOVES, THINLY SLICED

SEA SALT TO TASTE

RED RADISHES CUT INTO DECORATIVE SHAPES FOR GARNISH

1. Cut the salmon fillet into 6 to 8 pieces using a sharp knife at a 45- degree angle to slice through the flesh. Place on plate and season to taste with the pepper. Squeeze on the lemon juice, then drizzle on the tamari and sesame oil. Turn pieces over to coat all surfaces. Set aside while you prepare the greens.

2. Wash the chard and cut or strip the leaves from the stalks (see page 75). Slice stalks crosswise into ¼-inch pieces. Set aside. Chop the leaves coarsely; set aside, separate from the chopped stalks.

3. In a large skillet, heat 2 teaspoons of the oil over medium-high heat. Add the onion and sauté for 5 to 7 minutes, until soft and translucent. Reduce heat if onions are cooking too fast. Add garlic and cook for 1 minute.

4. Stir in chard stems and 2 to 3 tablespoons water. Cover and cook for 2 minutes. Stir greens into onion mixture, cover, and

cook for 3 to 5 minutes, stirring frequently. When ready, greens should be tender and still bright green. Sprinkle with a pinch of salt and stir. Remove to a platter.

5. In a skillet, heat the remaining 2 teaspoons oil over medium-high heat. Add the salmon pieces in a single layer and cook for 1 to 2 minutes a side; do not overcook. Pour any extra juices from plate onto cooking salmon. When salmon is cooked, place on top of greens. Serve immediately, garnished with the red radishes.

Greens:
A Nutritional Profile

Dark leafy green vegetables pack a powerful nutritional punch you could not fully replicate by taking nutritional supplements. This is because greens contain not only traditional nutrients important in maintaining good health, but also a lengthy list of micronutrients—often called phytochemicals—thought to protect against cancer and other diseases.

A number of the leafy greens are members of the *Brassica*—or *Cruciferae*—family, which has gotten a lot of attention from researchers for its role in disease prevention. Cruciferous leafy greens include kale, collards, cabbage, bok choy, mustard and turnip greens, and watercress. Most leafy greens contain very high amounts of vitamin A, as well as vitamins C and E, all considered antioxidant nutrients in the body that may help neutralize unstable, cancer-promoting oxygen molecules known as free radicals.

Leafy greens are a good source of fiber and essential minerals, especially calcium and iron.

"Greens are a very substantial source of calcium," says Louise Gittleman, nutritionist and author of *Supernutrition for Women* (New York: Bantam, 1991). "We make the mistake of thinking there is only dairy calcium. There are some wonderful sources of nondairy calcium, and greens are a very good high source. Some of the greens I'm fond of that have appreciable amounts of calcium include cooked beet greens, kale, dandelion greens, collards, parsely, turnip greens, and watercress."

Greens also supply magnesium, which Gittleman says we are "notoriously deficient in." Magnesium is involved in more biochemical responses in the system than any other mineral, she says. "It is also a helper to calcium."

Leafy greens are also cited as a source for folacin (folic acid), which helps prevent neural tube defects in newborns.

A host of other micronutrients in greens may also be responsible for preventing disease, but researchers have not yet been able to isolate and identify these key compounds. The compounds—called phytochemicals—include indoles and flavonoids, as well as carotenoids, a family of nutrients that includes beta-carotene.

Until recently, scientists had focused on beta-carotene as a supernutrient with a multitude of health benefits. Now there is thought that it may not be beta-carotene alone, but beta-carotene working in combination with its carotenoid relatives (phytochemicals) that provides these health benefits.

"When we eat leafy greens it's not just beta-carotene we're getting but a whole bunch of carotenoids," says Norman Krinsky, an authority on antioxidants and professor of biochemistry at Tufts University School of Medicine in Boston. "Beta-carotene is only about 20 percent of total carotenoids in green leafy vegetables."

There are 500 to 600 carotenoids, including beta-carotene and others that include lutein, lyocene, and zeaxantin, found in plants. Researchers are looking at these nutrients for their antioxidant properties, their effect on the immune system, and their cancer-prevention properties.

Carotenoids are prominent in many leafy greens. The ten top sources of carotenoids include cooked kale, collard greens, Swiss chard, and cooked and raw spinach. "The darker green the vegetable, the richer in carotenoids," says Gene Giunti, a registered dietitian from Boston. Other sources include carrots, tomatoes, sweet potato, and watermelon. Researchers believe that carotenoids may work in the body in tandem with other phytochemicals to boost the activity of enzyme systems that detoxify carcinogens.

Although researchers and scientists can point to many studies showing that consumption of fruits and vegetables reduces the risk of cancer and other illnesses, they cannot accurately identify which of these micronutrients in specific fruits or vegetables play a part in preventing diseases.

"There are a variety of compounds and we're not sure what are the protective factors," says Dr. Regina Ziegler, who studies the relationship between carotenoids and cancer at the National Cancer Institute in Bethesda, Maryland. "Until we have them identified, we have to eat a variety of fruits and vegetables."

These benefits will more likely come from eating the whole fruit and vegetable rather than from taking a supplement, suggests nutritionist Giunti. "You can't really isolate these compounds from vegetables and expect them to work. There are literally hundreds of these phytochemicals. To really get the maximum benefit, you want to eat the whole foods. There could be a synergy occurring that's not yet known."

Chinese Greens

THE GREAT DIVERSITY AMONG CHINESE VEGETABLES GIVES the cook new flavors and new challenges. We found some delicious-tasting and beautiful-looking varieties in Asian markets in ethnic neighborhoods, at farmstands and farmer's markets, and even in supermarkets. We tended to cook many in a wok because that is the quintessential Chinese method of cooking vegetables. Plus it's quick and easy. Almost all these greens can be stir-fried by themselves or in combination with other vegetables. It's easy to become overwhelmed with the multitude of names (many for the same vegetable) and varieties, so just start with one or two and move on from there. Be adventurous!

Bok Choy

Bok choy, also commonly called pak choi, has long ivory (celery-like) stalks and dark green leaves that are loaded with calcium, the antioxidant vitamins A, C, and E, and with folic acid. Besides the commonly available white-stemmed bok choy, there are several other types, including a light-green, stemmed type called Shanghai pak choi and a variety referred to as "soup spoon" because of its ladle-shaped stalks. Both are considered to have a better flavor than ordinary bok choy. "Baby" bok choy may be any one of these types, harvested after only a month or so, resulting in a tiny, tender, and delicately flavored vegetable.

Bok choy has a high water content, especially in the white leaf stalks, and lends itself to quick-cooking techniques, such as stir-frying. In 3 to 4 minutes you can have a side dish of stir-fry bok choy with ginger, garlic, and red pepper. In cooking, the white of bok choy remains crisp yet succulent, and the leaves become tender but remain bright green. The taste and texture of the vegetable goes well with Asian seasonings such as tamari or shoyu (naturally brewed soy sauce), toasted sesame oil, and hot red peppers.

Bok choy can be sliced and eaten raw in salads, or simmered in soups as well. In China, bok choy is dried and used to flavor soups. See page 34 for recipes.

Choy Sum

One of the most popular vegetables in China, choy sum is a flowering *Brassica* that resembles a bunch of thin broccoli stalks topped with dark green rounded leaves interspersed with tiny yellow flowers. *Choy* is the Chinese word for vegetable; *sum* means "flowering stem." Members of this family include Chinese oil vegetable and Chinese flowering cabbage.

The tender stalks are the favored part of the vegetable, but all parts—leaves and flowers—are edible. Choy sum is quick and easy to prepare and requires little fat or flavorings to be delectable. It can be stir-fried by itself in a little oil, steamed or boiled in a small amount of water, or stir-fried with other vegetables or meat.

Chinese Broccoli

Chinese broccoli is another Asian vegetable with edible stalks, leaves, and flowers, close in appearance to choy sum. Chinese broccoli has thicker, meatier stalks, ½ to ¾ inch wide. And its flowers are larger and usually white. It is also known as white flowering broccoli, or gai lan.

We love to stir-fry Chinese broccoli, either by itself—to serve with a black bean sauce—or with other vegetables, chicken, or meat. It has a delicate flavor, without a hint of bitterness. Better than regular broccoli!

Chinese Cabbage

There are two types of Chinese cabbage, both easily recognized and available in supermarkets: napa, which has a barrel-shaped head, and Michihili, which has a taller and thinner cylindrical head.

Napa has pale green and white overlapping leaves that are sometimes wrinkled, with wide leaf stalks. Michihili, often labeled as Chinese cabbage in markets, has elongated light green leaves.

All parts—the leaf, midrib, and white base—are tender and edible. These Chinese cabbages have a light, mild taste. Thinly sliced, they make a delicious and crunchy salad vegetable dressed with Asian flavorings such as sesame oil, rice vinegar, and soy sauce. We also like Chinese cabbage stir-fried with garlic, ginger, and a touch of soy sauce or toasted sesame oil. More delicate than European cabbages, Chinese cabbage should be quick-cooked (not boiled) to maintain its flavor.

The leaves can be kept whole and used to wrap fish for vegetables or shredded for soups.

Pea Shoots

A delicacy, in both Western and Asian cuisines, pea shoots are the tendrils and top leaves of the snow pea plant. Tender and delicious with a fresh pea flavor, they can be used raw in salads or lightly sautéed or stir-fried. Sautéed pea shoots make a tasty bed for fish or chicken.

Tatsoi

Tatsoi is a beautiful vegetable with tiny paddle-shaped leaves (similar in color to bok choy leaves) and pale greenish-white stalks. Also known as flat cabbage or rosette pak choi, it grows close to the ground, sometimes flat, in concentric circles like rose petals.

Tatsoi is so compact that you can stir-fry it whole, without cutting the leaf from the stalk, for a stunning presentation. We cooked it in this manner with sesame oil, ginger, and garlic with shrimp and a light sauce. We have also grilled tatsoi pieces and drizzled them with a bit of salad dressing.

Tender young tatsoi is often part of a mesclun salad mix. It is also added to soups. A cold-resistant vegetable like kale, tatsoi may taste best in the fall after a frost.

Mustard Greens

Chinese mustard greens come in a number of varieties and all manner of shapes and sizes. They have a characteristically sharp flavor, mellowed by cooking.

We are particularly enamored with a Japanese variety called red giant mustard, still uncommon outside of farmers' markets and home gardens. It has a lovely purplish-red-and-green color, and resembles a romaine lettuce leaf in size and shape. In cooking, it retains its color, and is more tender and less stringy than the more common Western mustard greens. We sautéed red giant mustard with just garlic and olive oil with great results. It has a spicy, mustard flavor that is somehow more appealing than other mustard varieties. The young and tenderest red giant mustard leaves are commonly found in mesclun salad mixes. The baby red giant leaves make a nice addition to sandwiches. "Better than mustard from a jar," reports Shepherd's garden seed catalog.

Mizuna

Mizuna is a mustard green of Chinese origin, but has been grown for hundreds of years in Japan and is considered a Japanese vegetable. It is a feathery and elegant leafy green, with thin white juicy stalks and deeply cut, dark green serrated leaves. Mizuna means "water/juicy vegetable" in Japanese. It is milder and more delicate tasting than other mustards, but still packs enough flavor to make it noticeable. You can add mizuna to salads of all kinds. It brings a mild mustard taste, and a beautiful texture. From Shepherd's: "Once you try mizuna, your salads will seem incomplete without it." Mizuna can also be added to stir-fries and soups.

Water Spinach

Although unrelated to spinach, Asian water spinach has reminiscent elongated, arrowhead-shaped leaves and long, hollow stalks. The Mandarin name for water spinach, *kong xin cai*, translates into "empty heart/stem vegetable." It is also called kangcong or swamp cabbage because it thrives near water. It is very perishable and should be used within 1 or 2 days for best results.

Both the stalks and leaves are eaten, but the crisp stalks take longer to cook. The leaves can be separated for cooking, and, like spinach, shrink considerably when cooked. You can add the leaves to miso broth or other soups. The Chinese flavor water spinach with garlic or a sauce and serve it with beef, pork, or shrimp.

Chinese Cabbage and Collard Greens

A nice contrast in color and texture. Caramelized onions contribute a rich, deep flavor that brings East and West together.

SERVES 3 TO 4

2 TABLESPOONS EXTRA VIRGIN OLIVE OIL

3 MEDIUM ONIONS, SLICED

1 GARLIC CLOVE, MINCED

1 BUNCH COLLARD GREENS, WASHED, STEMMED, AND SHREDDED TO EQUAL 4 CUPS (SEE PAGE 117)

4 CUPS CHOPPED CHINESE CABBAGE (NAPA OR CELERY CABBAGE)

SALT TO TASTE

1. In a large skillet, heat the oil over medium heat. Add the onions and cook for 20 to 30 minutes to caramelize. Do not burn. Reduce heat if necessary. Add garlic and sauté for 1 to 2 minutes.

2. Precook the collard greens by bringing 2 cups water to a boil in a large skillet that has a tight-fitting lid. Add the shredded collards and cook for 7 minutes. Add the Chinese cabbage and cook for an additional minute.

3. Remove greens with a slotted spoon to rid them of any excess liquid. Add to caramelized onions. Toss and heat through.

4. Season to taste with salt and serve hot.

Chinese Cabbage Salad

Colorful and crunchy, this salad is best served the day it's made to preserve its crisp texture. Jicama, a brown root vegetable the shape of a large turnip, has a crisp, juicy flesh like that of an apple, and flavor as mild as the cabbages. Both benefit from the assertive sesame flavoring. Don't forget the sesame seeds!

SERVES 4 TO 6

DRESSING:

4 TABLESPOONS RICE OR WHITE WINE VINEGAR

2 TABLESPOONS LIGHT SESAME OIL

2 TEASPOONS TOASTED (DARK) SESAME OIL

3 TEASPOONS TAMARI OR SHOYU

1 CUP THINLY SLICED RED CABBAGE

2 CUPS JULIENNED JICAMA

1 CUP JULIENNED CARROTS

3 CUPS THINLY SLICED NAPA OR CHINESE CABBAGE

2 SCALLIONS, WHITE AND GREEN PARTS, THINLY SLICED ON THE DIAGONAL

2 TABLESPOONS TOASTED SESAME SEEDS

1. In a bowl, whisk together the vinegar, sesame oils, and soy sauce.

2. Add the sliced red cabbage to the dressing for 15 to 20 minutes to marinate and soften while you cut the other vegetables.

3. Peel jicama and slice into ⅛-inch slices. Stack a couple of slices and cut into matchsticks about ⅛-inch wide. Peel carrots and cut thinly on the diagonal. Cut each diagonal into matchsticks. Combine the jicama, carrots, Chinese cabbage, and scallions in a bowl. Add the sliced red cabbage and dressing and mix well. Top with toasted sesame seeds.

TOASTING SESAME SEEDS

Toasting brings out the flavor of sesame seeds. Heat a heavy-bottomed skillet or cast-iron pan over medium-high heat. Add one layer of seeds (no need to add oil) and stir constantly until seeds darken slightly, begin popping, and emit a fragrant sesame aroma. This takes 5 to 7 minutes.

Chinese Broccoli with Black Bean Sauce

Chinese broccoli, also called flowering broccoli or gai lan, is a delicious green with edible stalks, leaves, and white flowers (resembling thinner-stalked broccoli or broccoli rabe). The sauce uses fermented black beans, which you can purchase very cheaply at the Asian market when you are buying greens.

SERVES 4

1 BUNCH CHINESE BROCCOLI

2 TABLESPOONS RINSED AND FINELY CHOPPED FERMENTED BLACK BEANS

½ CUP CHICKEN OR VEGETABLE STOCK

1 TABLESPOON SESAME, PEANUT, OR CANOLA OIL

2 TEASPOONS MINCED FRESH GARLIC

2 TEASPOONS MINCED FRESH GINGER

2 TEASPOONS ARROWROOT OR KUZU

3 TABLESPOONS WATER

2 TEASPOONS PURE MAPLE SYRUP OR OTHER SWEETENER

2 TEASPOONS SHOYU OR TAMARI (NATURALLY BREWED SOY SAUCE)

1. Before washing Chinese broccoli, cut off the bottom ½ to 1 inch of the stalks and discard. Plunge the remaining bunch into a bowl of cold water, swish around and drain in a colander. Cut all of the broccoli—florets, stalks, and any leaves on the stalks— into 1-inch pieces.

2. Assemble and prepare all the ingredients before stir-frying. Use a mortar and pestle, blender, or the back of a fork to press the black beans into a paste. Gradually incorporate the chicken or vegetable stock. Set aside.

3. In a large wok, heat oil and swirl to coat pan. Add the garlic and ginger and stir-fry for 15 seconds. Add the Chinese broccoli, florets, stalks, and leaves and stir-fry over high heat for 1 to 2

minutes. Add black beans and chicken or vegetable stock, cover, and cook for 4 to 5 minutes, until tender but still slightly crunchy and bright green.

4. Dissolve the arrowroot or kuzu in the water. Add sweetener and shoyu to the arrowroot mixture.

5. When the greens are cooked, stir in the arrowroot or kuzu mixture over high heat. Stir for another minute until sauce is thickened and glossy. Add more tamari to taste, if desired. Serve immediately.

ARROWROOT AND KUZU

Arrowroot and Kuzu are interchangeable thickening agents used as an alternative to cornstarch. They are dissolved in cold water and then heated to thicken. Kuzu lends a glossier appearance to sauces, and reportedly has medicinal properties. It is imported only from Japan and is very expensive.

Quick and Easy Choy Sum (Chinese Flowering Cabbage)

Chinese flowering cabbage is a tender, leafy green that is quick and easy to prepare and requires little fat or flavoring to be delectable. The variety used in this recipe measures 12 to 15 inches and the stalks are greenish and slightly grooved. They offer a crisp tender contrast to the wilted green leaves when cooked quickly. The recipe can also be made with another variety of Chinese flowering cabbage, Chinese broccoli, which measures 6 to 7 inches high and has white, slightly grooved stalks.

VARIATION

Add a slightly hot dimension with hot chili peppers such as jalapeño. Mince pepper and stir-fry in oil for 15 seconds before adding the Chinese flowering cabbage.

SERVES 3 TO 4

1 BUNCH CHINESE FLOWERING CABBAGE

EXTRA VIRGIN OLIVE OIL, CANOLA OR LIGHT SESAME OIL

SALT TO TASTE

1 TABLESPOON WATER, OR CHICKEN OR VEGETABLE STOCK

1. Wash the cabbage well in a large basin of cold water. Lift greens from water and drain in a colander.

2. Chop greens and stalks into ½-inch pieces and set aside.

3. Heat a large wok over high heat. Lightly brush the wok with the desired oil and immediately add the greens. Stir-fry continuously to cook the greens evenly, about 2 minutes. Season with salt, stir to distribute salt, and add the water. Cover the wok and cook for another minute or so, until the green leaves are wilted and the stalks crisp-tender.

4. Taste and adjust seasonings if necessary. Serve hot.

Red Giant Mustard Greens Divine

Red giant mustard greens are very delectable. The leaves are more tender than those of the more common curly edged green mustard greens, and the flavor is a little less pungent. The red giant leaves are variegated green and purple; some leaves are even almost completely dark purple. Combined with a bit of garlic and extra virgin olive oil, these greens are fabulous and require no precooking. The taste is mustardy and rich.

SERVES 2

1 POUND RED GIANT MUSTARD GREENS

1 TABLESPOON EXTRA VIRGIN OLIVE OIL

1 TEASPOON MINCED GARLIC

PINCH OF SALT

1. Wash greens well and remove and discard stalks. Coarsely chop. Set aside.

2. Heat a large skillet that has a tight-fitting lid over medium-high heat. Add the olive oil and swirl to coat pan. Add garlic and cook briefly, about 30 seconds. Do not burn.

3. Add prepared greens, with the water still clinging to leaves. Stir to coat with the oil and garlic. Cover and cook over medium heat until wilted and tender but still bright in color, 4 to 5 minutes, stirring occasionally.

4. Season to taste with salt and serve hot or at room temperature.

Sesame Pasta Salad
with Mizuna

Japanese udon noodles, shaped like fettuccine, are made from soft wheat flour rather than durum wheat. Their smooth but firm texture won't break apart in a pasta salad. Other pasta substitutes will also work.

SERVES 4

2 CUPS MIZUNA LEAVES THAT HAVE BEEN WASHED AND STEMMED

1 CARROT

¼ CUP THINLY SLICED SCALLIONS, WHITE AND GREEN PARTS

1 RED PEPPER, CORED AND SEEDED

1 8-OUNCE PACKAGE UDON NOODLES

2 TABLESPOONS LIGHT SESAME OIL

1 TABLESPOON TOASTED (DARK) SESAME OIL

1 TEASPOON FRESH GINGER JUICE (OPTIONAL, SEE PAGE 63)

2 TABLESPOONS TAMARI SOY SAUCE

2 TABLESPOONS TOASTED SESAME SEEDS

1. Chop mizuna into pieces about 1 inch long. Cut the carrot on a sharp diagonal into ⅛-inch rounds and chop each round into ⅛-inch matchsticks (or shred). Slice the scallions on the diagonal. Thinly slice red pepper.

2. Bring a large pot of water to a boil. Add udon and cook according to package directions. Drain the pasta and rinse under cold water until totally cooled. Drain again.

3. Place pasta in a large mixing bowl and toss with carrot, mizuna, red pepper, and scallions. Mix in sesame oils, ginger juice, soy sauce to taste, and sesame seeds.

4. Taste and adjust seasonings. Place in a serving bowl.

Stir-Fry Napa Cabbage with Ginger

This is a side dish Elizabeth Germain makes in her cooking classes, based out of her Cambridge, Massachusetts, home. We love the crunchiness of the napa cabbage and sesame seeds. Plus, it's easy to make and low in fat!

SERVES 3 TO 4

1 SMALL HEAD NAPA CABBAGE (6 TO 7 CUPS, CHOPPED)

1 CARROT

3 SCALLIONS

1 TEASPOON CANOLA OIL

1 TABLESPOON MINCED GINGER

PINCH OF SEA SALT

1 HANDFUL OF CILANTRO LEAVES

½ TEASPOON TOASTED (DARK) SESAME OIL

2 TABLESPOONS TOASTED SESAME SEEDS

1. Cut the cabbage lengthwise into quarters. Thinly slice each quarter on the diagonal. Cut the carrot on a sharp diagonal into rounds and chop each round into matchsticks. Thinly slice top green parts of the scallions on the diagonal (save the white part for another use).

2. Heat a wok over high heat. Add canola oil and swirl to coat the pan. Add the ginger and stir-fry for 30 seconds. Add the carrot and stir-fry for 1 minute. Add the cabbage and a pinch of salt. Stir-fry for 2 to 3 minutes, until the cabbage has wilted but is still crisp.

3. Remove wok from flame and toss in scallions and cilantro leaves. Sprinkle the toasted sesame oil and toasted sesame seeds over the top. Serve immediately.

Stir-Fried Shrimp with Tatsoi

*This attractive dish will be devoured by adults and children alike.
Tatsoi is a lovely plant that has a rosette shape. Sometimes tatsoi is
called Chinese flat cabbage because it grows close to the ground,
sometimes flat, and its leaves form themselves into
concentric circles like rose petals.*

SERVES 4

1 BUNCH TATSOI

4 TEASPOONS LIGHT SESAME OIL

2 TEASPOONS MINCED GARLIC

2 TEASPOONS PEELED, MINCED FRESH GINGER

1 POUND MEDIUM SHRIMP, PEELED AND DEVEINED

1 RED PEPPER, CUT INTO ¼-INCH STRIPS

¼ CUP MINCED SCALLIONS, WHITE AND GREEN PARTS

SAUCE:

2 TABLESPOONS TAMARI (NATURALLY BREWED
  SOY SAUCE)

2 TABLESPOONS MIRIN OR SHERRY

1 TEASPOON TOASTED (DARK) SESAME OIL

½ CUP SHRIMP, VEGETABLE, OR CHICKEN STOCK

1 TABLESPOON ARROWROOT POWDER

1. Separate tatsoi leaf stalks from base, and use whole, leaving
the leaf attached to the stalk. Wash well.

2. In a large, 13-inch wok, heat 2 teaspoons of the oil over high
heat. Do not let it smoke. Add 1 teaspoon each of the minced
garlic and ginger. Add shrimp and stir-fry until just pink, 2 to 3
minutes. Remove shrimp to a bowl.

3. Add 1 more teaspoon oil to the wok; add another teaspoon
each of the garlic and ginger, then the red pepper and scallions.

Stir-fry for 5 seconds. Toss in the tatsoi and stir-fry for 2 minutes, until wilted. Do not overcook because this can make the vegetable tough. Remove to the bowl with the shrimp.

4. Place sauce ingredients in the wok and cook until clear and thickened, about 1 minute. Return shrimp and vegetables to wok and toss to combine with sauce.

5. Serve hot over rice.

VARIATIONS

❖ *Add red pepper flakes for a spicier taste.*

❖ *Add chunks of fresh pineapple with some juice for a sweet taste. Or use pineapple juice instead of stock.*

Stir-Fry Tatsoi with Three Peppers

Bright and colorful, this dish makes a nice addition to any meal. Even if you have only one color of sweet pepper, the taste will be delicious. This is a good preparation also for bok choy, baby bok choy, or Shanghai pak choi.

ORIENTAL VEGETABLES

To help you through the maze of more than 100 varieties of Chinese and Japanese vegetables, we recommend Joy Larkcom's book Oriental Vegetables: The Complete Guide for Garden and Kitchen *(New York: Kodansha, 1991). It's quite instructional, not only for growing and cooking the vegetables, but also for learning their origins, names, and customary uses.*

SERVES 2 TO 3

2 TEASPOONS LIGHT SESAME OIL

½ SWEET RED PEPPER, JULIENNED

½ YELLOW PEPPER, JULIENNED

½ ORANGE PEPPER, JULIENNED

1 TEASPOON MINCED GARLIC CLOVES

1 TEASPOON MINCED FRESH GINGER

1 BUNCH TATSOI, WASHED WELL, LEAVES LEFT WHOLE WITH 1 TO 2 INCHES OF STALK ATTACHED

SALT TO TASTE

1. Heat a large wok over high heat. Add oil, swirl to coat wok, and immediately add the peppers and cook for 1 minute.

2. Add garlic and ginger and cook for 30 seconds, stirring constantly.

3. Add tatsoi, mix well to coat with oil, cover, and cook for 2 to 3 minutes, or until crisp-tender. Do not overcook.

4. Season with 2 pinches of salt and serve hot.

Tatsoi on the Grill

*This recipe goes well with grilled chicken kabobs or grilled polenta.
As part of a grilled vegetable platter, this tatsoi dish will
serve more than two to three people.*

SERVES 2 TO 3

1 BUNCH TATSOI

EXTRA VIRGIN OLIVE OIL OR CANOLA OIL

FAVORITE SALAD DRESSING AS DESIRED

1. Wash the bunch of tatsoi in a large basin of cool water. Make
sure there is no dirt lodged at the base of the stalks. After assessing the size of the tatsoi, cut into halves or quarters lengthwise so
that you have a nice group of leaves together, still joined at the
root end.

2. Preheat your grill—either outdoor or stovetop.

3. Brush tatsoi sections with oil. Place on hot grill and cook until
slightly tender, wilted, and browned here and there. Taste for
tenderness. Do not overcook.

4. When ready, brush lightly with salad dressing to serve hot or
at room temperature.

INDOOR GRILLING

*Le Creuset makes a
fantastic cast-iron
stovetop grill that works
great when the weather
is too cold to grill
outside. The grill covers
two burners and reverses
to a griddle on the other
side. It works on gas or
electric. We use it to
grill fish, meat, greens,
and other vegetables all
year.*

Shanghai Pac Choi with Carrots and Daikon

Shanghai pac choi is a light green, stemmed variation of bok choy. Bok choy, baby bok choy, or tatsoi would all work in this stir-fry. Be careful not to overcook. For optimum flavor, choose apple cider, if available, for the sauce.

SERVES 2 TO 3

1 BUNCH PAC CHOI, WASHED WELL

SAUCE:

⅓ CUP APPLE CIDER OR APPLE JUICE

2 TABLESPOONS SHOYU OR TAMARI (NATURALLY BREWED SOY SAUCE)

1 TEASPOON BROWN RICE VINEGAR

1 TABLESPOON ARROWROOT POWDER

1 TABLESPOON CANOLA OIL OR LIGHT SESAME OIL

2 TEASPOONS MINCED FRESH GINGER

2 GARLIC CLOVES, MINCED

1 CUP JULIENNED DAIKON RADISH

1 CUP JULIENNED CARROT

1 CUP MUNG BEAN SPROUTS

1. Separate stalks of the pac choi and slice leaves from the stalks. Cut stalks into ½-inch pieces and slice leaves into ½-inch ribbons. Set aside.

2. Combine the apple cider, soy sauce, vinegar, and arrowroot in a medium-size bowl. Set aside while you prepare the ginger, garlic, daikon, and carrot.

3. Heat a large wok over high heat. Add the oil and swirl to coat wok. Add the ginger and garlic and stir-fry for 10 seconds. Add the daikon, carrots, and pac choi stalks. Stir-fry for 1 minute.

4. Stir in the greens with 1 tablespoon of water, if necessary, to prevent burning. Cover and cook over high heat for 2 to 3 minutes, stirring frequently. Stir in bean sprouts.

5. Recombine sauce ingredients and add to vegetables. Cook just until clear and thickened. Serve immediately.

Both shoyu and tamari are traditional Japanese soy seasonings. We prefer them to commercial supermarket soy sauce, which is quickly made using hydrolized vegetable protein (from soybeans) and hydrochloric acid. Commercial soy sauce usually contains preservatives, caramel coloring, salt, and corn syrup for flavor and coloring.

Shoyu and tamari are traditionally made using soybeans, salt, water, and a soy-derivative called koji, and are aged for a year or two. Like wine, there are varieties of shoyu and tamari with a range in flavors.

Shoyu and tamari can be used interchangeably, although tamari is stronger and generally used more in cooking than for table use. Tamari is fermented with soy koji rather than wheat koji, which is why you will see "wheat free" varieties.

Collard Greens

Outside the South, few people have adopted this healthy, strapping green into their cooking repertoire. We've found very few recipes aside from the traditional southern "mess of greens": 1 to 3 hours of cooking ample quantities of collard greens in a large pot of water flavored with smoked ham or ham hock. Not a task geared to busy people looking for a quick greens side dish for dinner. Luckily, there are quick, easy, and low-fat ways to cook collards that taste great, too.

Nutritionally, collards are a goldmine. According to the USDA Composition of Foods, collard greens outrank broccoli, spinach, and mustard greens in nutritional value. A cruciferous, cancer-fighting vegetable along with kale and broccoli, collard greens are low in calories, high in fiber, and rich in beta-carotene, vitamin C, calcium, and B vitamins.

Depending on the cooking method, collards can have a mild, likable taste—though not as sweet as kale. There's no bitterness to them. We asked a longtime South Carolina collards grower to describe the taste of collards, and she had a hard time. "Hmm," she said hesitating. "I don't know; just say they taste good."

We find collard greens taste too grassy to eat raw in a salad. Undercooking can also produce a grassy taste. Collard greens taste great simply prepared with olive oil and onions, leeks, or garlic. Strong flavorings such as hot pepper, ginger, curry, vinegar, hot sauce, and bacon also enhance the flavor. Slivered collard greens taste good in soups and bean stews.

What is the best way to turn out delicious collard greens? Surprisingly, not by steaming. We have found, through comparison tests, that steamed collard greens are hard to chew and almost unpalatable. Boiling them in a large pot of water, southern style, turns out a limp mass of mild-tasting greens that have lost their distinctive flavor. It is also time-consuming and makes for a greater loss of nutrients.

The method we use is quick-cooking in a small amount of water as a preliminary step before sautéing. Bring about 2 cups of water to a boil in a skillet large enough for the greens to spread out. Add the chopped greens to the boiling water, cover, and cook on high "fast and furiously" for 8 to 10 minutes. Cooking greens quickly preserves both nutrients, color, and taste. The cooked greens can then be drained (save the broth!) and sautéed in a little oil with other vegetables and flavorings. The cooking broth is a delicious, nutritious beverage to enjoy while you finish your preparations.

Alternatively, you can sauté the collards. These greens will be a little chewier and stronger tasting than precooked collards, but slightly quicker to cook. Start with onions or leeks and garlic in a small amount of oil. Add the sliced collards and enough water to keep the greens from sticking to the pan and burning, about ½ cup per bunch. Cook the greens for the same amount of time, up to 10 minutes. This method saves the step of precooking.

The following recipes use both cooking methods, so experiment to find which you like best.

SHOPPING TIPS

Look for smooth, green leaves without any yellowing or insect holes. Avoid wilted greens; they have already lost some flavor and vitality. Try to find young or small collard leaves. They will be more tender than large leaves.

STORAGE

Store unwashed in a clear plastic bag, not tightly sealed, in the refrigerator. Store in the crisper to prevent additional moisture loss. Collards are best used within 2 to 3 days.

PREPARATION

The large and sturdy fanlike collard leaves are attached to a thick, heavy stalk and midrib that is best removed and discarded. You can do this by folding each leaf in half, vein or underside out, and pulling the stalk and rib away from the leaf. Move your hand down the leaf as you pull the stalk to avoid losing more leaf than is necessary. Or you can use a knife to slice leaves from the rib.

Wash collards by plunging them into a large bowl of cold water. Lift greens out of water to a colander and check bottom of bowl. If there is any sand, discard the water and repeat the process.

To chop, stack 4 to 5 collard leaves on top of each other and roll into a fat cigar shape. Using a large knife, slice crosswise into strips. Experiment with different widths, from slivers to slices ½ inch wide, and see what best fits what you are cooking. Slices about ¼ inch wide make an attractive presentation.

Collard Greens and Caramelized Onions

"A great accompaniment to any meal," said one of our testers.

SERVES 2 TO 3

¾ POUND COLLARD GREENS (6 OR 7 CUPS, CHOPPED)

1 TABLESPOON EXTRA VIRGIN OLIVE OIL

3 ONIONS, SLICED INTO THIN CRESCENTS

3 CLOVES GARLIC, MINCED

SALT TO TASTE

VARIATION

Add 2 tablespoons raisins for the last 3 minutes of cooking.

1. Wash collards, remove stalks and stack 4 to 5 leaves. Slice into strips, approximately ¼ inch wide (see page 117). Set aside.

2. In a large skillet or cast-iron pan, heat oil over medium heat. Add onions and sauté for 15 to 20 minutes, until golden and sweet. Take care not to burn. Add garlic and sauté for another 2 to 3 minutes, until golden.

3. While the onions are cooking, bring 2 to 3 cups of water to a boil in a 10- to 12-inch skillet with a lid. Add collards, cover, and cook over high heat for 8 to 10 minutes, stirring occasionally. The greens are cooked when they are tender but still bright green. Drain in a colander and set aside.

4. Add greens to onions and garlic. Season with salt to taste and cook for another 1 to 2 minutes to heat through. Serve hot, drizzled with additional olive oil if you dare.

Collards with Dill and Parsley

Quick, easy, and delicious. Sometimes no one in my family says anything about a dish of greens. It is just all gone before I get to have a second serving. Darn!

SERVES 2 TO 3

¾ POUND COLLARD GREENS (6 OR 7 CUPS, CHOPPED)

2 TEASPOONS EXTRA VIRGIN OLIVE OIL

2 CARROTS, CUT DIAGONALLY INTO ¼-INCH OVALS

½ CUP WATER

PINCH OF SALT

2 TEASPOONS CHOPPED FRESH DILL

¼ CUP MINCED FRESH PARSLEY

1 TABLESPOON FRESHLY SQUEEZED LEMON JUICE

1. Wash collard greens in a large basin of cool water. Trim stalks from greens (see page 117) and discard. Lay several leaves one on top of the other, roll into a fat cigar shape, and slice crosswise into ¼-inch strips. Set aside. Repeat with remaining leaves.

2. Heat the oil in a large skillet. Add the carrots and cook for 2 minutes, stirring frequently.

3. Add prepared collard greens and toss to coat with the oil, about 1 minute. Add water, cover, and cook for 8 to 10 minutes over medium-high heat. Check tenderness of greens, and sprinkle with a pinch of salt.

4. Stir in dill and parsley and cook for 1 minute. Season to taste with the lemon juice and serve immediately.

Southern-Style Black-Eyed Peas, Collard Greens, and Roasted Red Peppers

Black-eyed peas and collards taste delicious together. Black-eyed peas do not need to be soaked overnight, and are quick-cooking for an easy and satisfying vegetarian dinner. Serve with corn bread.

SERVES 6

2 TABLESPOONS OIL

2 CUPS THINLY SLICED ONIONS

1 TABLESPOON MINCED FRESH GARLIC

3 CELERY STALKS, CUT INTO 1/2-INCH DICE

1½ CUPS DRIED BLACK-EYED PEAS

7 CUPS WATER

2 BAY LEAVES

½ TEASPOON DRIED THYME

½ TEASPOON PAPRIKA

¼ TEASPOON RED PEPPER FLAKES

2 CUPS SLIVERED COLLARD GREENS

1 TO 2 TEASPOONS SALT

1 RED PEPPER, ROASTED, PEELED AND DICED (SEE PAGE 46)

2 CUPS COOKED LONG-GRAIN BROWN OR BASMATI RICE

HOT SAUCE TO TASTE AND/OR BALSAMIC OR APPLE CIDER VINEGAR, OPTIONAL

1. Heat oil in a heavy-bottomed soup pot over medium-heat. Add onions and cook for about 15 minutes, until soft and golden. Add garlic and cook for 1 minute.

2. Add celery, black-eyed peas, water, bay leaves, thyme, paprika, and red pepper flakes. Bring to a boil. Reduce heat, cover, and simmer for 25 minutes. If necessary, add more water during cooking to keep peas covered—the dish should have "gravy" when finished.

3. While this is cooking, prepare collard greens by plunging them into a basin of cool water. Remove entire rib by stripping leaves from stalks (see page 117). Stack 4 to 5 leaves, roll into a cigar shape, and cut into slivers, ⅛ inch or smaller. Add to pot and continuing cooking until the beans are soft, 15 to 20 minutes. Avoid overcooking the black-eyed peas; they can become mushy very quickly.

4. When the beans are cooked, add salt, dried red pepper, and cooked rice. Season with apple cider or balsamic vinegar and/or hot sauce if you wish.

VARIATIONS

❖ *Instead of mixing the rice into the dish, you can serve the black-eyed peas with rice on the side—and corn on the cob or corn bread.*

❖ *Stir in 1 to 2 cups fresh corn kernels during the last 5 minutes of cooking for added color and crunch.*

Quick Southern-Style Collards and Bacon

Another take on southern-style greens.

We love the flavor of bacon, so when we occasionally cook with it, we buy a good quality. We have found at least one company in Vermont that cures its bacon with pure maple syrup and does not add sodium nitrates or nitrites, which have been linked to the development of cancer. Ask your local market to carry bacon from The Pork Schop of Hinesburg, Vermont, (802-482-3617) if it doesn't already.

SERVES 2 TO 3

3 BACON STRIPS

¾ POUND COLLARD GREENS (6 OR 7 CUPS, CHOPPED)

2 CUPS WATER

1 TABLESPOON BACON DRIPPINGS

1 CUP THINLY SLICED LEEKS OR ONIONS

PINCH OF SALT OR TO TASTE

1. Heat a 10-inch cast-iron skillet. Fry the bacon until golden and fat is rendered. Remove bacon from fat to paper toweling to drain. Pour off rendered fat to a metal container to reserve. Wipe out pan.

2. Wash collards, remove stalks, and stack 4 to 5 leaves. Roll like a cigar and slice into thin strips, approximately ¼ inch wide (see page 117). In a large skillet with a lid, bring water to a boil. Add the greens and cook on high heat, covered, for 8 to 10 minutes for tough, older greens, 4 to 6 minutes for tender baby greens. Cooked greens should be tender but still bright green. Remove greens from cooking liquid to a bowl, using a slotted spoon. Save "pot likker" to drink.

3. In a large skillet, heat 1 teaspoon of the bacon drippings over medium heat. Add leeks and sauté for 5 to 8 minutes, until softened. Stir in collards to coat with leeks and drippings.

4. Season with salt, if desired. Crumble cooled bacon over the hot greens.

Southern-Style (but Low-Fat) Collard Greens

Traditionally in the southern United States, greens are cooked for at least 45 minutes and up to 3 hours with a ham hock and possibly salt pork to render extremely tender, juicy greens. Unfortunately, this makes for a rather fatty dish and greens that are really too soft for our taste. We have come up with a healthier version that gives a delicious smoky taste but contains little fat. The greens are cooked in lightly salted chicken broth with some liquid smoke to give that authentic taste. We tried using salted water rather than the chicken stock, but feel that the chicken stock lends a depth of flavor not achieved with water alone. Serve with the traditional corn bread to soak up the "pot likker." Oooohhhh so good!

SERVES 2 TO 3

¾ POUND COLLARD GREENS (ABOUT 6 CUPS, CHOPPED)

4 CUPS LIGHTLY SALTED CHICKEN STOCK

1 TEASPOON LIQUID SMOKE

APPLE CIDER OR HERBAL VINEGAR

MELINDA'S EXTRA HOT SAUCE

1. Wash collards, remove stalks, and stack 4 to 5 leaves. Roll like a cigar and slice into strips approximately ½ inch wide (see page 117).

2. Bring the chicken stock to a boil in a 3- to 4-quart saucepan that has a tight-fitting lid. Add the liquid smoke.

3. Add the collard greens to the stock, pushing the greens down to submerge. Return to the boil, reduce heat to a slower bubble, cover, and cook for 10 minutes.

4. With a slotted spoon, lift the greens from the stock and place in a bowl. Divide the greens between two plates and let each person season to taste with the vinegar and hot sauce. Serve the "pot likker" on the side with warm corn bread.

LIQUID SMOKE

Liquid smoke is the flavor of hickory, mesquite, or other aromatic wood captured in water. It takes only a spray or as little as a teaspoon of the smoke-flavored water to impart a light smoky flavor to foods. You can find liquid smoke in gourmet shops, and some supermarkets, or by mail. Desert Mesquite of Arizona sells a Mesquite Smoke Flavoring by mail and can be reached at (602) 437-3135.

Georgia Collards with Leeks, Corn, and Peanuts

Collards perk up with the combined sweetness and flavor of leeks and corn.

Corn Off the Cob

We love using fresh corn in many of our recipes—all year. It's colorful, sweet, and crunchy. Removing the corn kernels from the cob is easy. After you husk the corn, stand the ear on one end in a large bowl. Take a large sharp knife and slice down the cob from top to bottom, right along the edge. The whole kernels will fall in the bowl. You can use the back of the knife to scrape any remaining pulp from the cob.

SERVES 4 AS A SIDE DISH

1 POUND COLLARD GREENS (ABOUT 9 CUPS CHOPPED)

3 CUPS WATER

2 CUPS FRESH CORN KERNELS

1 TABLESPOON PEANUT OR CANOLA OIL

2 LEEKS, WHITE AND LIGHT GREEN PARTS ONLY, WASHED AND SLICED

¼ TEASPOON RED PEPPER FLAKES

SALT TO TASTE

⅓ CUP CHOPPED ROASTED PEANUTS

HOT SAUCE TO TASTE

1. Wash collards, remove stalks, and stack 4 to 5 leaves. Roll like a cigar and slice into strips, approximately ¼-inch wide (see page 117).

2. Bring water to a boil in a 10- to 12-inch skillet with a lid. Add collards, cover, and cook over high heat for about 6 minutes, stirring occasionally. Add fresh corn and cook for 2 to 3 more minutes, until collards are tender. Drain in a colander and set aside.

3. In the same skillet, heat oil over medium-low heat. Add leeks and pepper flakes and sauté for about 5 minutes.

4. Stir in cooked collards, season with salt, and cook for 2 minutes until greens are hot. Sprinkle with peanuts. Serve with hot sauce.

Quick Collards with Portobello Mushrooms

Instead of the traditional ham bone for collards, the portobello mushroom lends its "beefy" taste to flavor the collards in this dish.

SERVES 3 TO 4

¾ POUND COLLARD GREENS (6 OR 7 CUPS, CHOPPED)

2 CUPS WATER

2 TEASPOONS EXTRA VIRGIN OLIVE OIL

1 TEASPOON MINCED GARLIC

⅓ CUP THINLY SLICED SCALLIONS, WHITE AND
GREEN PARTS

2 PORTOBELLO MUSHROOMS, STEMS REMOVED AND CUT
INTO SLICES ABOUT 1 INCH LONG

SALT TO TASTE

1. Wash collards, remove stalks and stack 4 to 5 leaves. Roll like a cigar and slice into ribbons, anywhere from ¼ to ½ inch wide (see page 117).

2. To cook collards, place water in a 10- to 12-inch skillet with a lid. Bring to a boil and add the prepared collards. Cover and cook over high heat for 8 to 10 minutes, stirring occasionally. Drain in a colander and set aside.

3. Heat the oil in the same skillet over medium heat. Add the garlic and scallions and sauté for about 30 seconds. Turn the heat to medium-high and add the mushrooms and a pinch of salt to draw out some liquid. Cook for 5 to 6 minutes, stirring constantly, until mushrooms are tender.

4. Reduce heat to low, stir in the cooked collards, cover, and cook for 1 to 2 minutes, until hot.

VARIATION

Substitute any kind of mushroom or combination of mushrooms, plus ⅓ cup of scallions, for the portobello mushrooms.

PORTOBELLO MUSHROOMS

Portobello mushrooms are the giant mushrooms in supermarkets: dark brown with a flat, circular top and a thick tough stem that is discarded or used for stock. The thick caps have delicious flavor— many say beefy—and are good grilled, sautéed, or added to soups. These big mushrooms combine nicely with many cooking greens, adding a satisfying richness.

Collards, Burdock Root, and Shiitake

In this recipe the collard greens are shredded very fine, both for quick cooking and for aesthetic reasons. They look nice this way with the julienned carrots and burdock root. Light textures, hearty flavors.

SERVES 4

2 TEASPOONS UNSALTED BUTTER OR LIGHT SESAME OIL

4 TO 6 FRESH SHIITAKE MUSHROOMS, STEMMED AND CUT INTO THIN STRIPS

1 BURDOCK ROOT

2 CARROTS

1½ CUPS WATER

2 TEASPOONS TAMARI (NATURALLY BREWED SOY SAUCE)

1 TEASPOON TOASTED (DARK) SESAME OIL

4 CUPS VERY FINELY SHREDDED COLLARD GREENS THAT HAVE BEEN WASHED AND STEMMED (SEE PAGE 117)

1 TABLESPOON TOASTED SESAME SEEDS

1. In a large skillet over medium-high heat, heat 1 teaspoon of the butter or oil. Add the shiitake mushrooms and cook for 2 minutes to brown lightly. Remove from pan and set aside.

2. Peel burdock root. Cut root on a sharp diagonal into very thin oval slices. Stack 2 or 3 slices and cut into ⅛-inch wide matchsticks. Repeat process with carrots.

3. Heat remaining 1 teaspoon butter or oil in the skillet and add the burdock. Stir to coat all pieces, cooking for about 1 minute to brown lightly and release the flavor. Add the water and bring to a boil. Reduce heat to a simmer, cover, and cook for 10 minutes.

4. Add carrots and mushrooms and cook for 3 minutes, uncovered. Season with the tamari and toasted sesame oil.

5. Stir in the shredded greens and cook, covered, for 7 to 9 minutes until the greens are tender. Serve hot, garnished with the toasted sesame seeds.

BURDOCK ROOT

Burdock is a brown-skinned root vegetable shaped somewhat like a long, slender carrot. It has an earthy, mellow flavor and is known in herbal traditions to increase vitality and cleanse the blood. Peel or scrub the rough outer skin and slice, dice, or julienne for use in soups, stems, or sautéed vegetables.

Dandelion Greens

WHAT MAY BE AMERICA'S MOST HATED BACKYARD WEED—
the dandelion—is a well-loved edible green in dozens of
countries around the world.

No one knows this better than Peter Gail, who has been collecting dandelion recipes for the past twenty years. He now has
more than 680 recipes, a number of which are printed in his book
The Dandelion Celebration: A Guide to Unexpected Cuisine (Cleveland: Goosefoot Acres Press, 1994). We turned to Gail for his
tips on the best ways to cook and prepare dandelion greens.

To begin, he says, "Dandelions are inherently bitter. You
need to know that from the start."

But the significant nutritional profile of dandelions, he says,
makes it worthwhile to find ways to mask or reduce the bitterness.

Dandelion greens can be enjoyed cooked or raw. How you
prepare them may depend on whether you harvest them wild,
buy cultivated dandelions in the market, or grow them from
seed.

From wild sources, pick dandelion greens in locations where
the air and soil are relatively unpolluted. They are best picked in
the spring and before the flowers blossom, or in the fall from
new shoots after the plant has been cut back. At these two times
of year the greens will be the least bitter and best for adding to
salads.

Cooking in the following ways can reduce the bitterness of
dandelion greens. Gail's basic method is as follows: Wash the
greens thoroughly in warm water. Cut off any roots or tough
stems and sprinkle the greens with salt. Cook the greens in a
covered skillet, with just the water clinging to the washed leaves,
for 5 to 10 minutes. Drain and chop. At this point, sauté and add

your seasonings, or add the greens to a particular dish such as lasagne or quiche.

According to Gail, the foods that complement and best reduce the bitterness of dandelion green are olive oil, garlic, pork fat in some form, eggs, vinegar, lemon juice, cheese, tomatoes, and bread.

Another way to precook the dandelions is to blanch them in boiling water for 2 to 5 minutes. Some of the green's bitter compounds will leach into the water, making the greens more palatable. Use from 2 cups to 2 quarts of water, depending on your tastes. The more water, the milder the taste. Adding the greens to boiling water, rather than bringing them to a boil, also helps preserve nutrients.

After the greens are precooked, using either method, a simple preparation is to sauté them in garlic and olive oil. You can vary the taste by using a nut-flavored oil, and dress the greens with lemon juice, balsamic vinegar, or any other flavored vinegars. Dandelions with a creamy tahini sauce taste great. The Amish serve dandelions in a salad with a hot sweet and sour dressing made with vinegar, brown sugar, and hot bacon drippings.

"Serving dandelion greens on bread, for some reason which I cannot explain, completely eliminates the bitterness," says Gail. One of his favorite ways of eating dandelions is to make a broiled dandelion pizza sandwich out of bread, tomato sauce, chopped raw or cooked dandelions, and cheese. We also like to serve sautéed dandelions on top of hot polenta, the Italian dish made from cornmeal or corn grits, with a little grated cheese.

SHOPPING TIPS

Dandelion greens are grown commercially and are available in some supermarkets. Often, Gail says, the longer and bigger commercial dandelions, 12 to 14 inches long, are actually chicory hybrids.

Without paying high costs that supermarkets charge, you can pick dandelion greens free of charge each spring and fall. Or transplant wild plants to the outskirts of your garden. "Dandelions grown in good fertile soil are always sweeter and less bitter," says Gail.

STORAGE

Store dandelion greens loosely wrapped in a plastic bag in the crisper section of the refrigerator.

PREPARATION

To wash, fill a large bowl with cool water. Add greens and swish around to dislodge dirt. Remove any old or discolored leaves. Lift greens out of water to a colander and check bottom of bowl. If there is any sand, discard the water and repeat the process. Cut off the roots and tough stalks of the dandelion.

Polenta Topped with Dandelion Greens

You can make the polenta a day in advance or use leftover polenta to make this dish.

SERVES 4 AS A SIDE DISH

3½ CUPS WATER

1 CUP WHITE OR YELLOW CORN GRITS

2 CUPS WATER

2 BUNCHES DANDELION GREENS (TO EQUAL 4 CUPS CHOPPED) THAT HAVE BEEN WASHED, STEMMED, AND CHOPPED (SEE PAGE 131)

2 TEASPOONS OLIVE OIL

2 TEASPOONS MINCED GARLIC

SALT AND PEPPER TO TASTE

⅓ CUP PECORINO ROMANO OR PARMESAN CHEESE

LEMON WEDGES

1. In a large, heavy-bottomed pot, bring water to a boil. Slowly whisk in corn grits and salt, and stir continuously until mixture thickens. Turn heat to low and cook uncovered for 20 to 30 minutes, stirring often to prevent sticking. Polenta is ready when mixture pulls away from sides and a wooden spoon will stand up in the center. Spread polenta into an 8 by 8-inch pan or a pie plate. Refrigerate (uncovered) until polenta cools—at least half an hour, until it is firm and can be cut with a knife.

2. In a large skillet with a lid, bring 2 cups of water to a boil. Add chopped dandelion greens and boil quickly for 3 to 4 minutes. Drain and set aside, saving cooking liquid for drinking.

3. Wash and dry skillet. In the same skillet, heat oil over medium heat. Add garlic and sizzle for 30 seconds to 1 minute. Add cooked dandelion greens and salt and stir to coat greens with garlicky oil. Cover and cook for 1 minute, until greens are hot.

4. To grill polenta, brush a stove-top grill or cast-iron skillet with olive oil. Cut polenta into 2- by 3-inch strips and grill for 3 to 4 minutes on each side. Polenta strips should be crispy golden and hot.

5. To serve, place grilled polenta on plates and distribute dandelion greens along the center of the polenta. Sprinkle with the cheese. Serve with lemon wedges.

POLENTA

Polenta is a traditional Italian dish made from dried, ground corn cooked with water and salt. Polenta can be served as a creamy, soft side dish or cooled, sliced, and sautéed in olive oil as it is in the recipe on this page.

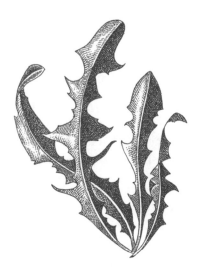

Frittata with Red Potatoes and Dandelion Greens

A satisfying brunch dish. Serve with crusty bread and sliced tomatoes.

SERVES 4

4 SMALL, RED-SKINNED POTATOES (ABOUT ⅔ POUND),
SCRUBBED

3 CUPS DANDELION GREENS THAT HAVE BEEN WASHED,
STEMMED, AND CHOPPED (SEE PAGE 131)

2 TABLESPOONS EXTRA VIRGIN OLIVE OIL

1 MEDIUM ONION, SLICED INTO THIN CRESCENTS

2 GARLIC CLOVES, MINCED

SALT AND PEPPER TO TASTE

6 LARGE EGGS

1 TEASPOON CHOPPED FRESH THYME (IF AVAILABLE)

FRESHLY GRATED PARMESAN CHEESE (OPTIONAL)

1. Preheat oven to 350°F.

2. Steam potatoes in a steamer basket until tender when pierced with a fork, about 20 minutes. Remove potatoes from water and set them aside.

3. Bring 2 cups water to a boil in a medium-size saucepan. Add dandelion greens and cook briefly, 3 to 4 minutes. Set aside.

4. Heat 1 tablespoon of the oil in a medium-size skillet over medium heat. Add onion and cook until soft and translucent, about 10 minutes. Add garlic to onion and cook for 1 to 2 minutes longer. Remove mixture to a bowl and set aside.

5. Remove skins from potatoes. Cut in half and slice each half into ¼-inch pieces. Warm the remaining oil in the skillet and add the potato slices. Toss to brown lightly over medium-high heat, about 5 minutes. Season with salt and pepper.

6. Lightly oil a 9-inch cast-iron skillet. Layer the onions, potatoes, and dandelion greens in the pan.

7. Using a fork, beat the eggs with thyme, salt, and pepper. Pour over the potato mixture and sprinkle with Parmesan cheese, if desired. Bake, uncovered, for 20 to 30 minutes, or until eggs are set. Serve hot.

DANDELION
DELICACIES

Beside enjoying the delicacy of dandelion greens, aficionados relish the roots and flowers of the dandelion in such concoctions as dandelion flower muffins and dandelion coffee ice cream. For these and more than 70 other recipes, you can mail-order The Dandelion Celebration: A Guide to Unexpected Cuisine, *from Goosefoot Acres Press, P.O. Box 18016, Cleveland, Ohio, 44118, (216) 932-2145.*

Dandelion with Spaghetti

This is one of Peter Gail's many recipes for dandelion greens. The author of The Dandelion Celebration, *Gail says that in combination with certain foods—such as tomatoes, olive oil, garlic, and cheese in this recipe—dandelion greens will lose their edge of bitterness. Precooking in water also helps.*

SERVES 2

3 TABLESPOONS OLIVE OIL

3 GARLIC CLOVES, MINCED

PINCH OF HOT PEPPER FLAKES

1 16-OUNCE CAN STEWED TOMATOES WITH JUICE

SALT TO TASTE

½ POUND SPAGHETTI

1 POUND DANDELION GREENS, WASHED, STEMMED, AND CHOPPED INTO BITE-SIZE PIECES (SEE PAGE 131)

GRATED ROMANO OR PARMESAN CHEESE

WHICH PASTA?

Any shape of pasta works well with this recipe, but our favorite is long, thin spaghetti.

1. Heat olive oil in a large skillet, and sauté garlic and a pinch of hot pepper flakes until garlic is golden, 1 to 2 minutes. Add tomatoes. Simmer, covered, for 10 to 15 minutes. Season with salt.

2. Cook the spaghetti in boiling water for 3 minutes less than directed on the package. Add the dandelion greens and continue cooking until spaghetti is done. Make sure that the dandelion leaves are submerged in the water during cooking. Drain well.

3. Combine tomato sauce, pasta, and dandelion greens. Heat and serve with grated cheese.

Creamed Sesame Dandelions

Elizabeth Germain, a natural-foods cooking instructor, uses calcium-rich tahini, a paste made from sesame seeds, to create a quick and creamy sauce for dandelion greens.

SERVES 2

2 CUPS WATER

1 POUND DANDELION GREENS, WASHED, STEMMED, AND CHOPPED INTO 1-INCH PIECES (SEE PAGE 131)

2 TEASPOONS EXTRA VIRGIN OLIVE OIL

2 CLOVES GARLIC, THINLY SLICED

SALT TO TASTE

2 TABLESPOONS TAHINI

3 TABLESPOONS WATER

½ TEASPOON TAMARI (NATURALLY BREWED SOY SAUCE)

FRESHLY SQUEEZED LEMON JUICE

1. Bring the 2 cups of water to a boil in a large 10- or 12-inch skillet that has a tight-fitting lid. Add chopped dandelions and cook for 2 to 3 minutes. Drain the cooked dandelion greens (saving the liquid broth to drink) and set aside.

2. Heat oil over low-to-medium heat in the skillet and sauté the garlic slices for 1 to 2 minutes, until light golden. Stir in the pre-cooked dandelions and a pinch of salt. Cover and cook over low heat for 1 to 2 minutes, to let the flavors mingle.

3. In a small bowl, combine tahini, water, and tamari and mix until creamy. Pour sauce into the pan with cooked greens and stir until thoroughly mixed. Serve hot with a squeeze of lemon juice, if desired.

Endive and Chicory

LIKE LETTUCE, ENDIVE AND CHICORY ARE MEMBERS OF THE daisy or thistle family. They share the same Latin name, *Cichorium*, because they are really the same plant, endive being the shoot of the chicory plant. Known to the Egyptians, Greeks, and Romans as a salad vegetable, endive and chicory have long been popular in Europe, especially with the French and Italians. Escarole, a type of chicory, may have also been a part of the "bitter herbs" used in Jewish tradition at Passover.

All chicories, with the exception of endive, provide lots of vitamins, especially vitamin C, when eaten raw, and the bitter factors have a tonic and diuretic effect. They are low in calories. Many countries considered the chicories to be medicinal well before they became culinary stars. Let's take a closer look at these interesting greens.

Escarole

Believed to be a native of India, escarole is a broad-leaved, slightly bitter green. Although the shape of the loosely packed head resembles that of some lettuces, its leaves are thicker than lettuce and pleasantly bitter. The plant can withstand more heat in the garden than lettuce and thus it makes a useful salad green to have on hand in the summer garden as well as at other times of the growing season.

The Italians often use escarole, *scarola*, in soups, such as our Garlic Escarole Soup with Rice (see page 146), or as a green filling for *calzone*, a type of folded-over stuffed pizza, or *torta pasqualina*, an Italian Easter pie. We find it equally delicious with pasta or broccoli rabe; we blanch the escarole for 1 to 2 minutes before using it with the pasta or rabe. Because escarole has a rather assertive taste, it goes well with oil-cured olives and anchovies and other strong flavors.

We also serve escarole raw in salads for an interesting contrast in taste and texture. And if you can't find Belgian endive for that special recipe, you can often substitute the heart of escarole, the tender inner leaves. The color is pale yellow and the taste is similar to that of Belgian endive, just not quite so delicate.

Chicory

In this country, chicory, or curly endive, is a variety of endive with a taste and texture similar to that of escarole. The plant forms a loose head of deeply cut leaves with masses of curly edges. We have found it to be slightly more bitter than the broad-leaved escarole. A smattering of chicory in a salad adds a distinctly strong taste that is refreshing and definitely not boring. Curly chicory can also be cooked like escarole.

Frisée

One of our favorite chicories is frisée, an easy-to-grow, beautiful, and delicate-looking variety. The leaves are deeply cut and very curly or frizzy at the edges. The best-tasting varieties have skinny leaves that form a beautiful curly head, with leaves radiating out from a center of pale yellow inner leaves to emerald green outer leaves. The taste is delicately bitter. Frisée is often found in mesclun mixes. It adds an interesting, sharp look to the rounder shape of the baby lettuces, chards, and mustard greens.

Belgian Endive

Also known as Witloof chicory, Belgian endive is the forced shoot of *Cichorium intybus*, a herbaceous plant found growing along roadsides and in fields of Europe and America. If you have ever walked along a rather "untidy" stretch of street you many have seen a tall, wiry stalk of a plant with lovely, pale blue daisy-like flowers emerging at various spots along the stalk. This is wild chicory, which has a little base of leaves at the bottom. These leaves can be picked and eaten before the stalk shoots up.

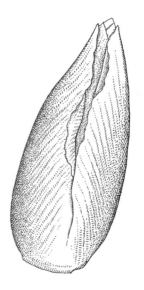

The forced shoot, Belgian endive, is grown mainly in northern climes where there might be a lack of salad vegetables in the winter. These plants are forced from chicory roots that have grown outside during the summer. In the fall, the tops are cut off about an inch above the root and the roots are buried in peat or dirt in a large pot and grown in the dark. The lack of light produces very pale whitish leaves tinged with pale yellow at the edges. The pointed leaves form a small, tight, elongated head, 4 to 5 inches long. This blanching, or lack of light by growing in the dark, produces leaves that are crisp in texture and delicately bitter in taste.

When you find Belgian endive at the market, it should not be green. If it is, it has been exposed to too much light, which allows the chlorophyll to form in the leaves. The leaves of Belgian endive are very beautiful with their elongated, pointed tips. They make an excellent composed salad that shows off this feature. The leaves are also excellent cut crosswise or lengthwise into strips and added to salads. The light color brightens and lightens. Belgian endive can also be cooked; it is most commonly braised with butter and Parmesan cheese. This can get a bit expensive because you need quite a few heads for a cooked dish.

Radicchio

Indigenous to Italy, radicchio is another variety of chicory. It is absolutely gorgeous. The bright magenta-and-white leaves make it very noticeable, both at the market and in a salad. The most common variety of this very popular northern Italian vegetable, Verona chicory, is a round, rather compact head, 3 to 5 inches in diameter. It is usually found near the Belgian endive and lettuces at the market. The outer leaves, which may have some green coloring, have been stripped off to reveal the interior blanched head with which we are becoming more and more familiar here in America. Red Treviso chicory is a nonheading variety of radicchio with elongated red-and-white leaves. There are also varieties that have green leaves streaked or speckled with wine-red.

Radicchio is grown outdoors as well as indoors in the dark, like Belgian endive. The indoor method produces a less bitter taste and absolutely no green in the leaves. In Italy, where the climate is often mild, several varieties of radicchio are sown outside in the autumn, grown in winter, and harvested for early spring markets. These types have a variegated red-and-green leaf, the green often predominating.

Radicchio is one of our favorite vegetables. It is a light-textured, bright way to dress up a salad. It is also excellent grilled, then brushed with a bit of olive oil and salt or your favorite vinaigrette. The color will no longer be bright, but the taste is superb, especially alongside other grilled vegetables and polenta, or poultry.

SHOPPING TIPS

When purchasing any loose-headed chicory such as escarole, frisée, or curly endive, select for brightly colored, crisp, fresh-looking leaves. There should be no wilting and no brown or yellow discoloration, which indicates improper handling or old age. For heading varieties such as radicchio and Belgian endive, the heads should be firm but not heavy, and there should be no discoloration.

As for radicchio, if outer leaves look shelf-worn, peel back to see if they reveal a good-quality leaf that is not wilted. You should feel free to have the produce manager trim away bad leaves.

Belgian endive should be pale yellowish at the edges, and white in the central part of the leaf. If it has become green, it has been in the light too long. It is still edible at this point, but may not be what your recipe requires. Some vegetable markets sell Belgian endive in its original shipping box, with the endive still covered with a bit of blue tissue paper. Voilà! If this is the case, your produce manager really knows what he or she is doing!

STORAGE

Store all chicories in a plastic bag in the refrigerator. If you should wash too much to use at one time, dry the leaves in a salad spinner and store the excess ones wrapped in a damp paper towel in the bag to keep leaves moist but not to the point that they will rot. Of the chicories, radicchio keeps the best—up to 1 week. Belgian endive should be used within 2 to 3 days because the outer leaves discolor quite quickly. Since both of these vegetables are rather expensive, it is important to keep them within easy reach in the refrigerator so they do not go unnoticed. Escarole, curly endive, and frisée keep for 3 to 5 days if properly stored. They are more durable than lettuce.

PREPARATION

Because Verona chicory or radicchio is the inner heart of a head of chicory, it usually does not need washing, nor does Belgian endive. Outer leaves can be trimmed if blemished.

Escarole, however, often hides sand in its base. To wash, cut off the base and separate the leaves. Fill a large bowl with cool water and add the escarole. Swish around, then lift leaves out of water to a colander and check bottom of bowl. If there is any sand, discard the water and repeat the process.

Pasta with Escarole and Roasted Red Pepper

A satisfying main dish pasta, appealing to adults and kids alike.

SERVES 4 TO 6

1 LARGE HEAD ESCAROLE (7 TO 8 CUPS CHOPPED)

1 QUART WATER

1 TEASPOON SALT

1 POUND FETTUCCINE

2 TABLESPOONS EXTRA VIRGIN OLIVE OIL

7 TO 8 OUNCES OYSTER MUSHROOMS, COARSELY CHOPPED

2 TABLESPOONS CHOPPED GARLIC CLOVES

1 ROASTED RED PEPPER, DICED (SEE PAGE 46)

1 BUNCH SCALLIONS, WHITE AND GREEN PARTS, THINLY
SLICED CROSSWISE

FRESHLY GRATED PARMESAN CHEESE

1. Wash the escarole well in a large basin of cool water, making sure there is no dirt or sand at the base of the leaves. Chop coarsely.

2. Bring the water to a boil in a large pot. Add salt and plunge in the escarole. Push down to submerge. Cook for 2 minutes. Lift greens out with a slotted spoon and set aside.

3. Bring greens cooking water to a boil and cook the pasta according to package directions.

4. Meanwhile, heat the olive oil in a large skillet over high heat. Add mushrooms and cook briskly, stirring constantly, for 2 minutes to brown slightly. Reduce heat slightly and add garlic. Cook for 20 seconds more, taking care not to burn.

5. Add roasted red pepper and scallions and cook for 2 minutes. Stir in blanched escarole and salt to taste, and toss to heat through.

6. Toss pasta with vegetables and garnish with freshly grated Parmesan cheese.

Scarola Con Olive e Uva Passa
(Escarole with Olives and Raisins)

SERVES 4

1 LARGE HEAD ESCAROLE (7 TO 8 CUPS, CHOPPED)

1 TABLESPOON EXTRA VIRGIN OLIVE OIL

3 GARLIC CLOVES

⅓ CUP RAISINS

10 OIL-CURED OLIVES OR GREEK BLACK OLIVES

FRESHLY GROUND BLACK PEPPER

1. Wash the escarole well in a large basin of cool water, making sure there is no dirt or sand at the base of the leaves (see page 143). Chop coarsely.

2. Bring a large pot of water to a boil. Add a pinch of salt and the escarole. Blanch for 1 minute. Remove and drain in a colander.

3. Heat oil in a large skillet over medium heat. Add the garlic and sauté for about 2 minutes, until softened. Do not burn. Stir in the greens and raisins and cook, covered, for 3 minutes.

4. Add the olives and heat through. Season to taste with pepper and serve as a side dish.

Garlic Escarole Soup with Rice

Sometimes chicken stock is essential to a recipe, and canned stock does not taste the same. Make ahead and freeze, to have on hand.

1 WHOLE CHICKEN OR
   4 POUNDS POULTRY
   PARTS, SKIN
   REMOVED

4 CELERY STALKS, DICED

4 CARROTS, DICED

2 ONIONS, DICED

1 LEEK, SLICED

1 BAY LEAF

6 PEPPERCORNS

HANDFUL OF PARSLEY

3 FRESH THYME
SPRIGS (IF AVAILABLE)

Place all ingredients in a large stockpot. Cover with cold water and bring to a boil. Simmer, partially covered, for 2 to 3 hours. Strain stock. Cool and refrigerate or freeze.

This satisfying soup is redolent with garlic. Arborio rice gives it an added dimension that makes you come back for seconds. Don't leave out the Parmesan cheese.

SERVES 4 TO 6

1 TABLESPOON EXTRA VIRGIN OLIVE OIL

3 MEDIUM ONIONS, THINLY SLICED

4 GARLIC CLOVES, MINCED

8 CUPS CHICKEN STOCK

1 TEASPOON SALT, OR TO TASTE

½ CUP ARBORIO RICE

SHREDDED CHICKEN FROM STOCK (OPTIONAL)

1 MEDIUM HEAD ESCAROLE, WASHED AND ROUGHLY
   CHOPPED (ABOUT 5 CUPS) (SEE PAGE 143)

GRATED PARMESAN CHEESE TO TASTE

1. Heat the oil in a large soup pot over medium-high heat. Add onions and cook, uncovered, for 15 to 20 minutes, until caramelized. Reduce heat to low, add garlic, and cook for another 5 minutes.

2. Add chicken stock and bring to a boil. Add the salt and rice and cook for 5 minutes.

3. Add shredded chicken meat, if using, and escarole. Simmer, covered, for about 10 minutes, until rice and escarole are tender. Season to taste with salt.

Radicchio on the Grill

A traditional salad green, radicchio takes on a wonderful flavor when grilled and brushed with a light dressing. It loses some of its brilliant burgundy coloring with grilling, but after tasting you won't care.

SERVES 3 TO 4

4 SMALL TO MEDIUM HEADS RADICCHIO
EXTRA VIRGIN OLIVE OIL FOR GRILLING

DRESSING:
1 TABLESPOON BALSAMIC VINEGAR
2 TABLESPOONS EXTRA VIRGIN OLIVE OIL
1 TABLESPOON CHOPPED FRESH BASIL
½ TEASPOON DIJON MUSTARD
SALT TO TASTE
3 TO 4 DROPS MELINDA'S HOT SAUCE TO TASTE

1. Remove any wilted outer leaves of the radicchio. Slice the entire head in half lengthwise and then into quarters, keeping the base intact.

2. In a small bowl, whisk together the vinegar, oil, basil, mustard, salt, and hot sauce. Set aside.

3. Heat a stove top or outdoor grill. Brush radicchio with oil and grill for 3 to 4 minutes a side, until base is tender when pierced with a fork.

4. While radicchio is still on the grill, brush with dressing. Serve immediately or at room temperature.

Pear, Radicchio, Mizuna, and Belgian Endive Salad

Beautiful colors and the sharp flavor of the mizuna and radicchio come together with the sweetness of pears and the salty richness of imported Parmesan. The dressing is light and slightly tangy.

SERVES 4

1 SMALL HEAD RADICCHIO

1½ CUPS MIZUNA WASHED AND ROUGHLY CHOPPED, TOUGH STEMS REMOVED

3 SMALL HEADS BELGIAN ENDIVE, CUT INTO HALVES LENGTHWISE AND THEN THIRDS, TO EQUAL APPROXIMATELY 2 CUPS

DRESSING:
½ TEASPOON DRY MUSTARD

1 TABLESPOON LEMON JUICE

1 TABLESPOON HERBED WHITE VINEGAR

½ TEASPOON MAPLE SYRUP

PINCH OF SALT

FRESHLY GROUND WHITE PEPPER

4 TABLESPOONS WALNUT OR CANOLA OIL

1 PERFECTLY RIPE ANJOU PEAR, HALVED, CORED, AND SLICED VERTICALLY INTO ¼-INCH WEDGES

12 WIDE SHAVINGS OF PARMIGIANO-REGGIANO

1. Slice radicchio head in half lengthwise, then thinly slice on either side of core. Place radicchio, endive and mizuna in a salad bowl.

2. In a small bowl, whisk together the mustard powder, lemon juice, vinegar, maple syrup, salt, and pepper. Drizzle in the walnut oil, whisking constantly to emulsify dressing.

3. To serve, toss greens with the dressing and place on individual salad plates. Top with pear slices and 3 shavings of Parmesan cheese for each serving.

Spaghetti with Caramelized Red Onions, Tomatoes, and Escarole

The slightly bitter flavor of escarole is offset by the sweet onions, tomatoes, and raisins.

SERVES 4

1 TABLESPOON EXTRA VIRGIN OLIVE OIL

3 CUPS THINLY SLICED RED ONION (1½ LARGE RED ONIONS)

1 POUND SPAGHETTI

2 TO 3 CUPS CHOPPED TOMATOES, OR 1 14-OUNCE CAN

1 TEASPOON DRIED BASIL, OR 2 TO 3 TABLESPOONS CHOPPED FRESH BASIL

2 HEADS ESCAROLE, WASHED AND COARSELY CHOPPED (10 TO 12 CUPS) (SEE PAGE 143)

3 TABLESPOONS RAISINS

SALT AND FRESHLY GROUND PEPPER TO TASTE

2 TABLESPOONS TOASTED PINE NUTS

1 TABLESPOON EXTRA VIRGIN OLIVE OIL (OPTIONAL GARNISH)

1. Heat 1 tablespoon olive oil in a large skillet over medium heat. Add onions and cook uncovered for 15 to 20 minutes, until caramelized. Do not burn. Adjust heat as necessary.

2. Meanwhile, bring a large pot of water to a boil for the pasta. Add 1 teaspoon salt and the pasta. Cook until *al dente*. Drain, saving ½ cup of the cooking liquid. Return pasta and liquid to pot and stir. Cover and set aside.

3. Add tomatoes and basil to caramelized onions and cook for 10 more minutes.

4. Meanwhile, bring 2 cups water to a boil in a large pot. Add a pinch of salt and all of the escarole, pressing it down to submerge all the leaves. Cook for 1 to 2 minutes. Drain. Add to tomato mixture with raisins. Cover and cook for 5 minutes. Season to taste.

5. Toss pasta with escarole mixture, garnish with the toasted pine nuts, and drizzle on the additional olive oil, if desired.

Choosing the Best-Tasting, Healthiest Greens

When it comes to buying greens for freshness and taste, you need to look for several things. The most obvious is the condition of the greens: Are they vibrant looking? Are they free of yellowed or withered leaves? Are they free of holes left by hungry insects? Several not-so-obvious factors also determine the taste of greens, and therefore the dish you make with them: Is the produce organic? Is it grown locally? Is it in season?

Our first recommendation is to buy organic whenever possible. We think organic greens taste better. They are certainly better for you. Organic greens are grown without chemical pesticides and are shipped without any longevity-enhancing chemicals. "They've got to get to the market more quickly and sold more quickly. The taste difference is noticeable," says David Steinman, author of the *Safe Shopper's Bible* (New York: Macmillan, 1995) and *Diet for a Poisoned Planet* (New York: Ballatine, 1992).

Steinman has been researching pesticides in foods for more than a decade. He has found that some greens including spinach, collard greens, and mustard greens generally contain higher levels of pesticides than other greens. "They tend to act like sponges, and consequently they tend to accumulate more pesticide residues. I give them the highest possible warning. That means watch out."

Sixteen samples of spinach tested by the U.S. government had ninety-five pesticide residues, Steinman reports. "Conventionally grown collard greens are rich in A and B vitamins, but unfortunately are pesticide saturated." Some of the pesticide residues found in chemically farmed greens include DDT, dieldrin, and heptachlor—all known cancer-causing chemicals.

The bottom line is that you can't really go wrong buying organic greens, says Steinman. They generally do not cost more than conventionally grown greens. "They taste better, they are available year-round. It's just a good deal for the farmer, for the consumer, for the children."

Organic food also has better nutritional value, according to one study published in *The Journal of Applied Nutrition*. Tests conducted over a two-year period at Doctor's Data lab in West Chicago, Illinois, consistently found that organic fruits and vegetables were richer in nutrients than nonorganic produce.

"The purpose of the study was to document whether there is more nutrition in organic food. I found in many cases there was nearly twice the level of nutritional elements in the organically grown," said Bob Smith, president of Doctor's Data and author of the study. On average, organic produce analyzed contained 63 percent more calcium, 59 percent more iron, 78 percent more chromium, and 60 percent more zinc than nonorganic produce. Levels of selenium, one of the minerals the body uses to defend itself from toxic elements in the environment, were several hundred percent higher, said Smith.

In addition to the benefits of buying organic, the locality and the season can determine the quality of leafy greens. The vegetables we buy from Hutchins farmstand, a 60-acre organic farm in nearby Concord, Massachusetts, are among the best we've ever had, better tasting than the organic greens we buy in local stores. The greens grown there—kale, arugula, broccoli rabe, red giant mustard, tatsoi—are crisp, vibrant, and perfect looking. Common sense says these vegetables are going to taste as good as they look. And they do.

Locally grown produce usually means it's fresher, says Elizabeth Germain, spokesperson for sustainable agriculture for Oldways Preservation & Exchange Trust. "The freshness of food really makes a difference, especially with greens. I think they lose part of their flavor and vitality, their life force, quicker than other vegetables."

"It's not enough to say if it's organic, it will taste better. There are a host of other considerations," says Deborah Madison, coauthor with Edward Brown of *The Greens Cookbook* (New York: Bantam, 1987). "I've had organic food that doesn't taste as good because it was old. Freshness counts. A particular farm also counts— as do the conditions in which it's grown, and whether it was over irrigated, or under irrigated. Good farming practices are also part of the picture."

Both Germain and Madison are part of a new movement of chefs and food professionals around the country emphasizing and seeking out "locally grown, seasonally fresh, and whole or minimally processed ingredients." Some of the country's best chefs are turning to local, often organic, farms to supply their restaurants.

You don't have to be a top chef, however, to enjoy the flavor and vibrancy of local, organic produce. "The first place to look during the growing season is at farmers' markets and farmstands," says Germain. "Community Supported Agriculture, farms that sell shares in exchange for food, is another excellent option." She also suggests shopping at natural food stores and food cooperatives that bring in and sell fresh produce from local farmers during the growing season.

"The supermarkets are usually the last place you go to seek out local and organic," says Germain. "They usually have established year-round arrangements that preclude a local farmer getting into the supermarket." Germain suggests asking produce managers to stock local, preferably organically grown, food.

Kale

KALE IS HIGHLY VALUED FOR ITS HEALTH-GIVING PROPERTIES. Called the "king of calcium" and a "heavy-hitting crucifer," kale is often placed on the list of the top 10 healthiest foods you can eat. One cup contains more than 5 grams of fiber (more than a serving of oat bran cereal) but only 43 calories. That same cup provides the daily requirement for vitamins A and C, and 134 milligrams of calcium.

Kale tastes good, too! Once cooked, the leaves that appear formidable and tough on the produce shelf become tender and sweet tasting. Kale has a pleasantly mellow flavor of its own, not quite so mild as spinach or Swiss chard, but not so strong tasting as mustard greens. The way it is cooked can enhance its flavor.

We find that kale benefits from a quick precooking in a small amount of water. Steaming—or wilting the kale in a skillet with only the water clinging to its washed leaves—tends to concentrate any strong flavor in the green and robs the vegetable of its bright green color. Although kale is one of the least bitter of the leafy cooking greens and can be steamed without disastrous results, the quick-boiling method results in a much better taste and makes the green less "chewy." To achieve the taste and texture we like, we cook kale in about 2 cups of boiling water for 4 to 5 minutes. To test for doneness, use a pair of tongs or a slotted spoon and sample a piece, as you would a strand of pasta. Kale is done when the leaves are tender to chew, while still remaining bright green. For a softer green, you can cook a few minutes longer, depending on the age of the green and your own preference.

Precooking in boiling water, like steaming, will rob kale of some of its minerals and vitamin C. But you can regain any lost minerals by saving and drinking the cup or so of tasty broth, or "pot likker," that remains after cooking.

As you will see from the following recipes, kale tastes delicious in soups, stir-fries, even grilled. We don't recommend eating kale raw, even shredded in salads, unless it's very tender, garden-grown baby kale.

With kale, simple enhancements go a long way. Precooked kale tastes good with olive oil and garlic, leeks, or onions, or it can be cooked with sweet vegetables such as carrots and corn. Serve with a splash of flavored oil, fresh lemon juice or vinegar, and a pinch of salt. Combine kale with "white" foods such as potatoes, white beans, and pasta. The following recipe for Potato Kale Soup (see page 168) is a variation of a traditional Portuguese soup (*caldo verde*), which combines kale, potatoes, and sausage. In Scotland, kale soup was so popular, that "kale" even meant "soup" in general.

Look for the different varieties of kale at farm stands or farmer's markets. Red Russian kale has purple-red stems and a toothy but less curly leaf. Italian kale has dark blue-green crinkled leaves. If we have a choice we buy these varieties first for the sweet taste. The two can be used interchangeably with any recipes calling for kale. Flowering kales— white, red, and red-on-green varieties— are striking in appearance and taste good if harvested young. The next wave from California will be mixes of young "teenage" greens (the stage between the baby greens used in mesclun and the mature plants), which will feature some of the flowering kales, for quick braising or stir-frying.

SHOPPING TIPS

Choose kale that has unwilted, uniformly colored, dark green or green-and-purplish leaves that have no yellowed edges. The greens should look fresh and well cared for by the produce department because they will last longer if they are fresh when you buy them. Kale is a cold-tolerant plant and will actually taste sweeter if picked after a frost.

If you need only a small bunch of kale, ask your friendly produce manager to split a bunch, but keep in mind that the kale will cook down significantly. One large bunch of kale weighs 1 to 1 ¼ pounds and cooks down to approximately 4 cups, which will serve 3 to 4 people.

STORAGE

Store unwashed kale in a clear plastic bag, not tightly sealed, in the refrigerator. Store in the crisper to prevent additional moisture loss. Sturdy kale keeps pretty well; use in 3 to 4 days for the best flavor.

PREPARATION

To wash kale, fill a large stainless steel bowl with cool or tepid water, plunge in the greens to rinse, then lift greens out of the water and place in a colander. Kale usually needs only one wash.

We have found the most efficient way to remove the stalks from kale leaves is by stripping. Use one hand to hold the stalk of an individual leaf, rib side up. Use the other hand to strip the leaf off the stalk with one quick motion.

Some people prefer to chop kale's center rib into small pieces and cook it along with the leaves for a crunchy kale. We generally choose to remove and discard the midrib for a more pleasant texture. If you want thin shreds, pile several leaves on top of one another, roll into a cigar shape, and thinly slice with a chef's knife.

Basic Kale

Once you've mastered this basic recipe, you are all set to serve kale as is or to use it in many delicious recipes. After conducting numerous tests, we find that this method results in the best-tasting kale: sweet, slightly al dente *texture, and earthy flavor. Of great importance is the size of the pan in which the kale is cooked. For a large bunch of kale, use a 10- or 12-inch skillet that has a tight-fitting lid. The advantages are that the water returns to a boil quickly and the kale can be spread out evenly. This ensures that the kale cooks properly in the required amount of time.*

SERVES 2 TO 3

¾ POUND KALE

2 CUPS WATER

PINCH OF SEA SALT

1. Fill a large bowl with cold water. Plunge in the kale and swish it around to loosen any dirt or sand. If you notice that there are any gray-green aphids on the kale, add a big pinch of salt to the water and swish again. Any dirt or sand should sink to the bottom and the aphids should come off. They are usually on the underside of the leaves. Check carefully.

2. Lift kale out of the water. If the water is dirty or there is sand on the bottom of the bowl, dump the water out, rinse the bowl, and repeat the process.

3. Use one hand to hold the stalk of an individual leaf, rib side up. Use the other hand to strip the leaf off the stalk with one quick motion. Discard or compost the stalks if tough. If stalks are tender, you can chop them and use them.

4. Chop or tear kale into bite-size pieces. Set aside.

5. Bring the water to a boil in a large skillet that has a tight-fitting lid. Add the prepared kale, return water to a boil, cover,

and cook over high heat for 4 to 5 minutes, stirring occasionally, until kale is tender. Take care that all the liquid doesn't evaporate. Season to taste with salt if desired.

6. Remove kale from the skillet with a slotted spoon. Cool in cold water if desired to stop cooking, or use immediately in your favorite recipe. Drink any remaining "pot likker" as a tonic!

BASIC KALE VARIATIONS

❖ *Sauté 2 minced garlic cloves in 2 teaspoons olive oil, add cooked kale, and a pinch of salt, and heat through.*

❖ *Drizzle cooked kale with olive oil and fresh lemon juice.*

❖ *Drizzle cooked kale with toasted sesame oil, toasted sesame seeds, and a pinch of salt.*

❖ *Use as a bed for grilled fish or chicken.*

Basic No-Fat, No-Fuss, Colorful Kale

So many recipes, even ours, start with heating oil or butter and sautéing onions. But most often, we avoid extra fat and want a tasty, quick recipe. This fits the bill. Johnna's kids love it because it includes their favorite vegetables: kale, corn, and carrots. Cooking the carrots and corn kernels in the water before the kale sweetens the cooking liquid, making it quite delectable to drink.

SERVES 3 TO 4

¾ POUND KALE (ABOUT 6 CUPS, CHOPPED)

2 CUPS WATER

3 CARROTS, PEELED AND QUARTERED LENGTHWISE

3 EARS OF CORN, KERNELS CUT FROM COBS

SALT TO TASTE

1. Wash kale and strip leaves from stalk (see page155). Discard stalks and chop leaves into bite-size pieces. Set aside.

2. Bring water to a boil in a large skillet that has a tight-fitting lid.

3. Meanwhile, cut the quartered carrots into ½-inch pieces. Place carrots and corn kernels in the boiling water, reduce heat, cover skillet, and simmer for 5 minutes.

4. Add prepared kale to carrots and corn. Cover and cook for 4 minutes. Water should be bubbling rather vigorously but not boiling over.

5. Sprinkle on salt to taste, stir to combine, and remove to a serving dish with a slotted spoon. Serve hot. Drink the "pot likker!"

Kale with Raisins and Toasted Pine Nuts

Sautéing the raisins briefly gives them a glossy look and caramelized taste. Combined with the nutty flavor and soft texture of the pine nuts, this dish is a hit every time it's served. It tastes delicious over pasta, too.

SERVES 2 TO 3

¼ CUP TOASTED PINE NUTS

¾ POUND KALE (ABOUT 6 CUPS, CHOPPED)

2 CUPS WATER

2 TEASPOONS EXTRA VIRGIN OLIVE OIL

2 GARLIC CLOVES, MINCED

⅓ CUP RAISINS

SALT TO TASTE

1. To toast pine nuts, place them on a pie tin or cookie sheet and bake at 325°F for 5 minutes, or until golden brown. Take care not to burn the nuts. Set aside.

2. Wash kale and strip the leaves off the stalks (see page 155). Discard stalks and roughly chop kale. Bring the water to a boil in a 10- or 12-inch skillet that has a tight-fitting lid. Add the kale and cook, covered, over high heat, stirring occasionally, until tender, approximately 5 minutes. Remove and drain, saving the cooking liquid to drink.

3. Rinse out and dry the skillet, then use it to heat the olive oil over medium heat, lifting and tilting the pan to coat. Add garlic and sauté for 15 seconds. Add raisins and sauté for 30 seconds to 1 minute, stirring constantly to prevent browning or burning. Raisins should be glossy and slightly puffed.

4. Add greens and stir to combine. Season with salt to taste and cover for a minute until greens are heated through. Serve hot, garnished with the toasted pine nuts.

PINE NUTS AND GREENS

We usually keep a small amount of pine nuts around for a last-minute addition to greens dishes. They provide additional crunch, texture, and contrast. A little plumper than sunflower seeds, pine nuts are grown in the Southwest and in the Mediterranean, where they are used in many dishes. They are rich in flavor and oil, contain more protein than any other nut, and are high in vitamin A, the B-complex vitamins, and minerals. Store in the freezer to avoid rancidity.

Lemon-Basil Kale

This light, summer side dish has a subtle flavor of basil and a zip of lemon juice. Try the variation also, adding 1 cup fresh corn for additional flavor, color, and crunch.

SERVES 2 TO 3

¾ POUND KALE (ABOUT 6 CUPS CHOPPED)

2 CUPS WATER

2 TEASPOONS EXTRA VIRGIN OLIVE OIL

2 GARLIC CLOVES, FINELY MINCED

15 FRESH BASIL LEAVES, WASHED AND CUT INTO
    FINE RIBBONS

SALT TO TASTE

2 TEASPOONS FRESHLY SQUEEZED LEMON JUICE

VARIATION

Add 1 cup fresh corn kernels with the kale in step 1. Cook along with kale for 4 to 5 minutes. Continue with recipe.

ACIDS AND GREENS

The addition of lemon, balsamic vinegar, and other acidic flavorings often picks up the flavor of leafy greens, as does a pinch of salt. It is important to add lemon or vinegar after the greens are cooked and just before serving. If you cook greens with an acid you turn bright green vegetables into a drab army green color.

1. Wash kale and strip the leaves off the stalks (see page 155). Discard the stalks. Chop the kale into bite-sized pieces. Bring the water to a boil in a 10- to 12-inch skillet that has a tight-fitting lid. Add the kale, cover, and cook over high heat, stirring occasionally, until tender, approximately 5 minutes. Remove and drain, saving the cooking liquid to drink.

2. Rinse out and dry the skillet, then use it to heat the olive oil over medium heat, lifting and tilting the pan to coat. Add garlic and sizzle for 15 to 30 seconds, stirring constantly to prevent browning or burning.

3. Add basil and sauté for 15 seconds more. Add kale and stir until heated through. Season to taste with the salt. Stir in lemon juice and serve immediately.

Kale Celery Sauté

The color and flavor of the celery complements the dark green of the kale and the red pepper, whether hot and spicy or sweet, provides a splash of brightness.

SERVES 2

¾ POUND KALE (ABOUT 6 CUPS CHOPPED)

2 TEASPOONS EXTRA VIRGIN OLIVE OIL

2 CELERY STALKS, CUT IN HALF LENGTHWISE AND THINLY SLICED ON THE DIAGONAL (1 CUP)

1 TEASPOON MINCED FRESH GARLIC

1 HOT RED CHERRY PEPPER, SEEDED AND CUT INTO SMALL DICE, OR ¼ CUP FINELY DICED SWEET RED PEPPER

PINCH OF SALT, OR TO TASTE

1. Wash kale and strip the leaves off the stalks (see page 155). Discard the stalks and coarsely chop kale. Bring 2 cups water to a boil in a 10- to 12-inch skillet that has a tight-fitting lid. Add the kale and cook, covered, over high heat, stirring occasionally, until tender, approximately 5 minutes. Remove and drain, saving the cooking liquid to drink.

2. Rinse out and dry the skillet, then use it to heat the olive oil over medium heat, lifting and tilting the pan to coat. Add celery and sauté for 3 to 4 minutes.

3. Stir in garlic and red pepper. Cover and cook over medium heat for 2 minutes. Stir in precooked kale and cook to heat through.

4. Season to taste with a pinch of salt and serve hot.

KIDS AND KALE

Of all the leafy cooking greens, kale stands out as Johnna's children's favorite. Its mellow yet distinctly sweet taste is a welcome change from the ubiquitous broccoli. Plus, it's a great way for them to get a good dose of calcium, potassium, vitamins A and C, and even some protein and iron. Her kids regularly eat Basic Kale (see page 156) with no complaints, but really enjoy kale sautéed with olive oil, garlic, and celery.

Cajun Kale Salad

This unusual salad shows off kale in a different way. Unlike spinach, kale keeps its shape after cooking, so it is suitable in salads. Here its dark, bright color is set off by the colorful peppers and corn. The spices add a dimension of excitement. Just be sure to sprinkle on the lemon juice not more than 10 minutes before serving. Otherwise the kale will turn a drab shade of army green. Without the oil, this salad is deliciously fat-free.

SERVES 4 TO 6

4 EARS SWEET CORN, SHUCKED

¾ POUND KALE (ABOUT 6 CUPS, CHOPPED)

1 LARGE RED PEPPER, DICED

1 GREEN PEPPER, DICED

1 SMALL VIDALIA ONION OR RED ONION, MINCED

1 SMALL GARLIC CLOVE, FINELY MINCED

1 TO 1½ TEASPOONS CAJUN SPICE MIX OR TO TASTE

SEA SALT TO TASTE

CAJUN SPICE MIX:

2 TEASPOONS PAPRIKA

½ TEASPOON CAYENNE

¼ TEASPOON FRESHLY GROUND BLACK PEPPER

¼ TEASPOON ALLSPICE

½ TEASPOON DRIED THYME LEAVES

¼ TEASPOON FRESHLY GROUND WHITE PEPPER

2 TABLESPOONS FRESHLY SQUEEZED LEMON JUICE

2 TABLESPOONS EXTRA VIRGIN OLIVE OIL (OPTIONAL)

1. To cook corn, bring 2 cups water to a boil in a large pot. Add corn. Cook for 5 minutes until bright yellow. Remove corn from water with a slotted spoon, saving a cup of the cooking liquid. Cool corn and cut kernels off the cobs. Place in a large mixing bowl.

2. Wash kale and strip the leaves off the stalks (see page 155). Discard stalks and chop kale leaves into medium-fine pieces. Bring saved corn cooking liquid to a boil, add chopped kale leaves, and cook for 4 minutes, or until kale is just tender and still bright green. Remove from cooking liquid with a slotted spoon to a large plate to cool quickly.

3. To prepare Cajun Spice Mix, combine paprika, peppers, all-spice, thyme, and white pepper in a small bowl or dish.

4. When kale has cooled, toss with the corn, red pepper, green pepper, onion, garlic, and desired amount of Cajun Spice Mix.

5. Just before serving, sprinkle on the lemon juice for a nonfat salad, or whisk together the lemon juice and olive oil and toss with vegetables. Season to taste with a pinch of sea salt.

USES FOR CAJUN SPICE MIX

❖ *Sprinkle on fish before grilling*

❖ *Sprinkle on roasted or baked potatoes*

❖ *Toss with shrimp, garlic, and oil and sauté*

❖ *Mix with butter for corn*

Chicken Stir-Fry with Cauliflower and Kale

Lots of vegetables make for a nutrient-dense stir-fry. A few leaves of kale are added for texture and color and make a nice change from broccoli. Although the recipe looks long, it is really quite easy to make and very tasty to eat.

3 BONELESS, SKINLESS CHICKEN BREAST HALVES, CUT INTO ¾-INCH CUBES

1 TABLESPOON TAMARI (NATURALLY BREWED SOY SAUCE)

1 TABLESPOON BALSAMIC VINEGAR

1 TEASPOON TOASTED (DARK) SESAME OIL

3 TEASPOONS CANOLA OIL OR LIGHT UNREFINED SESAME OIL

3 QUARTER-SIZE SLICES FRESH GINGER

2 GARLIC CLOVES, PEELED AND CUT INTO VERY THIN SLICES

1 CELERY STALK, THINLY SLICED ON THE DIAGONAL

1 MEDIUM CARROT, PEELED AND SLICED ON DIAGONAL

2½ TO 3 CUPS CAULIFLOWER FLORETS

4 TO 6 KALE LEAVES, WASHED, STEMMED, AND CHOPPED (SEE PAGE 155)

1 SMALL RED PEPPER, HALVED AND SLICED VERTICALLY INTO MATCHSTICKS

SALT TO TASTE

SAUCE:

¾ CUP WATER

1 TABLESPOON TAMARI

1 TABLESPOON KUZU OR ARROWROOT (SEE PAGE 103)

½ TEASPOON TOASTED (DARK) SESAME OIL

1. Place the chicken cubes in a medium-size bowl. Sprinkle on the 1 tablespoon tamari, balsamic vinegar, and 1 teaspoon toasted sesame oil. Marinate while you continue with recipe.

2. In a large wok, heat 1 teaspoon of the canola or light sesame oil. Add the ginger and garlic and cook for 30 seconds. Add celery and carrot and toss to coat with oil. Cover and cook for 1 minute.

3. Add cauliflower and kale and toss to combine. Cover and cook for 2 minutes, adding 1 to 2 tablespoons water to help create steam. Remove cover to stir vegetables and to make sure they are not burning.

4. Add the red pepper and a pinch of salt. Cover and cook 1 more minute. Remove vegetables to a plate and keep warm.

5. In the same wok, heat the remaining 2 teaspoons canola or light sesame oil. With a slotted spoon, remove half the chicken from the marinade and stir fry over high heat for 4 to 5 minutes, or until meat is cooked. Check center of a cube to make sure. Remove to the plate with the vegetables. Repeat with the remaining chicken. You need not add any extra oil because the oil in the remaining marinade will be sufficient to lubricate the wok.

6. In a small bowl, stir together the sauce ingredients. Add to the wok and cook until clear and thickened. Return the vegetables and cooked chicken to the wok and heat through. Serve immediately with more tamari, if desired.

VARIATIONS

Try using mushrooms, bean sprouts, bamboo shoots, or water chestnuts in the stir-fry.

Curried Potatoes with Kale

Kale's natural affinity for potatoes shines through in this filling side dish. The squeeze of lime juice adds sparkle. If you like a more spicy flavor, increase the amount of the curry powder.

YUKON GOLD AND YELLOW FINN POTATOES

Whenever possible, we choose these deep-yellow-fleshed varieties of potato for boiling, baking, or mashing. They have a creamy texture and a taste so rich that little or no butter is needed. In fact, it seems as if it has already been added.

SERVES 4

2 POUNDS WHITE, YELLOW FINN, OR RED POTATOES, PEELED

1 TABLESPOON CANOLA OIL

2 TEASPOONS CURRY POWDER

1½ CUPS CHOPPED ONION

SALT TO TASTE

1½ CUPS WATER

¾ POUND KALE (ABOUT 6 CUPS CHOPPED)

FRESHLY GROUND BLACK PEPPER TO TASTE

1 LIME, CUT INTO 6 WEDGES

1. Cut the potatoes into ¾-inch cubes and set aside.

2. Heat a 10- or 12-inch skillet over medium heat. Add the oil and swirl in pan. Add the curry powder and cook for 1 minute, taking care not to burn it. Add the onions and sauté over medium heat for 5 minutes, or until they begin to soften.

3. Add the potato cubes and toss to coat with the curry and oil. Season lightly with salt, add the water, and bring to a boil. Reduce heat, cover, and simmer for 15 to 20 minutes, until the potatoes are tender.

4. Meanwhile, wash the kale well, then strip the leaves off the stalks (see page 155). Discard stalks and chop kale into bite-size pieces. Bring 2 cups water to a boil in a 10- to 12-inch skillet that has a tight-fitting lid. Add the kale and cook, covered, over high heat, stirring occasionally, until tender, approximately 5 minutes. Remove and drain, saving the cooking liquid to drink.

5. Stir cooked kale with the potatoes. Heat through and season to taste with freshly ground black pepper and additional salt if necessary. Serve hot with a squeeze of fresh lime juice.

Quick-and-Easy
Grilled Kale

*You need a stovetop grill or an enameled steel sheet with small holes
for your outdoor grill. We use a two-burner LeCreuset grill,
which works perfectly.*

SERVES 2 TO 3

OLIVE OIL TO BRUSH GRILL

¾ POUND KALE (ABOUT 6 CUPS CHOPPED)

2 TABLESPOONS WHITE WINE VINEGAR (HERB-FLAVORED
  IS DELICIOUS)

SALT AND FRESHLY GROUND PEPPER TO TASTE.

VARIATIONS

❖ *Use collards
instead of kale.
Chop into thinly
sliced ribbons for a
festive appearance.*

1. Heat grill to medium high. Wash kale and strip the leaves off
the stalks (see page 155). Discard stalks and roughly chop kale.

2. Brush grill with oil and add the greens. Using metal tongs,
quickly mix greens to allow all of them to cook, about 1 minute.
Add the vinegar, salt, and pepper and continue cooking for
another 2 or 3 minutes, until greens are wilted and tender.

3. Serve immediately.

❖ *Try various
flavored vinegars:
Herbes de Provence
vinegar, lemon-
basil vinegar, etc.*

❖ *Try flavored oils.
Consorzio makes
olive oils flavored
with basil, roasted
garlic, and hot
peppers.*

Potato Kale Soup

Make this soup when you want hot, soothing comfort food on a drizzly, cold day. It's such a simple combination, but so delicious. The whole carrots and celery are added to the soup as it cooks to give it flavor, and are then discarded.

KALE SOUP
VARIATIONS

❖ *Add 1 cup fresh corn kernels to soup when you add cooked kale. Simmer for 5 minutes.*

❖ *Add 1 cup cooked white beans or kidney beans when kale is added.*

❖ *Add cooked, sliced sausage to this soup—as the Portuguese do in a dish called* Caldo Verde.

❖ *Add all three of the above for a hearty dinner meal.*

SERVES 6 TO 8

1 TABLESPOON EXTRA VIRGIN OLIVE OIL

1 TABLESPOON UNSALTED BUTTER

2 CUPS CHOPPED ONIONS

2 LEEKS, WHITE AND LIGHT GREEN PART ONLY, WASHED AND THINLY SLICED

6 CUPS WATER

4 MEDIUM POTATOES, CUT INTO ¾-INCH CUBES (ABOUT 4 CUPS)

2 TABLESPOONS MINCED FRESH PARSLEY

3 CARROTS, PEELED

3 CELERY STALKS

2 BAY LEAVES

1 TEASPOON SALT

¼ TEASPOON FRESHLY GROUND PEPPER

½ POUND KALE (ABOUT 4 CUPS CHOPPED)

1. Heat oil and butter in a heavy-bottomed 7-quart soup pot over medium heat. Sauté onions and leeks for 10 to 15 minutes, until golden, soft, and sweet.

2. Add the water, potatoes, parsley, whole carrots, whole celery stalks, bay leaves, salt, and pepper. Bring to a boil. Reduce heat to medium low, cover and simmer for 45 minutes.

3. While soup is cooking, wash kale and strip the leaves off the stalks (see page 155). Discard stalks and chop leaves into bite-size pieces. Bring 2 cups water to a boil in a 10- to 12-inch skillet with a tight-fitting lid. Add the kale and cook, covered, over high heat, stirring occasionally, until tender, approximately 5 minutes. Remove and drain, saving the cooking water to drink.

4. Remove the carrot and celery pieces and bay leaves from the soup. Purée half the soup in a food processor or blender. Return blended portion back to the pot, stir in cooked kale, and heat through. Season to taste with salt and pepper and serve hot.

Stir-Fried Kale, Carrots, and Walnuts

Kale's versatility as a vegetable makes it a good choice for an easy stir-fry. The cooked kale will be slightly crunchy. Serve with steamed fish and rice for a pleasant contrast in texture and flavor. Our tester served this with black-eyed peas and corn bread. Yumm!

SERVES 3 TO 4

¾ POUND KALE

3 TEASPOONS CANOLA OIL

⅓ CUP WALNUTS, COARSELY CHOPPED

2 LARGE GARLIC CLOVES, PEELED AND COARSELY CHOPPED

2 QUARTER-SIZE SLICES OF FRESH GINGER

¼ TEASPOON RED PEPPER FLAKES, OR TO TASTE

2 CARROTS, PEELED AND CUT INTO THIN MATCHSTICKS

2 TO 4 TABLESPOONS WATER OR CHICKEN OR VEGETABLE BROTH (OPTIONAL)

Sea salt or soy sauce to taste

1. Wash kale and strip the leaves off the stalks, discard the stalks, then cut the kale into ⅛-inch strips (see page 155). Cut slices in half. Set aside.

2. Heat a large wok over medium-high heat. Add 1 teaspoon of the oil to the pan and swirl around to coat the bottom of the wok. Add the walnuts and toast, stirring constantly, for about 1 minute. Set aside to drain on a paper towel.

3. Add the remaining oil to the wok. Swirl again. Add the garlic and ginger and stir-fry for 10 seconds. Add the red pepper flakes and carrots and stir-fry for 1 minute.

4. Add the shredded kale and toss well to coat with oil. Press down on the kale, cover, and let cook for 30 seconds. Stir-fry again and then cover. Cook for 3 minutes longer, stirring con-

tents of pan about every minute to avoid burning the kale. The steam generated should be enough to complete the cooking process, but 2 tablespoons water or broth can be added during the cooking process, if desired, to increase steam and tenderness of kale. Taste and season with salt or soy sauce. Remove ginger slices and serve hot, garnished with the walnuts.

CUTTING

MATCHSTICKS

An easy way to cut carrots into thin matchsticks is first to cut the carrot on a sharp diagonal into oval slices. Then stack 2 or 3 slices and cut them into ⅛-inch-wide strips. These thin strips cook quickly and are nice for salads, too.

White Bean Soup
with Kale

This soup is adapted from a recipe by Rachel Reid, who has been cooking with natural foods for the past twenty years. Cholesterol-fighting beans team up with nutrient-dense kale for a deliciously warming autumn or winter soup. Leftovers make great eating with a thick slice of whole grain bread.

TO COOK
THE BEANS

Soak 2 cups of beans overnight in plenty of water to cover. Drain, add 5 cups fresh water, and bring to a boil. Reduce heat and simmer for 45 to 60 minutes, until done. Do not add salt until cooking is complete. Add more water, if necessary.

SERVES 6

1 TABLESPOON CANOLA OIL

2 ONIONS, PEELED AND CHOPPED

2 CLOVES GARLIC, MINCED

1 TABLESPOON CURRY POWDER

½ TEASPOON CUMIN

4 CUPS COOKED WHITE BEANS

1 TEASPOON DRIED SWEET MARJORAM OR BASIL

3 CUPS BUTTERNUT SQUASH, PEELED, SEEDED, AND CUT INTO ¾-INCH CHUNKS

2 TO 3 CUPS SHREDDED KALE, LEAVES ONLY

6 CUPS BEAN COOKING LIQUID, VEGETABLE STOCK, OR WATER

SEA SALT TO TASTE

FRESHLY SQUEEZED LEMON JUICE

1. Heat the oil in a large soup pot over medium heat. Add onions and sauté over medium heat for about 10 minutes, or until softened and translucent. Add garlic, curry, and cumin and sauté for an additional 2 minutes.

2. Add the cooked beans, marjoram or basil, squash, kale, bean cooking liquid (and stock, if necessary, to equal 6 cups). Bring to a boil, reduce heat, add salt, and cook for 20 minutes, until squash is tender.

3. Taste and adjust seasoning. Add lemon juice to taste before serving.

Sesame Kale

A quick and easy side dish.

SERVES 3 TO 4

¾ POUND KALE (ABOUT 6 CUPS), WASHED, STEMMED,
AND COARSELY CHOPPED

1 TABLESPOON SESAME OR OLIVE OIL

1 TO 2 TEASPOONS FINELY CHOPPED FRESH GARLIC

½ CUP CHOPPED SCALLIONS, WHITE AND GREEN PARTS

SALT TO TASTE

1 ½ TABLESPOONS TOASTED SESAME SEEDS

1. Bring 2 cups water to a boil in a large 10- to 12-inch skillet that has a tight-fighting lid. Add chopped kale and cook for about 5 minutes, stirring occasionally, until kale is tender. Remove cooked kale with slotted spoon to drain, saving cooking water to drink.

2. Rinse out and dry the skillet, then use it to heat the oil over medium-low heat. Add garlic and sauté for about 1 minute. Stir in scallions and cook for another minute.

3. Add cooked kale and salt to taste and stir to combine. Cover and cook for 1 to 2 minutes until kale is hot. Sprinkle with sesame seeds and serve immediately.

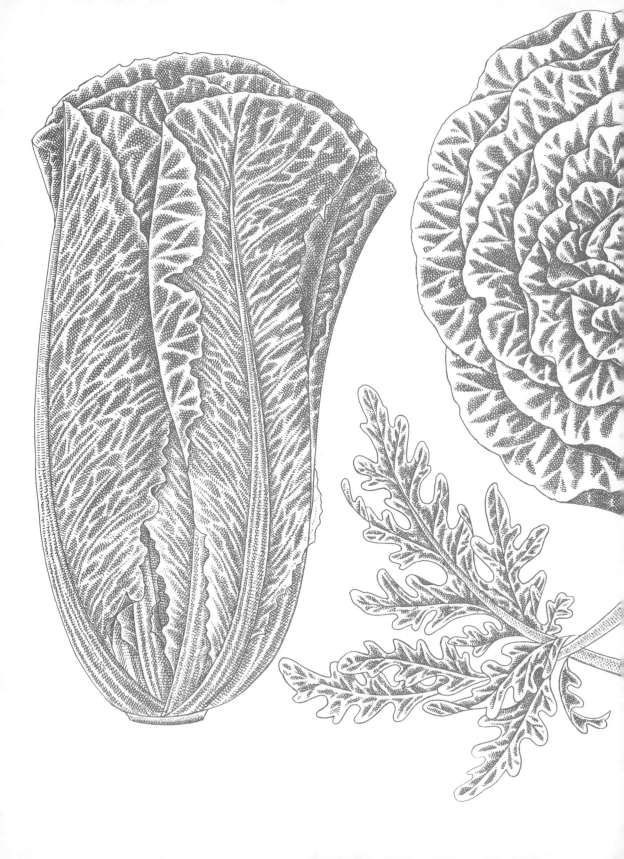

Lettuce and Salad Greens

THERE'S A PALETTE OF BRILLIANTLY COLORED SALAD GREENS, including radicchio, red romaine, and red orach, as well as wonderfully textured varieties, from soft Boston lettuce to wild curly frisée, being harvested across the country. You can use your artistic ability to create salads that taste and look spectacular. You no longer need carrots or peppers to add taste or nutrition to chunks of iceberg lettuce. You can choose from peppery arugula (high in calcium and vitamins) or red giant mustard and mild mustardlike mizuna, both cruciferous, cancer-fighting vegetables.

Typically, lettuces fall into several categories. Romaine lettuces have long broad leaves with a definite crunch. Butterhead lettuces form loosely folded rosettes with delicate, soft leaves. Loose-leaf lettuces include open-headed varieties like greenleaf and oakleaf. And, there's the country's most popular variety: the crisp iceberg lettuce, plain and crunchy.

Against this backdrop is a variety of other leafy greens that don't fall into the typical lettuce categories. Most are flavorful, colorful greens—arugula, mizuna, frisée, watercress, radicchio, red Belgium endive, and mâche.

Many are coming out of the biggest salad phenomenon of the past ten years: the introduction of salad mixes, or mesclun. Mesclun is a French term for a mixture of seedling or baby lettuces, herbs, and greens.

Mesclun mixes have evolved from four to five lettuces mixed with one or two greens into specialized combinations with Oriental greens, spicy greens, endives, radicchio, and cresses. "We as companies had to start being creative," said Karen Siske, director of commercial sales for Johnny's Selected Seeds. "One grower had to differentiate one mix from another, and we really had to hit the mat and look for other things." As a result, she says, specialty salad greens are booming, and there is now a market for greens such as purslane, miner's lettuce, chickweed, and red and green orach, among others.

Salads are a big part of our American food culture, especially during the spring and summer months. They are quick to make, crunchy, light, and delicious. Now we can enjoy this wide array of lettuces and greens to improve upon them.

Arugula

From mild and nutty to peppery, the small tangy arugula leaves add zest to any salad, even the blandest, and rate a 10 on the leafy-green nutrition scale. Arugula contains more vitamin C, calcium, and beta carotene than any other salad green. Arugula tastes delicious with butter lettuces, Bibb, and radicchio, and with walnuts, berries, citrus, tomatoes, and avocado. (For more on arugula, plus recipes, see chapter on arugula beginning on page 7)

Batavian

Batavian lettuces combine the crispness of romaine with the shape of a butterhead. They are good in salads of all kinds.

Butterhead

Butterhead encompasses Boston and Bibb lettuces. Soft, velvety leaves have a mild and delicate flavor, and balance nicely with nuttier or spicier greens such as arugula, radicchio, and watercress, both in flavor and color. They come alive with a balsamic vinaigrette.

Endive

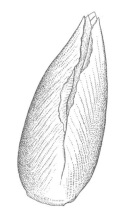

The creamy yellow-and-white blanched leaves of the Belgian endive are bittersweet and succulent. They combine very well with peppery greens such as arugula, radicchio, and watercress, as well as with other mixed greens, pears, apples, walnuts, and cheese. Endive adds a velvety crunch to any salad. The Red Belgium endive, a gorgeous leaf specimen with slightly more bitterness, can be used as you would regular Belgian endive. (Also, see chapter on endive and chicory, beginning on page 139)

Frisée

Also called curly endive, frisée is deliciously crisp with a bittersweet taste, which makes it a great textural addition to salads of all kinds, especially ones with mild lettuces. Like Belgian endive, frisée combines well with fruits, nuts, and cheeses. Its pale-colored, frilly leaves stand up well in warm salads.

Loose-Leaf

This type of lettuce consists of loosely connected leaves rather than a compact head. Mild and delicate tasting, loose-leafs include red leaf, green leaf, salad bowl, ruby, as well as green and red oakleaf. The red oakleaf is a particularly striking lettuce with a mild, nutlike flavor. Lollo rossa is a heavily ruffled Italian variety with green hearts and crimson-tipped leaves. Tango lettuce is crunchy with a distinct green flavor.

Mâche

Also known as corn salad and lamb's lettuce (not lamb's quarters), mâche is very succulent with attractive rounded leaves, which are harvested individually or in small bunches or rosettes. Its mildly nutty flavor and smooth texture go well with salads of all kinds. It is expensive and highly perishable, and therefore, not widely available.

Mesclun

Some greengrocers and even supermarkets now carry mesclun, a wonderful mixture of baby lettuces, herbs, and other greens. You might find mizuna (a variety of mustard greens), frisée (a type of endive), baby spinach, and assorted leaf lettuces. Mesclun is so full of flavor that often no other vegetable is needed in a meal.

Mesclun is quite pricey because the tender leaves are young and very perishable. But it is very lightweight, and a small amount is usually sufficient. If you can't find premixed mesclun, or if you want to cut the cost, make up a combination of your favorite tender greens or add the tender inner leaves of Bibb or Boston lettuce to a mesclun mix. Or grow your own! We each have a small mesclun bed near our kitchens for easy harvest. The marvelous mix of flavors and textures transports us to Provence, where mesclun is very popular.

Miner's Lettuce

Also called claytonia, miner's lettuce is an attractive salad green available for cultivation and from the wild. It is distinct looking with a leaf wrapped around a white-flowered stem. The blossoms are edible, too. Johnny's Selected Seeds describes the taste as "wild and fresh."

Mizuna

Mizuna is a Japanese green with a mild mustard taste. One of the most striking-looking salad greens, mizuna adds character as well as flavor to salads of all kinds. Use it in other vegetable or pasta salads, such as potato salad and sesame noodle salad, or as a base for grilled fish or chicken.

Purslane

Purslane is a wild edible plant also available for cultivation. Small, rounded, succulent leaves add a mildly tart taste to fresh salads.

Red Orach

A colorful salad ingredient, red orach is one of the newly available specialty greens and a member of the spinach family. It has historical use as a potherb. Its leaves, as well as those of green orach, contribute a tart tang.

Radicchio

Because of its brilliant magenta or cranberry color, radicchio can single-handedly improve the visual appeal of salads more than any other green. Native to Italy, from which it is sometimes exported, radicchio can be expensive, but a little goes a long way. It tastes best mixed with other greens because it is mildly bitter alone. Try it with any combination of butter lettuces, loose-leaf, arugula, or endive, and add cheese, nuts, berries, smoked meats, or chicken. (See more on radicchio in chapter on endive and chicory, page 139)

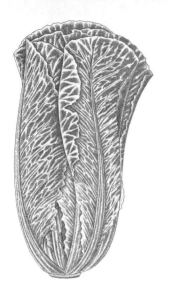

Romaine

Romaine lettuce has long, upright leaves with a thick, crisp texture. It is similar in texture to iceberg, but with a more distinctive lettuce flavor and up to six times as much vitamin C. The center leaves of romaine are the crispest and most flavorful part. The main ingredient in Caesar salads, romaine can be mixed with softer lettuces or used alone. Use a bold dressing. Red romaine is another strikingly colorful lettuce to mix with regular romaine or to add to sandwiches.

Watercress

Delicate with a delectable spiciness, watercress is a good choice with milder Boston or Bibb lettuces or endive. It is excellent combined with fruit, citrus, and tomatoes as well as with pasta, bean, and grain salads. Watercress is a member of the cruciferous family and a good source of calcium and vitamin C.

SHOPPING TIPS

Choose lettuce and salad greens that look fresh and crisp—never limp or wilted or dry or brown on the edges.

STORAGE

Store lettuce and salad greens in a plastic bag, not tightly closed, in the crisper drawer. Try to wash them just before using. If you do prepare them ahead, wash and thoroughly dry them, then wrap in a damp paper towel and store refrigerated in a plastic bag.

PREPARATION

With the exception of endive and radicchio, all salad greens should be washed well to remove any grit or sand. For headed varieties, such as loose-leaf and romaine, twist or cut off the stem and separate leaves before washing. Fill a large bowl with cold water. Plunge in the leaves and swish them around. Lift leaves out of water to a colander, and check bottom of bowl. If there is any sand or grit, discard the water and repeat the process.

For company, we even wash the prewashed mesclun, and have found sand at the bottom of the bowl. To crisp up slightly wilted mesclun leaves, one trick is to fill a bowl with very cold water and let the greens sit in the water for 10 to 15 minutes. (This cleans them, too.) Lift greens out and dry in a salad spinner.

A salad spinner is an inexpensive kitchen aid that really works to dry salad greens. It saves time and produces the crisp dry greens needed for a perfect salad.

Most lettuces are best torn by hand. We often do this while the greens are sitting in a bowl of water for cleaning. A few lettuces are better off being cut with a knife; endive and romaine are two. We also like the way radicchio looks in a salad when it is thinly sliced rather than torn by hands.

Mixed Greens with Creamy Lime-Fig Dressing

This dressing is made quickly in a blender. The figs give it a thick, creamy consistency as well as a sweetness that perfectly offsets the tang of the lime juice. Mirin, a Japanese sweet rice seasoning, helps round out the dressing, but it won't be harmed if mirin is not available.

SERVES 4

ABOUT FIGS

In this salad, you will get more calcium from the dried figs than from the greens (with the exception of arugula, if used). In addition to being high in calcium, figs are a good source of iron, potassium, and fiber.

DRESSING:

3 DRIED TURKISH OR CALMYRNA FIGS (STEMS REMOVED)

3 TABLESPOONS FRESHLY SQUEEZED LIME JUICE

1 TABLESPOON APPLE CIDER VINEGAR

1 TABLESPOON MIRIN, IF AVAILABLE

1 SMALL GARLIC CLOVE, MINCED

¼ CUP CANOLA OR OLIVE OIL

¾ CUP WATER

SALT TO TASTE

4 CUPS SALAD GREENS, SUCH AS RED LEAF LETTUCE, ARUGULA, BIBB, OR MESCLUN

1 YELLOW PEPPER, CORED, AND SLICED INTO VERY THIN STRIPS

3 DRIED FIGS, SLICED

1. To make the dressing, place figs, lime juice, vinegar, mirin (if using), garlic, oil, water, and salt in a blender. Blend for 2 to 3 minutes until smooth and creamy.

2. Wash salad greens and spin dry (see page 181). Tear into bite-size pieces. Just before serving, toss lettuce with dressing, using as much dressing as necessary to coat the greens. Garnish with yellow pepper and sliced figs.

Basic Balsamic Vinaigrette Over Mesclun

Homemade dressings like this one taste delicious and take only minutes to make. In addition to mesclun, use this balsamic vinaigrette with arugula, watercress, loose-leaf, or butterhead lettuces. It's also great as a dressing to brush on grilled vegetables.

SERVES 4

MESCLUN SALAD GREENS FOR 4 (4 TO 6 CUPS)

DRESSING:
1 SHALLOT OR 1 GARLIC CLOVE
2 TABLESPOONS BALSAMIC VINEGAR
1 TABLESPOON LEMON JUICE
2 TEASPOONS DIJON MUSTARD
1 TEASPOON MAPLE SYRUP OR OTHER SWEETENER
½ CUP EXTRA VIRGIN OLIVE OIL
¼ TEASPOON SALT, OR TO TASTE
FRESHLY GROUND BLACK PEPPER
4 TO 5 DROPS OF HOT SAUCE

1. To make dressing, place peeled shallot or garlic in the work-bowl of a food processor or blender. Process to mince. Add balsamic vinegar, lemon juice, mustard, sweetener, olive oil, and salt and process until emulsified, 1 to 2 minutes. Taste and season with additional salt, if needed, black pepper, and hot sauce.

2. To mix by hand, place minced shallot or garlic, vinegar, lemon, mustard, and sweetener in a medium-size bowl. Slowly whisk in olive oil. Taste and adjust seasonings.

3. Mix with greens just before serving. Save extra dressing for another salad.

"TEMPERS THE ARDORS OF VENUS"

Salads became the object of great admiration in Seventeenth- and Eighteenth-century France, according to Harold McGee in On Food And Cooking *(New York: Macmillan, 1984). French hygienists of the period recommended eating a salad at the end of every meal. One wrote that a salad "moistens, refreshens, frees the stomach, encourages sleep, tempers the ardors of Venus, and appeases the thirst."*

Rasperry-Orange Vinaigrette with Arugula, Raddichio, and Endive

This is a light and fruity dressing that works with most salad greens. If endive or radicchio is unavailable, try mixing the arugula with any loose-leaf lettuce. If arugula is unavailable, ask your produce manager to order some.

SERVES 4 TO 6

- 1 BUNCH ARUGULA (ABOUT 2 CUPS)
- 2 SMALL HEADS BELGIAN ENDIVE (ABOUT 2 CUPS)
- 1 TINY HEAD RADICCHIO (ABOUT 1 CUP)
- 1 SMALL HEAD BIBB OR BOSTON LETTUCE
- 1 ORANGE, HALVED AND SECTIONED USING A GRAPEFRUIT KNIFE
- ½ CUP RASPBERRIES (IF IN SEASON)

DRESSING:
- 3 TABLESPOONS RASPBERRY VINEGAR
- ⅓ CUP FRESHLY SQUEEZED ORANGE JUICE (1 TO 2 ORANGES)
- 1 TEASPOON HONEY OR OTHER SWEETENER
- 1 TEASPOON PREPARED MUSTARD
- 1 TABLESPOON CHOPPED SHALLOTS OR RED ONION
- ¼ CUP CANOLA OIL
- ¼ TEASPOON SALT

1. Wash arugula by plunging leaves into a bowl of cool water. Lift out into a colander or salad spinner. Remove stems up to leafy part and chop slightly if leaves are longer than 2 inches. To prepare endive, cut off base. Halve leaves lengthwise and slice crosswise about ½ inch thick. Slice or tear radicchio into bite-size pieces. Wash and dry Bibb or Boston lettuce (see page 181) and cut into small pieces.

2. To make the dressing, place raspberry vinegar, orange juice, honey, mustard, shallots, oil, and salt in a blender. Blend for 1 minute.

3. Just before serving, toss salad greens with just enough vinaigrette to coat the greens. Garnish with orange sections or raspberries.

Our pantry wouldn't be complete without a bottle of raspberry vinegar on hand. It has a delicious flavor— slightly sweet and slightly tart—perfect for fresh summer salad greens or wilted, hot greens. Raspberry vinegar is widely available, but a particularly wonderful mail-order source is Cheshire Gardens in Winchester, New Hampshire. Its Queen of Hearts Raspberry Vinegar is made with French white Bordeaux wine and wildflower honey. It's good enough to use directly on your salad without oil for a low-calorie dressing. Cheshire Garden's mail-order catalog (603-239-4173) also includes strawberry vinegar and an assortment of blended herb vinegars— all organic.

Dry Town Cafe's Sun-Dried Caesar Salad

Bob Skydell, chef-owner of The Dry Town Cafe on the island of Martha's Vineyard, off Massachusetts, serves this popular lunchtime Caesar salad made with crisp romaine lettuce, a sun-dried tomato dressing, delicious rosemary croutons, and freshly grated Parmesan cheese.

THE DRY TOWN CAFE

The Dry Town Cafe, one of Martha's Vineyard's best new restaurants, maintains a large kitchen garden full of leafy greens and other vegetables to supply the restaurant with fresh, seasonal produce. The changing nature of what becomes available at the peak of freshness dictates the food the restaurant serves and is a source of creative inspiration for the kitchen staff.

SERVES 4

1 LARGE HEAD ROMAINE LETTUCE

FRESHLY GRATED PARMIGIANO-REGGIANO

DRESSING:

½ CUP SUN-DRIED TOMATOES

2 TABLESPOONS RED WINE VINEGAR

½ CUP EXTRA VIRGIN OLIVE OIL

SALT AND PEPPER TO TASTE

ROSEMARY ROASTED CROUTONS:

⅓ OR ½ SOURDOUGH BAGUETTE

2 TABLESPOONS EXTRA VIRGIN OLIVE OIL

1 TABLESPOON FINELY MINCED FRESH ROSEMARY

SALT AND PEPPER

1. Cut or tear romaine lettuce. Wash and spin dry (see page 181).

2. Soak sun-dried tomatoes in hot water until hydrated, 20 to 30 minutes. Drain and discard soaking water.

3. In a food processor or blender, combine tomatoes and vinegar. While processor is running, add olive oil in a slow stream. Season with salt and pepper.

4. To prepare croutons, cube the baguette into ½-inch pieces. You should have about 3 cups. Toss lightly in olive oil, rosemary, salt, and pepper. Bake at 275°F until pieces are crisp and golden.

5. Place chopped romaine in a salad bowl. Add just enough dressing to coat leaves. Sprinkle with Parmesan cheese. Add the croutons and toss.

Zippy Watercress, Green Apple, and Feta Salad

Salads do not have to be boring. Here we combine the spiciness of watercress, the tartness of an apple, and the pungency of a red onion with the mild-tasting Boston or Bibb lettuce.

SERVES 4

1 HEAD BOSTON OR BIBB LETTUCE

1 BUNCH WATERCRESS LEAVES (ABOUT 2 CUPS)

1 GRANNY SMITH APPLE, CORED AND CUT INTO THIN SLICES

¼ CUP MINCED RED ONION

½ CUP SHEEP'S-MILK FETA CHEESE, CUT INTO
    ¼-INCH CUBES

DRESSING:

3 TABLESPOONS RED WINE VINEGAR

6 TABLESPOONS EXTRA VIRGIN OLIVE OIL

PINCH OF DRIED OREGANO

¼ TEASPOON SALT

1. Wash lettuce and watercress and spin dry (see page 181). Tear or cut lettuce into bite-size pieces. Remove watercress leaves from thick stems. Make a few random slices through the bunch. Toss lettuce and watercress with apple, red onion, and feta cheese.

2. In a medium-size bowl, whisk wine vinegar with the olive oil. Add oregano and salt to taste.

3. Just before serving, toss salad with just enough dressing to coat leaves.

FETA CHEESE

❖ *Sheep's-milk feta cheese is the smoothest flavored and richest of the feta varieties. It's our favorite, and a traditional cheese in Greece and France. You can find it in specialty cheese shops and gourmet delis.*

❖ *Goat's-milk feta is sharper and saltier than sheep's milk. It has a unique taste.*

❖ *Cow's-milk feta cheese is the most commonly used feta in this country. It is the saltiest feta by our taste, not as subtle as the sheep's-milk feta.*

Romaine, Mozzarella and Olives with Roasted Red Pepper Dressing

This dressing also works well on red or green leafy lettuces, arugula, or watercress—just about any combination of salad greens. It also doubles as a nice sauce for fish.

FRESH MOZZARELLA

Fresh mozzarella cheese, now sold packed in water in many supermarkets, is a soft, mild, and delicate cheese. It is not aged, and is more perishable than the traditional mozzarella commonly used on pizza. Fresh mozzarella perfectly complements fresh basil, red pepper, olives, and tomatoes.

SERVES 4

1 HEAD ROMAINE LETTUCE, WASHED, DRIED, AND CUT OR TORN INTO BITE-SIZE PIECES (SEE PAGE 181)

1 CUP FRESH MOZZARELLA, CUT INTO BITE-SIZE PIECES

¼ CUP FRESH BASIL, THINLY SHREDDED

20 OIL-CURED BLACK OLIVES, PITTED AND SLICED

DRESSING:

2 RED PEPPERS, ROASTED, PEELED, AND SEEDED (SEE PAGE 46)

2 TABLESPOONS WATER

1 TABLESPOON BALSAMIC VINEGAR

2 TABLESPOONS EXTRA VIRGIN OLIVE OIL

½ TEASPOON SALT

¼ TEASPOON FRESHLY GROUND BLACK PEPPER

1. To make dressing, place roasted peppers, water, balsamic vinegar, olive oil, salt, and pepper in a blender. Blend for 1 to 2 minutes, until smooth and creamy. Taste and adjust seasonings.

2. In a salad bowl, mix together the romaine lettuce, fresh mozzarella, basil, and olives. Just before serving, spoon the dressing on top of the greens, but do not mix in, for an attractive presentation. You will have enough dressing left over for another salad.

Raspberry-Flavored Shrimp Over Mesclun Greens

This is an elegant dish that takes only minutes to prepare. The mesclun mix of baby lettuces comes already washed, which adds to the ease in preparation. If you make this dish on a summer or fall evening in raspberry season, be sure to add some berries for an extra treat.

SERVES 2

3 CUPS MESCLUN MIX

½ POUND MEDIUM SHRIMP

3 TABLESPOONS EXTRA VIRGIN OLIVE OIL

2 TABLESPOONS FINELY MINCED SHALLOTS

4 TABLESPOONS RASPBERRY VINEGAR

SALT AND FRESHLY GROUND PEPPER TO TASTE

FRESH RASPBERRIES AS GARNISH (OPTIONAL)

1. Portion mesclun (1 to 1½ cups per person) onto individual plates. Set aside.

2. Peel shrimp—leaving the tails intact for a nicer presentation—and devein. Set aside.

3. Heat 1 tablespoon of the oil in a skillet over low heat. Add shallots and cook for 2 to 4 minutes, until soft and slightly golden.

4. Turn heat to medium high. Add 1 tablespoon of the raspberry vinegar and shrimp and cook until shrimp are pink, 2 to 3 minutes on each side. Season with salt and pepper. Remove shrimp and place on top of mesclun.

5. Deglaze skillet with remaining 2 tablespoons of olive oil and 3 tablespoons raspberry vinegar. Drizzle warm vinaigrette on top of shrimp and greens. Garnish with raspberries, if in season.

Sharp and Sweet Salad Greens with Creamy Lemon Walnut Dressing

The sharp taste of watercress and the bitter edge of Belgian endive and radicchio are set off by the mild flavor and soft texture of the Bibb lettuce. The smooth sweetness of the walnut dressing brings it all together. The combination makes a slightly exotic salad for entertaining.

WALNUT OIL

Used frequently by the French, walnut oil imparts the smooth, nutty flavor of walnuts to a salad. It makes a good accompaniment to more bitter salad greens such as arugula, endive, radicchio, and watercress. Look for cold-pressed varieties, which will have more flavor than commercially processed brands. Keep refrigerated after opening.

SERVES 4 TO 6

1 BUNCH WATERCRESS

1 SMALL HEAD RADICCHIO

8 TO 10 INNER LEAVES OF BIBB OR BOSTON LETTUCE

1 TO 2 HEADS BELGIAN ENDIVE

DRESSING:

⅓ CUP LIGHTLY TOASTED WALNUTS

2 TABLESPOONS WALNUT OR CANOLA OIL

2 TABLESPOONS FRESH LEMON JUICE

1 TABLESPOON WATER

½ TEASPOON DRY MUSTARD

1 TEASPOON PURE MAPLE SYRUP OR OTHER SWEETENER

¼ TEASPOON SEA SALT, OR TO TASTE

FRESHLY GROUND BLACK PEPPER TO TASTE

1. Strip the watercress leaves from tough stalks. Wash and spin dry. With a large knife, make a few random slices through the bunch before placing in a medium-size mixing bowl.

2. Peel off any wilted outer leaves of the radicchio. Slice in half and cut into thin strips. Add to watercress. Wash the Bibb or Boston lettuce and spin dry (see page 181). Tear into bite-size pieces. Mix with other lettuces and toss gently. Set aside.

3. To make dressing, first toast the walnuts. Preheat the oven to 325° F. Place walnuts on a cookie sheet and bake until lightly toasted, 5 to 7 minutes. Do not overcook or they will have a bitter taste. Remove from oven and cool. Rub the cooled nuts with your hands or place in a clean cotton towel to remove as much brown skin as possible.

4. Grind the nuts in a blender until finely chopped. Add the oil, lemon juice, water, dry mustard, maple syrup, salt, and pepper and blend until creamy. Taste and adjust seasonings.

5. To serve, separate the Belgian endive leaves from the main stalk and arrange attractively on a large platter or individual serving plates, pointed end toward the edge of the plate. Just before serving, dress the watercress, radicchio, and lettuce in a mixing bowl and place the greens mixture on the platter or plates, slightly overlapping the blunt ends of the endive.

VARIATIONS

You can make substitutions for different salad greens if you find the radicchio or endive unavailable or too expensive. Arugula and Bibb or Boston is a nice combination, as is watercress and loose-leaf lettuce or watercress and endive.

Skewered Chicken Teriyaki Over Frisée and Arugula

Arugula and light curly frisée make a nice bed of greens for chicken and a warm teriyaki dressing. You can use mesclun or any combination of salad greens.

SERVES 4

MARINADE:

4 TABLESPOONS SHOYU OR TAMARI (NATURALLY BREWED SOY SAUCE)

2 TABLESPOONS MIRIN OR SHERRY

2 TABLESPOONS HONEY

2 TABLESPOONS APPLE CIDER VINEGAR

2 TABLESPOONS LIGHT SESAME OIL

2 TEASPOONS FRESHLY GRATED GINGER

2 TEASPOONS MINCED GARLIC

4 BONELESS, SKINLESS CHICKEN BREASTS

2 CUPS WASHED AND DRIED ARUGULA

2 CUPS WASHED AND DRIED FRISÉE

1. In a medium-size bowl, mix together the tamari, mirin, honey, apple cider vinegar, oil, ginger, and garlic.

2. Cut chicken into 1-inch cubes and place in bowl with the marinade. Refrigerate, covered, for at least 30 minutes.

3. While chicken is marinating, prepare greens. Remove arugula stems, and chop or tear leaves into bite-size pieces. Remove any thick stems from frisée and chop roughly into pieces 1 to 2 inches long. Place greens on a serving platter.

4. Preheat the broiler. Drain marinade from chicken and save. Skewer the chicken and broil for about 5 minutes on each side. Chicken should be lightly browned and cooked through.

5. While chicken is cooking, place remaining marinade in a small saucepan or skillet. Cook over high heat until slightly thickened, about 10 minutes.

6. When chicken is done, place skewers on top of greens. Drizzle chicken and greens with the warm marinade.

MIRIN

A basic seasoning in Asian cooking, mirin is naturally brewed and fermented from sweet brown rice, water, and koji (a natural rice culture). The sweetness of mirin complements savory seasonings such as soy sauce and rounds out the flavor of many dishes. It can add depth of flavor to sautéed vegetables, sauces and vinaigrettes, broths, and barbecued dishes. It's available in whole foods and Asian markets.

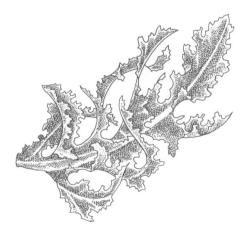

Broiled Salmon on Baby Greens

Mesclun serves as an excellent bed for rich, broiled salmon. The warm dressing is drizzled on the greens just before the fish is placed on top.

SERVES 4 TO 6

1½ POUNDS FRESH SALMON FILLETS

2 TABLESPOONS PLUS 1 TEASPOON DIJON MUSTARD

1 TEASPOON MAPLE SYRUP OR RICE SYRUP

3 TEASPOONS BALSAMIC VINEGAR

6 CUPS MESCLUN OR FRESH MIXED ORGANIC GREENS
(MIZUNA, ARUGULA, BOSTON LETTUCE, WATERCRESS,
RADICCHIO, FRISÉE)

5 TABLESPOONS EXTRA VIRGIN OLIVE OIL

4 TABLESPOONS WHITE OR RED WINE

½ TEASPOON MAPLE SYRUP

SALT AND PEPPER TO TASTE

1. Preheat the broiler.

2. Cut the fillets crosswise into 4 to 6 equal portions. In a small bowl, combine the 2 tablespoons Dijon mustard, sweetener, and 1 teaspoon of the balsamic vinegar. Spread mixture on the salmon fillets and set aside while you prepare the serving plates.

3. Clean and trim the greens. Combine in a salad bowl to distribute the varieties evenly. Arrange 1 to 1½ cups mixed spring greens on individual serving plates. Set aside while you cook the fish.

4. Broil the salmon fillets for 6 to 10 minutes, or until just cooked through and browned lightly. Take care to avoid burning. Lower the broiler rack if necessary.

5. While the fish is cooking, heat the olive oil, remaining vinegar and mustard, and the wine in a small skillet. When the fish is cooked to perfection, drizzle the warm dressing over the greens, lay a portion of fish on top of the greens, and serve immediately.

Greek Salad

*Make this in the summer when garden-fresh cucumbers
and tomatoes are abundant.*

SERVES 4 TO 6

2 CUCUMBERS

3 VINE-RIPENED TOMATOES

½ MEDIUM RED ONION OR 3 SCALLIONS, THINLY SLICED

3 TO 4 CUPS ROMAINE LETTUCE LEAVES THAT HAVE BEEN
   WASHED, DRIED, AND CUT

½ POUND SHEEP OR GOAT FETA CHEESE

½ CUP KALAMATA OLIVES, RINSED

DRESSING:

¼ CUP EXTRA VIRGIN OLIVE OIL

2 TABLESPOONS FRESHLY SQUEEZED LEMON JUICE

1 TABLESPOON RED WINE VINEGAR

2 TEASPOONS FRESH OREGANO, OR 1 TEASPOON DRIED

FRESHLY GROUND BLACK PEPPER TO TASTE

1. Place prepared lettuce in a salad bowl.

2. If cucumbers are waxed, peel them. Quarter lengthwise and
cut into ¾-inch chunks. Place in salad bowl with lettuce.

3. Quarter tomatoes and cut into chunks resembling cucumber
chunks. Add to salad bowl with sliced onions. Toss with lettuce.

4. Crumble or dice the feta cheese and add it to the salad, along
with rinsed olives.

5. In a small bowl, combine all dressing ingredients. Pour over
salad, toss lightly, and serve.

Mustard Greens

CREATING AN APPEALING DISH WITH MUSTARD GREENS IS A challenge. Sitting on produce shelves, mustard greens have a certain allure with their bright green and frilly-edged leaves and mustardy perfume. Once cooked, however, they often turn a drab green and have a rather stringy, thin texture. They hit the taste buds with a pungent, not altogether favorable, impression.

Restaurants don't seem to be experimenting with mustard greens as they are with other greens. And cookbooks rarely have tackled this cruciferous vegetable. Food writer Elizabeth Schneider, who has delved into the culinary history of greens, says she can locate very few world cuisines that make use of mustard greens. "Only in some areas of India, China, Africa, and the American South does the green seem to have met up with the saucepan or stewpot. And very, very few recipes exist even among those who take the green for granted."

So why bother? After experimenting with all types of cooking methods and combinations, we found that in certain combinations, mustard greens can offer a unique, delicious contribution. Served alone, the pungent mustard greens taste can be overwhelming. But mixed with other mellower greens, such as spinach, kale, and mizuna, mustard greens do much better. The less sharp or bitter greens tame the flavor of the strong mustard greens. And instead of a dominating mustardy flavor, you get hints of the nippy mustard taste, which now picks up the flavor of the blander greens. As an analogy, think of eating plain prepared mustard from a jar. Compare that to spreading it on a sandwich or adding it to a dressing. Mustard greens, the source of spicy seeds used to make mustard, can play a similar role in dishes.

We found mustard greens also combine well with beans (a bland partner) and other sweet vegetables such as carrots, corn, sweet potatoes, and leeks. We had much success adding mustard greens to soups, gumbos, or stews. Cooked mustard greens mellow, but still contribute that hint of spiciness.

Mustard greens take well to stir-frying and sautéing with other vegetables. Adding small amounts of water during cooking helps create enough steam to soften the mustard greens. While grilling works fine for some greens such as kale, collards, and radicchio, we didn't have much success with mustard greens. Likewise with steaming, which only increased the bitterness.

SHOPPING TIPS

Pick a bunch of mustard greens with uniformly colored green leaves without any yellowed or dry leaves.

STORAGE

Mustard greens yellow and dry out rather quickly in the refrigerator. They are best used within 1 or 2 days.

PREPARATION

Wash mustard greens by plunging them into a large bowl of cold water. Lift greens out of water to a colander, and check bottom of bowl. If there is any sand or dirt, discard the water and repeat the process. Strip or cut the leaves from the stalks. To chop, stack 4 to 5 leaves on top of each other and roll into a fat cigar shape. Using a large knife, slice crosswise into strips.

Sautéed Mustard Greens, Spinach, and Yellow Pepper

The spinach and sweet pepper nicely balance the strong flavor of the mustard greens. The onion and garlic round out this side dish.

SERVES 4 AS A SIDE DISH

1 POUND MUSTARD GREENS

1 POUND SPINACH

2 TABLESPOONS EXTRA VIRGIN OLIVE OIL

2 ONIONS, THINLY SLICED

1 TABLESPOON MINCED GARLIC

1 FRESH JALAPEÑO PEPPER, STEMMED, SEEDED, AND MINCED (OPTIONAL)

½ CUP WATER

1 YELLOW PEPPER, STEMMED, SEEDED, AND CUT INTO SMALL DICE

¼ TEASPOON SALT

1. Wash greens and cut or strip leaves from stalks (see page 199). Discard the stalks. Chop leaves into ½-inch strips. Cut roots and stalks from spinach bunches and wash in several changes of water (see page 223). Chop roughly. Set aside.

2. Using your largest skillet or stockpot, heat oil over medium heat. Add onions and sauté for 10 minutes, until soft and golden. Add garlic and jalapeño and sauté until cooked, 3 to 4 minutes longer.

3. Turn heat to medium high, and stir in mustard greens. Add the water, cover, and cook for 3 to 4 minutes. Stir in spinach and yellow pepper, cover, and cook for 3 to 4 minutes, stirring several times to cook greens evenly.

4. Season with salt and serve hot.

Stir-Fry of Mustard Greens, Kale, and Leeks

A treat for the taste buds with spicy mustard, mild kale, and sweet leeks and carrots.

SERVES 3 TO 4

- 4 CUPS MUSTARD GREENS
- 4 CUPS KALE
- 1 TABLESPOON PEANUT OR CANOLA OIL
- 2 LEEKS, WHITE AND LIGHT GREEN PARTS, WASHED AND THINLY SLICED
- SALT TO TASTE
- 2 LARGE CARROTS, PEELED AND CUT INTO MATCHSTICKS (SEE PAGE 171)

1. Wash the mustard greens and kale and strip or cut leaves from stalks (see pages 199 and 155). Roughly chop the kale and mustard greens into bite-size pieces. Measure 4 cups of each and set aside.

2. Heat a large wok. Add the oil and swirl to coat pan. Add the leeks and stir-fry for 1 to 2 minutes.

3. Add the kale, mustard greens, and a pinch of salt and stir-fry over high heat for 1 to 2 minutes. Add 3 to 4 tablespoons water plus the carrots, then cover and cook for 3 to 4 minutes, or until greens are wilted and tender. Check occasionally, adding more water if necessary to keep the greens from sticking to the wok.

4. Adjust seasonings and serve immediately.

Mustard Greens with Corn, Leeks, and Bacon

What a combo! Great flavor, and a real crowd pleaser.

SERVES 2 TO 3

1 POUND MUSTARD GREENS

2 TO 3 BACON STRIPS

2 TEASPOONS BACON DRIPPINGS

½ CUP THINLY SLICED LEEKS, WHITE AND LIGHT
    GREEN PART ONLY

1 CUP FRESH CORN KERNELS

SALT AND PEPPER TO TASTE

1. Wash the mustard greens and strip or cut leaves from stalks (see page 199). Discard the stalks. Roughly chop the leaves and set them aside.

2. Broil or fry the bacon until cooked. Drain on paper toweling, cool, and crumble. Set aside. Save 2 teaspoons of the fat.

3. Heat a large skillet that has a tight-fitting lid over medium-high heat. Add bacon drippings and swirl to coat pan. Add leeks and cook for 4 minutes, until soft and translucent. Reduce heat if necessary to keep leeks from sticking to the pan.

4. Add corn and cook over medium-high heat to brown slightly, about 2 minutes.

5. Add mustard greens, with the water still clinging to the leaves. Stir to coat with the oil, cover, and cook over medium-high heat for about 6 minutes, stirring occasionally. Add additional water if necessary to prevent sticking.

6. Season to taste with salt and black pepper and serve hot, garnished with the crumbled bacon.

Curried Chick-Peas with Mustard Greens and Sweet Potato

This dish forms a complete meal when served with rice and maybe some Indian-style bread.

SERVES 4

1 POUND MUSTARD GREENS

1 TABLESPOON CANOLA OIL

1½ CUPS CHOPPED ONIONS

1 TABLESPOON MINCED GARLIC

1 TEASPOON FINELY GRATED GINGER

2 TEASPOONS CURRY POWDER

2 CUPS BEAN COOKING WATER

1 CUP DRIED CHICK-PEAS (SOAKED OVERNIGHT), OR 2 ½ CUPS COOKED

1 CUP PEELED AND CUBED SWEET POTATO OR YAM

½ TEASPOON SALT, OR TO TASTE

LEMON WEDGES AND YOGURT (OPTIONAL)

1. Wash the mustard greens and strip or cut leaves from stalks (see page 199). Discard stalks. Shred leaves. You should have 5 to 6 cups.

2. Heat oil in a large soup pan or skillet over medium-high heat. Add onions and cook for about 10 minutes. Reduce heat if necessary to avoid burning.

3. Add garlic and ginger and cook for 30 seconds. Add curry powder and stir to combine well.

4. Add 2 cups bean cooking liquid, cooked chick-peas, sweet potato, and salt. Bring to a boil, reduce heat, cover, and simmer for 10 minutes. Taste and adjust seasonings.

5. Stir in mustard greens and cook until tender, 10 to 15 minutes. Serve hot with lemon wedges and yogurt, if desired.

TO COOK BEANS

Place chick-peas in a sieve or colander and sort through them, discarding any dirt or small stones. Rinse beans well under running water. Transfer beans to a large pot, cover with water, and soak overnight or for at least 4 hours. Discard soaking water. Add a bay leaf and 1 or 2 whole carrots or celery stalks to the beans and cover with water. Bring to a boil, reduce heat, and simmer for 1½ to 2 hours, until done. Add more water if necessary to keep beans covered. Do not add salt until cooking is complete. When beans are done, remove and discard the bay leaf and vegetables. Place a colander over a plastic or glass storage container and place both of these in the sink. Pour the cooked beans into the colander, saving the cooking liquid in the storage container. Prepare the beans in advance of making this or any other recipe requiring beans; beans store well for about 3 days in the refrigerator and longer in the freezer.

Red Lentil Soup with Mustard Greens

The goodness of lentils, vegetables, and greens—all in less than 1 hour.

SERVES 4 TO 6

½ POUND MUSTARD GREENS (2 TO 3 CUPS)

1 TABLESPOON CANOLA OR OLIVE OIL

2 CUPS CHOPPED ONIONS

2 CARROTS, PEELED AND CHOPPED

2 CELERY STALKS, CHOPPED

1 TEASPOON CUMIN SEED

1½ CUPS RINSED RED LENTILS

6 CUPS WATER

½ TEASPOON THYME

½ TEASPOON OREGANO

½ TEASPOON BASIL

1 TEASPOON TURMERIC

1 BAY LEAF

1 TEASPOON SALT, OR TO TASTE

LEMON JUICE OR UMEBOSHI VINEGAR (SEE PAGE 67), TO TASTE

VARIATION

Use chopped spinach or Swiss chard instead of mustard greens. Cook spinach or chard for 4 to 5 minutes.

1. Wash greens and cut or strip leaves from stalks (see page 199). Discard stalks. Coarsely chop the leaves and set them aside.

2. In a heavy-bottomed stockpot, heat oil over medium heat. Add onions and sauté for 10 to 15 minutes, until golden and sweet. Meanwhile, chop carrots and celery.

3. Add cumin to onions and stir for another 1 to 2 minutes until cumin smells fragrant. Add carrots, celery, lentils, water, thyme, oregano, basil, turmeric, and bay leaf and bring to a boil. Turn heat to medium-low and simmer, partially covered, for 25 to 30 minutes, stirring occasionally to prevent sticking.

4. When lentils are creamy looking, add the salt and chopped mustard greens. Simmer, covered, for about 10 minutes, until greens are tender.

5. Adjust seasonings, adding a squeeze of lemon juice or umeboshi vinegar.

RED LENTILS

Red lentils (which are really orange-red in color) are shaped like brown lentils, and are extremely quick cooking. In a soup, they break apart and become creamy in about 30 minutes. You get all the health benefits of the bean without the soaking or long cooking. The one drawback is that the pretty color fades during cooking.

Coconut-Flavored Sweet Potato with Mustard Greens

If your grocery store does not carry coconut milk, or if you can't find coconut milk without preservatives, you can make your own using unsweetened, shredded (dried) coconut. It takes minutes.

Mix 1 cup shredded coconut in a blender with 1 cup boiling water. Blend for 1 minute. Pour into strainer and press to force out liquid. Put pulp back into blender with ½ cup of boiling water. Drain and press again. Discard pulp. Yields 1 cup coconut milk.

Simmering mustard greens in coconut milk takes away their bitter edge. Serve this as a side dish or over white or brown basmati rice.

SERVES 4

2 TEASPOONS CANOLA OIL

1 MEDIUM ONION, CUT IN HALF AND THINLY SLICED

1 TEASPOON MINCED GARLIC

1 TEASPOON BROWN MUSTARD SEEDS

1 ½ CUPS COCONUT MILK

1 TEASPOON GROUND CORIANDER

⅛ TO ¼ TEASPOON CAYENNE

1 CINNAMON STICK, BROKEN IN HALF

3 CUPS PEELED AND CUBED SWEET POTATO

4 TO 5 CUPS MUSTARD GREENS (ABOUT ¾ OF A POUND)

SALT TO TASTE

5 CUPS MUSTARD GREENS

FRESH LEMON OR LIME JUICE TO TASTE

1. Heat oil in saucepan over medium heat. Add onion and sauté for about 5 minutes, until translucent. Add garlic and mustard seeds and sauté for another 2 minutes.

2. Add coconut milk, coriander, cayenne, cinnamon stick, and sweet potato to onion mixture. Cook, covered, over medium heat for about 10 minutes, until sweet potato begins to soften.

3. While the sweet potato is cooking, wash the mustard greens and strip or cut leaves from stalks (see page 199). Discard the stalks. Chop the greens into bite-size pieces.

4. Stir in mustard greens and simmer, covered, over medium-low heat for approximately 15 minutes. The greens should be tender and the sweet potato soft. Adjust salt level; remove cinnamon stick.

5. Just before serving, squeeze in lime juice or serve with lemon or lime wedges.

Mustard Greens with Spicy Hazelnuts

Our friend Anna Giacoma blanches mustard greens before adding a simple but spicy nut topping. Use the full amount of cayenne if you like it hot.

SERVES 2 TO 3

½ CUP HAZELNUTS

1 POUND MUSTARD GREENS

2 TEASPOONS CANOLA OIL

¼ TO ½ TEASPOON CAYENNE

1 TABLESPOON OLIVE OIL

2 TEASPOONS BALSAMIC VINEGAR

¼ TEASPOON SEA SALT

1. Preheat oven to 350°F. Toast the hazelnuts in a baking dish in the oven for 15 minutes, or until golden. Cool slightly and roll in a towel to remove skins. Chop coarsely.

2. While hazelnuts are toasting, prepare the greens. Wash mustard greens and cut or strip leaves from stalks (see page 199). Discard stalks. Coarsely chop the leaves into 2-inch pieces.

3. In a medium skillet, heat canola oil over medium-low heat. Add cayenne and toasted hazelnuts and sauté for about 2 minutes. Place in a bowl and set aside.

4. Bring a medium pot of water to a boil and add the greens and a pinch of salt. Cook for 2 to 3 minutes. Drain well, squeezing out as much moisture as possible.

5. Place greens in a bowl. Season with olive oil, balsamic vinegar, and salt. Top with spicy hazelnuts.

The Science of Cooking Greens

One of the biggest surprises in cooking leafy greens is how lousy they can taste when steamed. Since steaming is a healthy way to cook, and since greens are among the most nutritious vegetables, the two should make a perfect match.

In our tests at home, however, steaming produced greens that were grayer and more bitter than those cooked by other methods. When the more assertive greens such as mustard greens, broccoli rabe, and collards were boiled or blanched, they tasted and looked better. According to Harold McGee, author of *On Food and Cooking* (New York: Macmillan, 1988), leafy greens contain acids that, when heated, come into contact with the plant's chlorophyll and turn it gray. You can dramatize this effect by adding lemon or vinegar (both acids) to a pot of kale or chard—the bright green chlorophyll quickly turns an unappealing army green. When you steam greens, the same thing happens: The acid in the plant itself destroys its own color.

If you cook greens in a large pot of water, however, the acids are diluted and the vegetables stay bright green. It's simple science.

This same principle applies to the bitter compounds found in many greens. Steaming concentrates the bitterness. Cooking in a large pot of water (blanch-ing) diluted the bitterness and mellows the flavor of the greens as they cook. Hence, they will taste better as well as maintain a bright green color.

Before adding broccoli rabe or turnip greens to a pasta or potato dish, Italians will bring a pot of water to a boil, add the greens, and cook off the bitterness. They then drain the vegetable and add it to whatever dish they are preparing. Southerners traditionally boil greens for long periods of time in a large pot of water flavored with a ham bone.

In theory, blanching is a wonderful method when taste and appearance are paramount, but we didn't like the idea of losing nutrients by cooking for a long time in a lot of boiling water. We also didn't like waiting 15 to 20 minutes for a large pot of water come to a to boil.

We wanted to find another way to cook greens to preserve as many nutrients as possible while using enough water to leach out some of the acids and bitter compounds for great taste.

The answer was to boil or "shallow-blanch" the greens in a minimum amount of water. For best results, use approximately 2 cups of water for a bunch of greens, up to 1 pound. Bring the water to a boil, add the chopped greens, and cook in the boiling water until the green is tender. This takes from 3 to 10 minutes, depending on the type of green. A large skillet with a tight-fitting lid works best. This allows the greens to be spread out as much as possible for quicker cooking a large stockpot will also work. Cooking greens "fast and furiously" like this preserves nutrients, color, and taste.

It's best to bring the water to a boil first, before adding the greens. Boiling water helps neutralize enzymes in the vegetable that will destroy additional pigments and vitamins. These enzymes are active at low temperatures between 120°F and 160°F, but destroyed by boiling, according to McGee.

We use water to precook the more assertively flavored greens such as kale, collards, broccoli rabe, and turnip and mustard greens. (Milder greens such as spinach, chard, and beet greens can be cooked in water, but because they are mild to begin with and cook so quickly, steaming or wilting them in a skillet usually works fine.) You can vary the amount of water depending on the assertiveness of the green you are cooking and the end result you seek. The more water used, the more diluted the flavor of the green. If the broccoli rabe remains too bitter for your particular taste using only 2 cups of water, try using 1 or 2 quarts, as some cooks suggest. Don't forget to drink whatever cooking water remains (unless you're using quarts of water). This "pot likker" is a tasty broth that captures any minerals or vitamins lost in the cooking.

Does this mean you can't steam greens, blanch them in a large pot of water, or wilt them in a skillet? Of course not. We use this technique as a guideline because this is how we think greens taste best. By describing the technique and science behind it, you have the knowledge and the option to cook the greens to suit your own taste.

Parsley

BECAUSE OF ITS WIDESPREAD AVAILABILITY AND COMMON supporting role, parsley is not often praised for its many contributions to the food world. But it should be. As one of the world's most widely used herbs, parsley really is indispensable. What other green herb offers such a bright and fresh flavor but is easygoing enough to blend into hundreds of dishes?

There are about thirty-seven varieties of parsley. But we usually find two kinds in the supermarket: broad, flat-leaf parsley, and curly leaf parsley. There isn't an enormous difference between the two, but most cooks have a preference for one or the other. The flat-leaf variety, also referred to as Italian parsley, seems to be the preferred type. It has a slightly fuller, deep green flavor, which makes it excellent for seasoning and cooking. Flat-leaf parsley is also the choice for drying in bunches for year-round use.

The delicate, sweet taste of curly parsley makes it a good choice for fresh use in salads or as a flavor accent to pasta, vegetables, eggs, and potatoes.

SHOPPING TIPS

Buy the crispest, freshest-looking bunch available. There should be no yellowed or limp leaves.

STORAGE

To store parsley, wash well and dry. Store in a plastic bag, along with one or two paper towels to absorb any excess water, in the crisper section of the refrigerator. It will keep for about a week.

PREPARATION

Take special care to wash parsley. It can be very sandy. Fill a bowl with cold water, add the parsley, and swish it around vigorously. Lift parsley from the water into a colander. Repeat procedure at least one more time, until there is no sand or grit in the washing bowl when you remove the parsley. We like to remove parsley stems at this stage, while it is soaking in water.

Before chopping, dry parsley thoroughly in a salad spinner or on a towel. Wet leaves will cling to the knife and clump together. Use an 8- or 10-inch chef's knife to chop. Hold the point of the knife down and rock the blade up and down until the parsley is very fine.

We also find it convenient to chop a bunch of parsley in a food processor if the blades are sharp. Wash and dry thoroughly before adding to the processor.

The Best Pesto

Including parsley in your pesto helps preserve the green color. It also provides a depth of flavor that is hard to resist. You be the judge on how much oil to use in this recipe. Even though it is much less than in many other recipes, ⅓ to ½ cup of olive oil does pack a wallop of fat. But oh so delicious! A little pesto goes a long way.

MAKES 1 CUP

3 GARLIC CLOVES, PEELED

3 CUPS FRESH BASIL LEAVES, PACKED IN CUP

¾ TO 1 CUP FRESH PARSLEY LEAVES, PACKED IN CUP

¼ CUP PINE NUTS

⅓ TO ½ CUP EXTRA VIRGIN OLIVE OIL

⅓ CUP FRESHLY GRATED PARMESAN OR PECORINO
ROMANO CHEESE

SEA SALT AND FRESHLY GROUND BLACK PEPPER TO TASTE

1. Place peeled garlic in the workbowl of a food processor fitted with a metal blade. Process to chop. Add the basil and parsley leaves and process to chop.

2. While the motor is running, add the nuts and olive oil, starting with the lesser amount of oil. Add the cheese and process again. If the pesto seems too dry, add the rest of the olive oil.

3. Season to taste with salt and black pepper and serve on freshly cooked pasta, as a topping for baked fish, or in soup.

VARIATION

You can omit the cheese if you like. In that case, try adding a teaspoon or two of light miso along with the pine nuts and olive oil.

Ana Sortun's Parsleyed Olive Oil

This simple and delicious preparation from Chef Ana Sortun can be made in advance and used to drizzle over grilled fish or chicken or to use as a dip for crusty bread. The vitamin C will help keep the green color brighter longer. Use a blender to give a tighter purée— a food processor won't work.

BEST NEW CHEF

A Seattle native, Ana Sortun studied at La Varenne in Paris before moving to the Boston area and making a name for herself and the restaurants where she worked as head chef: 8 Holycoke in Cambridge and Aigo Bistro in Concord. Named Best New Chef in 1993 by Boston Magazine, she is now at Casablanca in Cambridge, Massachusetts.

MAKES 3 ½ CUPS

1 BUNCH FLAT-LEAF PARSLEY

3 CUPS EXTRA VIRGIN OLIVE OIL

SALT AND PEPPER TO TASTE

1 TABLET VITAMIN C, CRUSHED

1. Pick leaves off of parsley and save stems for soup or broth. Wash well and dry in a salad spinner.

2. Using a blender, purée parsley with oil, salt, pepper, and vitamin C. Turn on high speed and blend for 3 to 5 minutes, until parsley is completely liquefied and there are no "flecks." Check for seasoning and store in the refrigerator.

Green Goddess Dressing

Try this dressing over a salad or use it as a topping for baked fish.

MAKES 1 CUP

¾ CUP ORGANIC, LOW-FAT SOUR CREAM

½ CUP MINCED PARSLEY

2 TABLESPOONS EXTRA VIRGIN OLIVE OIL

2 TABLESPOONS FRESHLY SQUEEZED LEMON JUICE

2 TABLESPOONS FRESH DILL

1 TEASPOON MAPLE SYRUP OR SWEETENER

2 TABLESPOONS MINCED SCALLION,
   WHITE AND GREEN PARTS

¼ TEASPOON SALT

FRESHLY GROUND PEPPER TO TASTE

Combine all ingredients in a blender. Blend for 1 to 2 minutes.
Taste and adjust seasonings. Keep refrigerated until ready to use.

Poached Salmon Salad
with Gremolata

*Gremolata, a mixture of lemon, garlic, and parsley, makes a
refreshing addition to this salmon salad.*

SERVES 2 TO 3

1 CELERY STALK, SLICED

½ SMALL ONION, SLICED

1 CARROT, SLICED

½ CUP WATER, WINE, OR FISH STOCK

1 BAY LEAF

1 POUND FRESH SALMON FILLET, CUT FROM
MIDSECTION OF FISH

½ POUND GREEN BEANS, CUT INTO DIAGONAL
PIECES ½ INCH LONG

¼ MEDIUM RED ONION, SLICED INTO THIN CRESCENTS

6 OIL-PACKED SUN-DRIED TOMATOES, DRAINED AND CUT
INTO ¼-INCH STRIPS

GREMOLATA:
1 GARLIC CLOVE, MINCED

4 TABLESPOONS MINCED FRESH PARSLEY

GRATED RIND OF 1 ORGANIC LEMON

DRESSING:
2 TABLESPOONS EXTRA VIRGIN OLIVE OIL

3 TABLESPOONS FRESH LEMON JUICE

1 TEASPOON BALSAMIC VINEGAR

1 TEASPOON MAPLE SYRUP

PINCH OF SEA SALT

1. Place celery, onion, carrot, water, and bay leaf on bottom of a
saucepan just large enough to hold salmon. Bring liquid to a boil,
reduce heat, and lay salmon on top of vegetables, skin side down.
Poach, covered, for 5 to 8 minutes. Test with fork and knife by

cutting into flesh; it should flake easily, but not seem dry in the center. Let cool. Remove skin and cut fish into 1-inch chunks. Set aside.

2. Blanch cut green beans for 3 to 5 minutes in boiling water. They should be bright green and crisp-tender. Plunge into cold water to stop cooking. Drain.

3. Place sliced red onion, sun-dried tomatoes, and drained green beans in a large mixing bowl. Add cooled salmon pieces.

4. To make gremolata, combine garlic, parsley, and lemon rind. Chop together to help flavors mingle. Set aside.

5. To make dressing, whisk together olive oil, lemon juice, vinegar, and maple syrup in small bowl. Pour over vegetables and salmon and toss very gently with your hands. Arrange on an attractive plate and sprinkle gremolata over all. Serve immediately.

Pesto Pasta with Chicken and Sun-Dried Tomatoes

We like to marinate the chicken before cooking to give it a lemony rich flavor. But if you want to make it quick, just skip the marinating and go right to the cooking.

SERVES 4 TO 6

2 WHOLE BONELESS, SKINLESS CHICKEN BREASTS

PESTO (SEE RECIPE ON PAGE 213)

½ CUP SUN-DRIED TOMATOES

SALT AND BLACK PEPPER TO TASTE

1 POUND PASTA, SPIRALS OR PENNE

MARINADE:

JUICE OF 3 LEMONS

1 CUP WHITE WINE

1 TABLESPOON MINCED SHALLOTS

1 TEASPOON MINCED GARLIC

PINCH OF SALT

1. Combine marinade ingredients in a medium-size bowl. Cut chicken into strips, ½ inch wide and 1 to 2 inches long. Add chicken to bowl, and marinate for 2 hours at room temperature or for up to 8 hours refrigerated, covered.

2. Make the pesto. Boil water for pasta.

3. Place sun-dried tomatoes in a small bowl and cover with boiling water for 15 to 20 minutes, until softened. Drain water and cut tomatoes into strips.

4. Drain marinade from chicken. Heat a large, heavy skillet over high heat. Coat with a little olive oil and sauté chicken until brown on both sides and just turning from pink to white. Season with salt and pepper to taste. If you have a stovetop grill, grill the chicken.

5. Cook pasta according to package directions. Drain. Toss pasta with enough pesto to coat. Mix in chicken and sun-dried tomatoes and serve hot.

Spinach

SPINACH NEEDS LITTLE INTRODUCTION OR SALES PITCH. It is one of the most versatile and mild-tasting greens, which accounts for its popularity. It was being grown in America by the early 1800s, brought over from Europe.

There are two types commonly found in markets: the flat or smooth-leaved spinach and the savoy variety, with curly, crinkled leaves. Each has its own fans. The flat-leaf variety grows quickly and is easier to clean. It is bred for its smooth and delicate flavor and is sometimes preferred for fresh salads. Those who choose curly say it has more substance and works better in cooked dishes. New varieties, with slightly crinkled green leaves, combine the qualities of smooth and savoy. New Zealand "spinach" is a member of a different botanical family but good in salads.

The basic (easiest) preparation of spinach it to sauté it in a covered skillet with just the water from washing clinging to its leaves. It wilts and cooks in 2 to 4 minutes. We like spinach Italian-style with olive oil and garlic (sometimes with raisins and pine nuts too). Our favorite discovery was spinach cooked with sliced fennel and a squirt of fresh lemon juice. You can also use spinach to stuff chicken or fish, or you can make spinach pesto for use on pasta or fish. Add spinach to soups and grains for color, taste, and nutrition.

Spinach is high in vitamins A, C, and E, the antioxidant vitamins shown to reduce the risk of cancer. It also makes the top-10 list of fruits and vegetables with the highest sources of carotenoids, a large family of nutrients (that includes beta-carotene) being studied for preventing disease. Spinach also fulfills the daily requirement for folacin, and contains more iron than most greens. It also contains more oxalic acid than other greens, which, when released in cooking, binds with calcium and iron and makes it hard to assimilate these minerals in the body. Eating spinach with foods such as cheese, eggs, sunflower seeds (sources with fat) may counteract or act as a deterrent to oxalic acid present. Still, for the best sources of calcium and iron, include kale, turnip greens, and watercress in your diet.

SHOPPING TIPS

Pick bunches with crisp, vibrant, undamaged leaves. Loose spinach is usually fresher than packaged and easier to examine for quality. Pick spinach with thinner rather than thicker stems for younger plants.

STORAGE

Store fresh spinach by wrapping it in a paper towel or cloth to absorb moisture, then place it in a clear plastic bag in the refrigerator. It will keep for 3 or 4 days, depending on its condition when purchased.

PREPARATION

If you haven't already discovered, spinach is often very sandy. To wash, trim off the roots and the stems if they are thick and tough. Fill a big stainless steel bowl with cold water, add spinach and swish around, letting sand settle to the bottom. Place spinach in a colander while you change the water. Wash spinach in several changes of water until there is no sand left. If using for cooking, there is no need to dry the spinach. For a salad, dry leaves in a salad spinner for crispness.

Spinach Pesto

The addition of spinach and parsley plus a touch of lemon adds an exciting twist to traditional pesto. Delicious over pasta, and great as a topping for baked fish.

MAKES 1 1/2 CUPS

2 GARLIC CLOVES, PEELED

2 CUPS FRESH SPINACH LEAVES THAT HAVE BEEN WASHED AND DRIED (SEE PAGE 223) AND PACKED IN CUP

½ CUP FRESH BASIL LEAVES, PACKED IN CUP

½ CUP FRESH PARSLEY LEAVES, PACKED IN CUP

⅓ TO ½ CUP EXTRA VIRGIN OLIVE OIL

¼ CUP PINE NUTS

3 TABLESPOONS FRESHLY SQUEEZED LEMON JUICE

SEA SALT AND FRESHLY GROUND BLACK PEPPER TO TASTE

VARIATIONS

❖ *Add 2 tablespoons grated Parmesan cheese along with the pine nuts and olive oil.*

❖ *You can add a teaspoon or two of light miso for a different taste. Miso, a paste made from fermented soybeans, is a good alternative to cheese.*

1. Place peeled garlic in the workbowl of a food processor fitted with a metal blade. Process to chop. Add the spinach, basil, and parsley leaves and process to chop.

2. While the motor is running, add the olive oil and nuts, starting with the lesser amount of olive oil. Add the lemon juice and process again. If the pesto seems too dry, add the rest of the olive oil or additional lemon juice.

3. Season to taste with salt and black pepper and serve on freshly cooked pasta, as a topping for baked fish, or in soup.

Sautéed Spinach with Fennel and Onions

In this quick and easy side dish, spinach is highlighted by the licorice flavor of the fennel and sweet onions. Try it!

SERVES 4

2 TEASPOONS EXTRA VIRGIN OLIVE OIL

1 MEDIUM ONION, SLICED INTO THIN CRESCENTS

1 MEDIUM-SIZE FENNEL BULB

2 TO 4 TABLESPOONS WATER

2 POUNDS FRESH SPINACH (ABOUT 8 CUPS, CHOPPED)

SALT TO TASTE

FRESHLY GROUND BLACK PEPPER TO TASTE

LEMON WEDGES

1. In a large skillet with a lid, heat 1 teaspoon of the olive oil over medium heat. Swirl to coat pan. Add sliced onions and sauté for 10 minutes, until softened and very lightly caramelized.

2. While onions are cooking, prepare fennel. Cut off top stalks and discard (or save for vegetable stock). Slice bulb in half vertically and cut each half into ¼-inch-wide strips. Cut strips in half crosswise, so that they are 1½ to 2 inches long. Add to onions and stir to combine. Add 2 tablespoons water and cook, covered, over medium heat for about 5 minutes, stirring occasionally. Fennel should be tender.

3. Meanwhile, wash spinach well and drain it in a colander (see page 223). Discard thick stems and coarsely chop the leaves. Add spinach to fennel and onion mixture. Cover and cook for 3 to 5 minutes, until spinach is wilted. If mixture seems dry, add 2 more tablespoons water.

4. Season with salt and pepper and drizzle with remaining teaspoon olive oil. Squeeze a bit of lemon juice on top for added zip.

Uncle Eddie's Spiral Meatloaf with Mixed Greens

Uncle Eddie, a chef in the army, was Johnna's uncle. He was very creative and served this attractive meatloaf to family and friends. The beautiful spiral of greens makes a nice presentation. You can serve this on a roasted red pepper or tomato coulis.

SERVES 4

1 CUP WATER

2 CUPS KALE LEAVES THAT HAVE BEEN WASHED, STEMMED (SEE PAGE 155), AND CHOPPED

2 CUPS SPINACH LEAVES THAT HAVE BEEN WASHED (SEE PAGE 223), DRAINED, AND CHOPPED

1¼ POUNDS LEAN GROUND BEEF

½ CUP FINELY MINCED ONION

1 LARGE GARLIC CLOVE, PEELED AND MINCED

½ TEASPOON SEA SALT

20 GRINDS OF BLACK PEPPER

1 TEASPOON MINCED FRESH ROSEMARY

½ CUP CRUMBLED FRESH BREAD

1 TABLESPOON DIJON MUSTARD

½ TEASPOON MAPLE SYRUP OR HONEY

1. Preheat oven to 375°F.

2. In a medium-size skillet with a lid, bring the water to a boil. Add the chopped kale and cook for 3 minutes. Add the chopped spinach and continue to cook until greens have wilted, about 2 minutes. Remove greens with a slotted spoon to a colander to drain and cool slightly. Drink any remaining cooking liquid; it's full of vitamins and minerals. When the greens have cooled enough to handle, squeeze out any excess moisture. Set aside.

3. Place the ground beef, onion, garlic, salt, pepper, rosemary, and crumbled bread in a medium-sized bowl. Mix well with your

hands. Press mixture into a flattened 12 x 10-inch rectangle, about ½ inch thick, on a cookie sheet or clean counter top.

4. Distribute the cooked greens evenly over the meat rectangle. Roll up, starting with the 10-inch side, into a jelly roll shape. Place in a shallow baking dish.

5. In a small bowl, combine mustard and sweetener. Spread this mixture on top of the meatloaf. Place in the oven and bake for about 45 minutes, or until cooked through. Let cool for 5 minutes before slicing into ¾-inch-thick pieces.

Yellow Split Pea Soup with Spinach and Sweet Potatoes

Spinach is just the right touch for this hearty soup. Perfect for a fall or winter evening meal.

SERVES 6 TO 8

1 TABLESPOON OIL

1 LARGE ONION , CHOPPED

1 LEEK, WASHED AND SLICED

½ TEASPOON GROUND CUMIN

2 CUPS CHOPPED CARROTS

1 CUP CHOPPED CELERY

1½ CUPS YELLOW SPLIT PEAS, RINSED WELL

8 CUPS WATER

2 BAY LEAVES

½ TEASPOON DRIED THYME

½ TEASPOON BASIL

½ TEASPOON CELERY SEED

1½ CUPS PEELED AND DICED SWEET POTATO

4 CUPS SPINACH LEAVES THAT HAVE BEEN WASHED (SEE PAGE 223), DRAINED, AND CHOPPED (ABOUT 12 OUNCES)

SALT TO TASTE

UMEBOSHI VINEGAR (SEE PAGE 67) OR RED WINE TO TASTE (OPTIONAL)

1. Heat oil in a heavy-bottomed soup pot. Add onion and leek and sauté for about 10 minutes. Add cumin and cook for 1 minute longer.

2. Add carrots, celery, split peas, water, bay leaves, and herbs. Bring to a boil, lower heat to medium low, and simmer, partially covered, for about 50 minutes, stirring occasionally to prevent sticking.

3. Add the sweet potato and cook for another 20 minutes, until sweet potato can be pierced with a fork. Add chopped spinach and cook for 5 minutes. Season to taste with salt and umeboshi vinegar or wine.

Orzo with Spinach, Feta, and Olives

This salad is tasty and really hits the spot. Orzo is a melon-seed-shaped pasta that is popular in Greece.

SERVES 4 TO 6

12 OUNCES WHOLE WHEAT OR REGULAR ORZO

1 POUND SPINACH LEAVES THAT HAVE BEEN TRIMMED, WASHED, AND DRAINED (SEE PAGE 223), AND COARSELY CHOPPED

½ CUP CHOPPED RED ONION

½ CUP CRUMBLED FETA CHEESE

10 KALAMATA OLIVES, PITTED AND CHOPPED

⅓ CUP TOASTED PINE NUTS

¼ CUP EXTRA VIRGIN OLIVE OIL

3 TABLESPOONS BALSAMIC VINEGAR

½ TEASPOON SALT, OR TO TASTE

FRESHLY GROUND BLACK PEPPER TO TASTE

PINCH OF CAYENNE (OPTIONAL)

VARIATION

❖ *Add 1 diced garden-ripe tomato.*

❖ *Substitute cooked rice for orzo.*

1. Cook orzo according to package directions. Add spinach for the last minute of cooking. Drain and rinse with cold water to stop cooking.

2. Place red onion, feta, olives, and toasted pine nuts in a mixing bowl. Add orzo and spinach.

3. In a small bowl, whisk together the olive oil, vinegar, salt, pepper, and cayenne, if using. Pour over orzo mixture and toss to combine. Taste and adjust seasoning. Serve at room temperature.

Quinoa with Chick-Peas and Spinach

Quinoa (pronounced keen-wa*) has become our whole grain of choice because it tastes delicious, cooks in 15 minutes, and is more nutritious than brown rice. Paired with spinach, chick-peas, and spices, it makes a great luncheon salad or dinner accompaniment.*

SERVES 4

1 CUP QUINOA

1 CUP WATER

¾ CUP FRESHLY SQUEEZED ORANGE JUICE (ABOUT 2 ORANGES)

½ TEASPOON SEA SALT OR HERBAMARE VEGETABLE SEASONING SALT (SEE PAGE 29)

ZEST FROM 2 ORGANIC ORANGES

1 TABLESPOON EXTRA VIRGIN OLIVE OIL

2 MEDIUM ONIONS, CHOPPED

3 GARLIC CLOVES, MINCED

½ CUP ORGANIC RAISINS

1 CUP COOKED CHICK-PEAS

1½ POUNDS SPINACH LEAVES THAT HAVE BEEN TRIMMED, WASHED, DRAINED, AND DRIED (SEE PAGE 223) AND CHOPPED (ABOUT 6 CUPS)

SALT TO TASTE

½ TEASPOON CINNAMON

¼ CUP TOASTED PINE NUTS

1 ORANGE, CUT INTO WEDGES

1. Rinse the quinoa well and drain in a fine-mesh sieve. Combine water and orange juice (to equal 1¾ cups) and bring to a boil in a 1½- or 2-quart saucepan. Add the salt, orange zest, and the rinsed quinoa. Return to the boil, reduce heat, cover, and simmer for 15 minutes, or until all the liquid has been absorbed. Remove from heat and let sit, covered, for 10 minutes to fluff up.

2. While the quinoa is cooking, heat the oil in a large skillet that has a tight-fitting lid. Add the onions and sauté over medium-high heat for 10 minutes, until they have softened and started to brown a bit. Add garlic and sauté until golden.

3. Add raisins, chick-peas, and chopped spinach. Cover and cook over medium heat for 5 minutes, or just until the spinach has wilted. Adjust heat if necessary. Drain any excess water after cooking the spinach. Season to taste with salt.

4. To serve, fold the vegetables into the hot, cooked quinoa. Stir in cinnamon. Garnish with the toasted pine nuts and orange wedges for a final squeeze of orange juice.

Chicken Breasts Stuffed with Spinach and Wild Mushrooms

Slicing these spinach-stuffed chicken breasts makes an attractive presentation. Wild mushrooms and pecans add a complex flavor that is appealing to adults and children alike. Regular commercial mushrooms can be used if wild mushrooms are unavailable.

SERVES 2 TO 4

1 POUND SPINACH

1 TABLESPOON EXTRA VIRGIN OLIVE OIL

1 LEEK, WHITE PART ONLY, WASH AND FINELY SLICED

1 GARLIC CLOVE, FINELY MINCED

1 CUP FRESH OYSTER, CHANTERELLE, OR SHIITAKE MUSHROOMS, SLICED

2 TABLESPOONS WHITE WINE OR CHICKEN STOCK

GRATINGS OF FRESH NUTMEG

SALT OR HERBAL SALT SEASONING TO TASTE

FRESHLY GROUND BLACK PEPPER TO TASTE

½ CUP WHOLE MILK OR PART-SKIM RICOTTA

¼ CUP CHOPPED, TOASTED PECANS

2 WHOLE CHICKEN BREASTS, SKINNED AND BONED

FRESH LEMON JUICE

EXTRA VIRGIN OLIVE OIL

PAPRIKA

1. Preheat oven to 375°F. Oil a cookie sheet and set aside.

2. Trim spinach leaves and wash well (see page 223), drain them in a colander and chop into bite-size pieces. Heat a large skillet or stockpot over medium heat. Add chopped spinach with just the water clinging to the leaves, cover, and cook until wilted, about 5 minutes. Lift cover to stir occasionally. Remove spinach from pan, drain, and set aside.

3. Wipe out pan and heat the olive oil over medium heat. Add the leek and garlic and cook for 5 to 7 minutes, until softened.

4. Add the chopped mushrooms and sauté over medium-high heat for another 5 minutes, or until fragrant. Add the white wine and allow to almost evaporate. Remove pan from heat.

5. Stir in cooked spinach and season to taste with nutmeg, salt, and black pepper. Let cool to room temperature and stir in ricotta and chopped pecans.

6. Open chicken breasts into one piece, and cut out extra tenderloin piece. Flatten to an even thickness with a meat mallet or the bottom of a heavy skillet. Spread one half of the stuffing mixture onto the fillet side of one breast and roll up. Repeat with the remaining breast and stuffing.

7. Place stuffed breasts seam side down on the prepared cookie sheet. Drizzle with lemon juice, brush with olive oil, and sprinkle on a bit of paprika for color.

8. Bake for 25 to 35 minutes, or until chicken is cooked and filling is heated. Do not overcook. Let rest for 5 minutes before cutting.

9. To serve, cut diagonally into ½-inch slices and place attractively on a serving platter or on individual plates.

Spinach Salad with
Asian Pears

Soft leaves of raw spinach teamed with crisp, clean-tasting Asian pears make a delightful salad, especially when topped with sautéed raisins and cashews.

SERVES 4

1 BUNCH FRESH SPINACH (ABOUT ¾ POUND)

1 ASIAN PEAR, CORED AND THINLY SLICED VERTICALLY INTO WEDGES

1 TEASPOON CANOLA OIL OR GHEE (SEE PAGE 88)

3 TABLESPOONS RAW CASHEW PIECES

3 TABLESPOONS RAISINS

DRESSING:

2 TABLESPOONS RASPBERRY VINEGAR

1 TABLESPOON FRESHLY SQUEEZED LEMON JUICE

⅓ CUP EXTRA VIRGIN OLIVE OIL

SALT TO TASTE

1. Trim the stems from the spinach, wash well in several changes of cold water, drain and dry in a salad spinner or pat dry with a kitchen towel (see page 223). You should have 4 to 5 cups fresh leaves. Gently tear large leaves into 2 to 3 pieces and leave small leaves whole. Arrange the leaves on a large platter.

2. Arrange pear slices attractively around the edge of the platter on top of the spinach. Set aside.

3. Heat a small skillet over medium heat. Add the oil or ghee and the cashew pieces. Toast nuts, stirring frequently. When nuts have begun to brown, add raisins. Cook a bit longer, allowing the raisins to caramelize and brown slightly and puff up. Take care to avoid burning. Drain on a paper towel and set aside to cool.

4. In a small bowl, combine raspberry vinegar and lemon juice. Slowly whisk in olive oil. Season to taste with salt. Drizzle the dressing over the spinach and pears, sprinkle on the cashews and raisins, and serve immediately.

Note: Substitute Bosc or Anjou pears
if Asian pears are unavailable.

ASIAN PEARS

Asian pears—golden, brown-speckled, apple-shaped pears—appear in produce sections in late summer through early winter. They originated in China and are now grown in California. Although expensive, they are worth every penny. Crisp, sweet, and refreshingly juicy, they should be eaten when hard. Avoid pears that have begun to soften because they will be overripe and sickly sweet.

Winter White Bean Salad with Greens

This makes a nice luncheon salad.

SERVES 4 TO 6

1½ CUPS DRIED NAVY, OR GREAT NORTHERN BEANS

1 BAY LEAF

SALT TO TASTE

1 CUP DICED FENNEL

½ CUP MINCED RED ONION

2 TABLESPOONS MINCED FENNEL LEAVES

¼ CUP MINCED FRESH PARSLEY

2 FRESH SAGE LEAVES, MINCED (IF AVAILABLE)

¼ CUP PLUS 1 TABLESPOON EXTRA VIRGIN OLIVE OIL

3 GARLIC CLOVES, MINCED

1 SMALL BUNCH SPINACH OR CHARD (ABOUT ½ POUND), TRIMMED AND WASHED (SEE PAGE 223)

2 TABLESPOONS WHITE WINE VINEGAR

1 TABLESPOON BALSAMIC VINEGAR

1 TEASPOON DIJON MUSTARD

FRESHLY GROUND BLACK PEPPER

1. Soak beans overnight in 5 cups water. Drain and cover with fresh water. Bring to a boil, skim off foam, add 1 bay leaf, reduce heat, and cook, partially covered, over medium-low heat until beans are tender but not mushy, 30 to 40 minutes. When beans are perfectly cooked, add ½ teaspoon salt and cook for another 5 minutes. Drain, saving cooking water for another use, and rinse beans. Set aside to cool to room temperature. You should have 3 to 4 cups.

2. Place cooled beans, fennel, red onion, fennel leaves, parsley, and sage in a medium-size bowl. Set aside.

3. Heat the 1 tablespoon olive oil in a large skillet over medium heat. Add the garlic and sauté for 1 minute. Add spinach with water still clinging to leaves and stir to distribute oil and garlic. Cover and steam for 1 minute to wilt leaves. They should be just cooked but still bright green. Remove from heat.

4. Whisk together the ¼ cup olive oil, white vinegar, balsamic vinegar, and mustard. Pour over beans and vegetables. Toss gently to combine. Serve at room temperature with lots of black pepper.

Turnip Greens

To cook turnip greens, you first have to find them. They are not the most popular green, especially in the Northeast, where we live, and not all stores carry them. We found them in certain urban markets in ethnic neighborhoods

Turnip greens can be confused with mustard greens, which are in the same mustard family. Both are light green with curled edges, delicate looking with a light green stem. The taste is also similar, an assertive mustard flavor with a peppery kick. Turnip greens can be used in recipes that call for mustard greens and can also be mixed with other milder greens.

Both turnip and mustard greens are considered the most bitter of the dark leafy greens and therefore respond better to certain cooking techniques. Steaming turnip greens is not the best cooking method and should be avoided unless you want to suffer while you eat. Wilting the greens in a skillet with only the water clinging to the washed leaves produces the same unappetizing result. Cooking or blanching first with a couple cups of water or broth works best to rid the green of some of its bitterness. For a good example, try the Turnip Tops–Potato Sauté recipe (see page 241)—the greens are absolutely delicious.

Slivered turnip greens make a flavorful addition to all kinds of soups. To mellow the strong flavor of turnip greens, you can mix them with other milder greens in a side dish. Adding turnip greens to dishes adds not only bite but also vitamins and minerals. Turnip greens are one of the best sources of calcium among dark, leafy greens. Other key nutrients include fiber, vitamin A, vitamin E, iron, and potassium.

Unless you find a bunch of baby turnips, you will generally not find turnip greens with the roots attached. Some varieties are grown just for the tops. When purchasing, avoid bunches that have wilted or yellowed leaves.

STORAGE

Try to buy just before using; turnip leaves tend to turn yellow quickly. Store refrigerated in a plastic bag for no more than 2 days.

PREPARATION

Remove the stem from the turnip greens by one of two methods. For the hand-stripping method, use one hand to hold the stalk of an individual leaf, rib side up. Use the other hand to strip the leaf off the stalk. If the particular bunch you purchase has leaves that are reluctant to be separated from the stalk, lay the entire leaf with stalk on a cutting board and use a chef's knife to cut the rib away from the leafy part.

We find it is easier to cut the leaves before washing, rather than cutting a bunch of dripping greens. To cut, pile several leaves on top of one another, roll slightly, and slice with a chef's knife.

Turnip greens tend to hold dirt and sand, and need a thorough washing. Fill a large bowl with cool water, plunge in the greens to rinse, lift greens out of water to a colander, and check bottom of bowl. If there is any sand or dirt, discard the water and repeat the process.

Turnip Tops—Potato Sauté

This simple recipe is an Italian staple called frit gris *in Piedmont. Our friend Anna Giacoma, an Italian native and cook from the Piedmont region, says this is one of the ways her mother prepared turnip tops, as well as broccoli rabe. In Italy, it is served with polenta and/or sausages.*

SERVES 4

1 POUND TURNIP GREENS, STEMMED AND WASHED (SEE PAGE 240)

2 STEAMED OR BAKED POTATOES (ANY KIND EXCEPT RUSSET)

2 TABLESPOONS OLIVE OIL

4 GARLIC CLOVES, MINCED

SALT TO TASTE

VARIATIONS

❖ *Substitute broccoli rabe for turnip greens. Cut off 1 inch from bottom of head, wash well, drain (see page 43), and follow same instructions as for turnip tops.*

❖ *Include baby turnips if they are attached to turnip greens. Blanch turnips with the greens. Chop into small cubes.*

1. In a large stockpot or saucepan, bring 2 to 3 quarts of water to a boil. Add turnip tops to slightly salted water and blanch for 2 to 3 minutes. Drain and, when cool enough, coarsely chop them on a cutting board. Set aside.

2. Peel and cut the potatoes into small cubes. (They are better if they are left over from the day before.)

3. In a large skillet, heat the 2 tablespoons olive oil over medium-low heat. Add garlic, blanched greens, and diced potatoes. Stir gently for a couple of minutes, then cover and cook on a medium-low flame, for 20 to 30 minutes, stirring occasionally.

4. Stir in salt to taste and cook for 5 more minutes.

Smoked Turnip Greens

Turnip greens taste delicious simmered in a broth flavored with a smoked turkey bone. We like to use smoked turkey bone because it is less fatty than the ham hock or salt pork used traditionally to cook Southern-style greens.

QUICK SMOKED-TURKEY STOCK

Make ahead, then use during the week to cook turnip greens, collards, or kale. Or freeze leftover broth.

4 QUARTS WATER

2 TO 3 PIECES SMOKED TURKEY BONE

SALT TO TASTE

In a large soup pot, bring water and turkey bones to a boil. Simmer, partially covered, for 1 to 2 hours. Strain through a colander; discard turkey bone.

SERVES 3 TO 4

1 TABLESPOON OIL

2 ONIONS, THINLY SLICED

4 CUPS SMOKED TURKEY BROTH

1 TO 2 POUNDS TURNIP GREENS, STEMMED AND WASHED (SEE PAGE 240)

1 TEASPOON SALT, OR TO TASTE

1. In a large skillet with a lid, heat oil over medium heat. Add onions and sauté for 5 to 10 minutes, until golden and tender.

2. Add turkey broth and bring to a boil. Add greens and salt and simmer over medium-high heat for 7 to 8 minutes.

3. Remove onions and greens with a slotted spoon. (Discard broth.) Season with salt to taste.

Fall Root Soup with Turnip and Beet Greens

We like this soup because it combines the root vegetables with the leafy tops of the beets and turnips. Although the soup takes on the magenta beet color, each root vegetable retains its individual character. What a powerhouse of good nutrition and taste!

SERVES 6 TO 8

1 TABLESPOON EXTRA VIRGIN OLIVE OIL

2 MEDIUM ONIONS, THINLY SLICED INTO HALF-MOONS

1 LEEK, WHITE AND LIGHT GREEN PART, WASHED AND THINLY SLICED

1 TEASPOON MINCED GARLIC

1 SMALL BUNCH BEETS (ABOUT 1½ CUPS WHEN PEELED AND CUT INTO ¾-INCH DICE)

2 CUPS RUTABAGA, PEELED AND CUT INTO ¾-INCH DICE

1 CUP TURNIPS, PEELED AND CUT INTO ¾ INCH DICE

1 CUP CARROTS, PEELED AND CHOPPED INTO ¾ INCH PIECES

8 CUPS WATER

1½ TEASPOONS SALT, OR TO TASTE

2 CUPS BEET GREENS THAT HAVE BEEN WASHED, SLICED INTO ½-INCH RIBBONS, AND ROUGHLY CHOPPED (SEE PAGE 20)

2 CUPS TURNIP TOPS THAT HAVE BEEN WASHED, SLICED INTO ½-INCH RIBBONS, AND ROUGHLY CHOPPED (SEE PAGE 240)

YOGURT OR LOW-FAT SOUR CREAM (OPTIONAL)

1. In a heavy-bottomed soup pot, heat oil over medium heat. Add onions and sauté for 10 minutes. Add leeks and garlic and sauté for another 5 minutes, stirring often.

2. Add beetroots, rutabaga, turnips, carrots, water, and salt and bring to a boil. Cover and simmer over medium-low heat for about 20 minutes, until vegetables are tender but not mushy. Add the greens and cook for another 10 minutes, until tender.

3. Season with salt and serve hot. You can top with a dollop of yogurt or low-fat sour cream, if desired.

Shrimp and Greens Gumbo

We haven't come across many "green" gumbos, but this recipe has a mess o' greens and all the other components to make a filling and delicious gumbo. You can substitute chicken, sausage, or any seafood for the shrimp. Or make with vegetable stock and beans for a vegetarian gumbo.

SERVES 8 TO 10

10 CUPS MIXED, CHOPPED, RAW GREENS (INCLUDE AT LEAST 2 OF THE FOLLOWING: KALE, COLLARDS, MUSTARD GREENS, CABBAGE, OR TURNIP GREENS)

½ CUP FLOUR

⅓ CUP CANOLA OIL

2 CUPS CHOPPED ONIONS

1 TABLESPOON MINCED FRESH GARLIC

1 CUP DICED CELERY

2 RED PEPPERS, SEEDED AND DICED

9 CUPS HOT CHICKEN OR VEGETABLE STOCK

1 TEASPOON DRIED THYME

1 TEASPOON PAPRIKA

⅛ TO ¼ TEASPOON CAYENNE

2 DRIED WHOLE CHIPOTLE PEPPERS (DRIED, SMOKED JALAPEÑOS)

2 BAY LEAVES

1 28-OUNCE CAN CRUSHED TOMATOES WITH JUICE

2 CUPS FRESH CORN KERNELS

1 TABLESPOON GUMBO FILÉ (IF AVAILABLE)

1 POUND PEELED AND DEVEINED SHRIMP

SALT TO TASTE

HOT SAUCE TO TASTE

2 TO 3 CUPS COOKED RICE (BASMATI TASTES GREAT)

1. Wash greens thoroughly. Remove stems and midribs. Chop into bite-size pieces, no larger than a soup spoon. Set aside.

2. Make the roux. In a heavy 10-inch skillet or dutch oven, combine flour and oil and stir to make a paste. Place over medium-high heat and stir constantly until the roux is a dark rich brown (the color of a copper penny), 10 to 15 minutes. You must stir constantly or the flour mixture will burn.

3. Add the onions, garlic, celery, and peppers to the roux and sauté until the onions are transparent. Once you add the vegetables the roux stops cooking, but continue to stir occasionally because the mixture will be rather thick. (No need to add water.)

4. Transfer mixture to a stockpot. Gradually add the hot stock, stirring with a whisk until smooth. Add the thyme, paprika, cayenne, and whole chipotle peppers and bring to a boil. Reduce heat and simmer, covered, for 10 minutes.

5. Add the greens and bay leaves and simmer, covered, for 30 minutes. Stir occasionally to cook greens evenly. Skim off any oil that rises to the surface while cooking.

6. Add the crushed tomatoes, corn, and filé and simmer for 5 minutes.

7. Add shrimp and simmer until shrimp turns pink, about 5 minutes. (Do not boil or shrimp will toughen.)

8. Taste and adjust the seasonings. Remove and discard the chipotle pepper and bay leaves. Add the cooked rice and serve hot.

MAKING ROUX

A roux is a mixture of flour and fat cooked until it is browned. The browning of the flour gives it a nutty, roasted flavor that thickens and enriches gumbo. "No self-respecting Cajun would dream of making gumbo without a roux," says Gwen McKee, author of The Little Gumbo Book *(Brandon, Mississippi: Quail Ridge Press, 1986).*

Making a roux is not difficult. Typical proportions are equal amounts of flour to oil (butter, vegetable oil, or bacon drippings). The idea is to cook the roux to a dark, rich brown color without burning it. This can take 10 to 15 minutes of constant stirring, which is the secret: standing and stirring the entire time the roux is cooking.

Watercress

A MEMBER OF THE CRUCIFEROUS FAMILY OF VEGETABLES, watercress is incredibly nutritious. It is high in vitamins C, B_1, and B_2, has almost three times the calcium of spinach, and is comparable to the carrot as a source for vitamin A. It is also a source of copper, iron, and magnesium. Whew! Let's eat some right now!

Watercress, with its pungent flavor and beautiful dark green color, is a welcome addition to many recipes. Green salads perk up with a few sprigs of watercress, soups shine when watercress is stirred in at the last minute to offer a more subtle taste, and your taste buds sing when watercress is nibbled out of hand as you gather it wild from a clean, cold stream .

Watercress is a perennial aquatic plant with irregularly shaped, dark green leaves and hollow stems. It roots easily given the right conditions—lots of cool, flowing water, moist soil, and dappled sunlight. It is mildest in early spring and blossoms in June. At this time it becomes more pungent in flavor, and that characteristic continues through July. In August, older plants die back only to reveal new growth. It is often available just for the picking before the first frost comes.

We've harvested wild watercress from flowing streams on Martha's Vineyard, off Massachusetts, and icy streams in Colorado's high mountains. It grows wild in all fifty states. Wherever you get it, even the supermarket, it's wonderful!

Watercress's peppery and spicy leaves boost the flavor and appearance of salads with milder greens like endive, butter lettuces, or loose-leaf varieties. It goes well with citrus, nuts, and tomatoes. You can use it like parsley or arugula and mix it in with your favorite cold pasta or vegetable salads as a colorful herb.

SHOPPING TIPS

Choose bunches of watercress that are completely green with absolutely no yellowing of the leaves. It should look very fresh and perky as it is extremely perishable. If the bunches displayed are wilted, ask the produce manager to get you a fresh bunch. If you are lucky enough to pick your own watercress, pick the top four inches of the plants.

STORAGE

Watercress keeps best in a glass of water in the refrigerator, with the top covered loosely with a plastic bag. Supermarket watercress is more perishable than fresh-harvested, but is tasty nonetheless. Use in 1 or 2 days for best results.

PREPARATION

For salads, we prefer using just the watercress leaves and very thin stems. It may take a few minutes to strip the leaves from the tough bottom stems, but it's worth the effort. Strip leaves delicately by hand. Just hold the stem in one hand and gently strip the leaves away from the stem with the thumb, index, and third fingers of the other hand.

Wash leaves in a bowl filled with cool water. Swish around to dislodge any dirt or sand. Lift out and dry in a salad spinner. If you have picked off most leaves and only a few thin stems remain, just make a few random slices through the bunch before you add it to a salad. Since watercress is delicate, it's best washed and cut just before using.

Sweet Carrot and Watercress Salad with Orange-Mustard Dressing

Bright orange carrots and dark green watercress leaves make for a festive salad. Add a delicious, reduced-fat dressing made with freshly squeezed orange juice and you have a satisfying and cooling salad full of vitamins, crunch, and sweetness. Perfect for potlucks or as a substitute for coleslaw.

SERVES 6 TO 8

2 BUNCHES WATERCRESS (2 TO 3 CUPS)

6 CUPS PEELED AND SHREDDED CARROTS

3 CELERY STALKS, CUT IN HALF LENGTHWISE AND THINLY CUT ON A DIAGONAL

½ CUP FINELY CHOPPED RED OR VIDALIA ONION

1 CUP CURRANTS, OR ½ CUP RAISINS

DRESSING:

½ CUP FRESHLY SQUEEZED ORANGE JUICE

1 TABLESPOON DIJON OR WHOLE-GRAIN MUSTARD

1 TABLESPOON FRESH LEMON JUICE

1 TEASPOON MAPLE SYRUP

1 TABLESPOON CANOLA OIL

1 TABLESPOON OLIVE OIL

¼ TEASPOON SALT, OR TO TASTE

½ CUP SLICED ALMONDS

1. Strip the watercress leaves from large stems. Wash leaves in a bowl of cool water, lift out to drain, and spin dry. Chop delicately by making a few random slices through the bunch.

2. In a medium-size bowl, combine carrots, celery, onion, watercress, and raisins or currants. Mix gently.

3. Combine all the ingredients for the dressing in a jar and shake until mixed. Pour over salad. Adjust salt to taste.

4. Toast sliced almonds in a 350°F oven for 5 to 7 minutes. Use as a garnish.

MAKING CROUTONS

Croutons are as good as the bread they are made from, so try these with a favorite loaf.

1 MEDIUM-SIZE LOAF LIGHT-WHEAT, SOUR-DOUGH, OR FRENCH BREAD (ENOUGH TO MAKE 3 CUPS CROU-TONS)

1 TO 2 TABLE-SPOONS EXTRA VIRGIN OLIVE OIL

1/8 TEASPOON PAPRIKA

COUPLE PINCHES OF SALT

FRESHLY GROUND BLACK PEPPER

Cut bread into 1/2- or 3/4-inch cubes. Drizzle on olive oil and toss with paprika, salt, and pepper. Place on a baking tray and toast in a preheated 350°F oven for 10 minutes, or until bread is lightly crisped.

This light, refreshing salad is perfect for summer grilling and guests.

SERVES 4

1 LARGE OR 2 SMALL CUCUMBERS (ABOUT 3 CUPS CUBED)

2 CUPS WATERCRESS LEAVES (ABOUT 1 BUNCH)

1 CUP SLICED RADICCHIO LEAVES

DRESSING:

2 TEASPOONS FRESHLY SQUEEZED LEMON JUICE

2 TEASPOONS RED WINE VINEGAR

1/8 TEASPOON DRIED OREGANO, OR 1/2 TEASPOON FRESH

1/8 TEASPOON DRIED BASIL, OR 1/2 TEASPOON FRESH

1/4 TEASPOON SALT

3 TABLESPOONS EXTRA VIRGIN OLIVE OIL OR CANOLA OIL

FRESHLY GROUND BLACK PEPPER, TO TASTE

3 CUPS HOMEMADE CROUTONS

1. Peel cucumbers, slice in half lengthwise, and scoop out the seeds with a spoon. Cut each half into strips 1/2-inch wide, and then cut strips crosswise into 1/2-inch squares.

2. Strip the watercress leaves from large stems. Wash leaves in a bowl of cool water, lift out to drain, and spin dry. Chop slightly, so leaves are separated from other leaves but still whole. Slice radicchio into thin strips.

3. To make dressing, mix lemon juice, vinegar, oregano, basil, and salt in a medium bowl. Whisk in oil. Season to taste.

4. Just before serving, dress salad and toss with croutons.

Lemony Watercress Pasta Salad

This is one of our favorite springtime or summer pasta recipes—so fresh tasting with the lemon and Greek fare of feta cheese and olives. Arugula can be used in place of watercress.

SERVES 4 TO 6 AS A SIDE DISH

1 BUNCH WATERCRESS (ABOUT 2 CUPS)

8 TO 12 OUNCES PASTA

4 TABLESPOONS EXTRA VIRGIN OLIVE OIL

1 CUP FINELY CHOPPED ITALIAN PARSLEY

½ CUP THINLY SLICED RED ONION

20 TO 25 PITTED KALAMATA OR OIL-CURED OLIVES, CHOPPED

1 CUP SHEEP'S-MILK FETA CHEESE, CUT INTO SMALL CUBES

JUICE OF 1 LEMON

GRATED RIND OF 2 ORGANIC LEMONS

SALT AND FRESHLY GROUND BLACK PEPPER TO TASTE

1. Strip the watercress leaves from large stems. Wash leaves in a bowl of cool water, lift out to drain, and spin dry. Chop slightly, so leaves are separated from other leaves, but still whole.

2. Cook pasta until *al dente*. Drain and toss with 2 tablespoons of the oil. Let cool for 5 minutes.

3. Toss with remaining ingredients. Serve warm or at room temperature, garnished with lemon slices.

Note: If you serve this pasta salad the next day, perk it up with a sprinkling of extra lemon juice.

KING LOUIS IX AND WATERCRESS

Watercress has been awarded a spot on the coat of arms of the city of Vernon, France, along with the fleur-de-lis, the royal symbol. It is said that Louis IX of France, while hunting one hot summer's day, was overcome by thirst. Because no water was at hand, he was presented with a bunch of water-cress to chew. Refreshed, the king decided on the spot to honor the plant and the place it grew.

WHICH PASTA?

A tube-shaped, ridged pasta such as penne or ziti or rotelle will best distribute the chopped parsley and watercress in this Greek salad.

Kristen's Wilted Watercress Salad With Shiitake Mushrooms

Kristen Kinser, former owner of The Pig Bakery on Martha's Vineyard, brought us to a wild watercress patch on the Vineyard where we collected shopping bags full to test many of our watercress recipes. She also gave us this recipe for an Oriental-flavored, wilted watercress salad.

SERVES 4

4 CUPS WATERCRESS (ABOUT 2 BUNCHES)

1 CARROT

1 TABLESPOON CANOLA OIL

2 TEASPOONS FRESHLY GRATED GINGER

2 TO 3 CUPS THINLY SLICED FRESH SHIITAKE MUSHROOMS
(ABOUT ½ POUND), STEMS DISCARDED OR RESERVED
FOR STOCK

1/4 CUP THINLY SLICED SCALLIONS

1 TABLESPOON TOASTED DARK SESAME OIL

1 TEASPOON TAMARI (NATURALLY BREWED SOY SAUCE)

3 TABLESPOONS WATER

1 TABLESPOON MAPLE SYRUP

1 TABLESPOON PLUS 2 TEASPOONS BROWN RICE VINEGAR

TOASTED SESAME SEEDS TO GARNISH

1. Strip the watercress leaves from large stems. Wash leaves in a bowl of cool water, lift out to drain, and spin dry. Chop slightly, so leaves are separated from other leaves but still mostly whole. Peel carrot and slice on a sharp diagonal into ⅛-inch-thick ovals. Slice ovals into tiny matchsticks. Place the chopped watercress leaves and carrots in a large salad bowl or serving dish.

2. Heat canola oil in a large skillet over high heat. Sauté ginger and mushrooms for 4 to 5 minutes. Some bits will stick to the pan. Stir in scallions and cook for 30 seconds. Remove from pan and set aside.

3. To deglaze the pan, add the sesame oil, tamari, water, maple syrup, and brown rice vinegar. Cook together for 1 minute over low heat.

4. Pour hot dressing over watercress and carrot mixture. Toss gently and serve immediately, garnished with toasted sesame seeds.

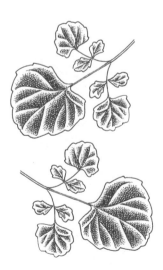

Watercress Corn Chowder

In this recipe, sweet fresh corn is combined with peppery green watercress to make a colorful summer vegetable soup. Instead of heavy cream or milk, the recipe calls for puréeing the potatoes and corn to create a creamy consistency.

SERVES 6 TO 8

1 TABLESPOON EXTRA VIRGIN OLIVE OIL

1 TABLESPOON BUTTER

2 CUPS DICED ONIONS

2 LEEKS, WHITE PART ONLY, WASHED WELL AND THINLY SLICED

7 CUPS WATER

4 MEDIUM POTATOES, PEELED AND CUT INTO ½-INCH DICE (ABOUT 4 CUPS)

3 CUPS FRESH CORN KERNELS (4 TO 5 EARS)

2 TABLESPOONS FINELY CHOPPED FRESH PARSLEY

2 BAY LEAVES

½ TEASPOON THYME

1½ TEASPOONS SALT

¼ TEASPOON FRESHLY GROUND WHITE OR BLACK PEPPER

"GUERRILLA" STOCK

2 CARROTS, PEELED

2 CELERY STALKS

4 CORNCOBS

2 CUPS COARSELY CHOPPED WATERCRESS

1. Heat the olive oil and butter in a heavy-bottomed 7-quart soup pot. Sauté onions and leeks for about 10 minutes, until soft and sweet, stirring to prevent burning.

2. Add water, potatoes, 1 cup of the corn kernels, parsley, bay leaves, thyme, salt, pepper, carrots, celery, and corn cobs. Bring to a boil, reduce heat, and simmer, covered, for 40 minutes.

3. Remove carrots, celery, and corncobs and discard. Purée the soup in batches in a blender until creamy. Return to soup pot.

4. Add remaining corn, bring to a boil, and simmer for an additional 5 minutes. Turn off heat; taste and adjust seasonings. Stir in watercress and serve hot.

"GUERRILLA" STOCK

Our "guerrilla" stock is a quick way to add flavor to your soups without making stock in a separate pot. Just add cleaned, whole vegetables: carrots, celery, corncobs (if corn is used), celery root, parsnip, etc. When the soup is finished, you can discard the whole pieces. Voilà! More flavor, less work. Keep the vegetables whole, or cut in half to make them easier to retrieve.

Watercress Tabouli

A member of the nasturtium family, watercress thrives in clean, cool water. If you are lucky and know some watercress aficionados, you might find out where to pick wild watercress as we did on Martha's Vineyard. We came prepared, plastic grocery bags in hand, to harvest an abundant amount to enjoy for several days. Supermarket watercress is very perishable, so be sure to use it in one or two days. In this recipe the pungent flavor of watercress is mellowed by an assortment of fresh vegetables. Roasted red pepper adds a deliciously interesting dimension, and quinoa is used instead of the traditional bulgur. It is light and refreshing.

SERVES 6 TO 8

1 CUP QUINOA, RINSED WELL AND DRAINED IN A
   FINE-MESH SIEVE

1¾ CUPS WATER

½ TEASPOON SALT

1 BUNCH WATERCRESS (ABOUT 2 CUPS CHOPPED)

1½ CUPS CHOPPED KIRBY CUCUMBERS

6 MEDIUM RADISHES, HALVED AND SLICED

1 CUP CHOPPED VIDALIA, WALLA WALLA, OR RED ONION

¾ CUP DICED OR COARSELY GRATED CARROTS

1 RED PEPPER, ROASTED, PEELED, AND DICED (SEE PAGE 46)

DRESSING:

¼ CUP FRESH LEMON JUICE

¼ CUP EXTRA VIRGIN OLIVE OIL

1 TEASPOON FINELY MINCED GARLIC

½ TEASPOON SALT, OR TO TASTE

1. Place the quinoa, water, and ½ teaspoon salt in a 3-quart pot. Bring to a boil, reduce heat, cover, and simmer for 15 minutes. Turn off heat and let stand for 10 minutes. Fluff with a fork and cool to room temperature. To speed cooling, spread quinoa on a large platter while you prepare the vegetables for the salad.

2. Strip the watercress leaves from large stems. Wash leaves in a bowl of cool water, lift out to drain, and spin dry. Chop slightly, so leaves are separated from other leaves but still whole.

3. In a large mixing bowl, combine the cucumbers, radishes, onion, watercress, carrots, and roasted red pepper. Stir in cooled quinoa.

4. In a small bowl, whisk together the dressing ingredients. Pour over quinoa and vegetables and toss gently to combine all ingredients. Serve at room temperature or chilled.

QUINOA: STILL A SUPERGRAIN

Quinoa, pronounced keen-wa, is a nearly perfect health food. We use this tiny South American grain more than rice in cooking. Deliciously nutty and ready in only 15 minutes, quinoa is also more nutritious than brown rice. The only grain that is a complete protein by itself, quinoa is also a great source for B vitamins, vitamin E, calcium, and iron.

Scrambled Eggs and Watercress

Simple, quick, and delicious, these scrambled eggs hit the spot any time of the day. For dinner, serve with crusty whole grain bread and sliced tomatoes.

SERVES 2

4 EGGS

SALT AND FRESHLY GROUND PEPPER TO TASTE

1 TABLESPOON CANOLA OIL

2 SMALL LEEKS, WHITE PART ONLY, WASHED WELL AND VERY THINLY SLICED

4 SMALL CARROTS, PEELED AND COARSELY GRATED

½ CUP COARSELY CHOPPED WATERCRESS

HOT SAUCE (OPTIONAL)

1. Break the eggs into a small bowl, beat lightly, and season with salt and pepper. Set aside.

2. Heat an 8- or 9-inch cast-iron skillet over medium heat. Add the canola oil and swirl to coat pan. Add the leeks and sauté for about 5 minutes. Take care to avoid burning. Add carrots, cover, and cook until softened, about 5 minutes. Remove vegetables to a plate.

3. In the same skillet, scramble the eggs over medium heat, until just cooked. Stir in leeks, carrots, and watercress and serve immediately, accompanied by hot sauce if desired.

Tomato and Watercress Salad with Creamy Watercress Dressing

Red and green. Tomatoes and watercress. Simple yet bold flavors combine in this salad topped with a soft, green-goddess-style dressing to make a dramatic presentation and taste sensation. Use the dressing within two days for best flavor; the watercress gets bitter quickly.

SERVES 4

1 BUNCH WATERCRESS (ABOUT 2 CUPS, CHOPPED)

3 RIPE GARDEN TOMATOES

DRESSING:

½ CUP WATERCRESS LEAVES, PACKED IN CUP

1/4 CUP PLAIN YOGURT

2 TABLESPOONS CHOPPED PARSLEY

1 SMALL GARLIC CLOVE

1 TABLESPOON RASPBERRY VINEGAR

¼ CUP EXTRA VIRGIN OLIVE OIL

1 TEASPOON HONEY OR MAPLE SYRUP

SALT AND PEPPER TO TASTE

1. Strip the watercress leaves from large stems. Wash leaves in a bowl of cool water, lift out to drain, and spin dry. Remove the leaves from the larger stems of watercress and break the topmost pieces into bite-size morsels. Arrange on a large platter in a layer that covers the platter completely.

2. Slice the tomatoes into ⅓-inch-thick slices. Cut slices in half and arrange attractively on top of the watercress. Set platter aside.

3. To make the dressing, place the watercress, yogurt, parsley, garlic, raspberry vinegar, olive oil, maple syrup, salt, and pepper in the jar of a blender. Blend until puréed.

4. To serve the salad, drizzle some of the watercress dressing over the tomatoes to make an attractive presentation. Serve the remaining dressing in a pitcher on the side.

Wild Greens

THERE IS A LOT TO BE SAID FOR PICKING AND EATING WILD greens, though it is not for everyone.

"Most people are trapped in a fast-paced lifestyle, so the idea of slowing down and taking time to gather their own food is just weird," says Russell Cohen, a Cambridge, Massachusetts, naturalist who has been leading edible wild plant walks for more than two decades.

But if you enjoy the outdoors and are interested in supplementing your diet with some new and delicious varieties of greens, then you may want to investigate this food source. "This is an opportunity to get exotic flavors you can't find in the supermarket," says Cohen. "Some of these plants have flavors where there are no cultivated counterparts."

Collecting wild greens can be quicker than going to the supermarket since a number can be found right in your backyard. Peter Gail, author of *The Dandelion Celebration*, (Cleveland, OH: Goosefoot Press, 1994) says his next book will profile twenty-six wild plants than can be found in yards and gardens across America. "These plants are not only tasty and nutritious, but they are in your backyard and *free*," he says.

Many of these backyard "weeds" are delicious leafy greens such as chickweed, lamb's quarters, amaranth, and curled dock. You can begin to identify these wild plants by taking a local class or nature walk, or by referring to one of the many books devoted to the subject.

Once you've learned to identify the various wild greens, cooking them is easier than you may think. According to Rosemary Gladstar, a well-known herbalist and teacher in Vermont, there are basically two kinds of wild foods cooking: survival cooking and gourmet wild foods cooking. "Survival cooking is what one does when one chooses or is forced to live off the land," Gladstar says. "The other type of wild food cooking involves combining wild plants with cultivated foods and adapting them to familiar recipes for family meals."

A basic knowledge of cooking conventional greens can help you in substituting and cooking greens you pick yourself. A wild green like lamb's quarters, for example, tastes as mild and delicious as spinach and can be used in any recipe that calls for spinach. Amaranth, another wild plant with edible leaves, is actually a wild beet plant whose tops can be cooked similarly to beet greens. Wild chicory and wild mustard greens can be treated as you would mustard greens bought in the supermarket.

"It's not some kind of arcane, complicated subject that needs to be intimidating," says Cohen. "You can substitute wild greens for conventional greens in almost any recipe. Usually, the result is that you will have a much more interesting flavor."

In addition to great flavor, wild greens often surpass their cultivated cousins in vitamins and minerals. "They've done all kinds of nutritional analysis and found the wild versions of almost any conventional counterpart have more vitamins," explains Cohen. Lamb's quarters, a wild spinach, outranks spinach in almost every category, including protein, fiber, calcium, and vitamins A and C. Amaranth has more calcium than collards, turnip greens, or kale. Dandelion and lamb's quarters top broccoli, spinach, and collards as a source for vitamin A. Aside from common nutrients, wild plants are commonly used medicinally to treat skin disorders, dispel toxins, regenerate the liver and kidneys, and treat other medical troubles.

We've listed some of the more commonly found wild greens along with their culinary uses. For additional reading, check out Lee Allen Peterson's *A Field Guide to Eastern Edible Wild Plants* (Boston: Houghton Mifflin Co., 1978); Roger Philip's *Wild Food: A Unique Photographic Guide to Finding, Cooking and Eating Wild Plants, Mushrooms and Seaweed* (Eureka, California: Mad River Press, 1986); and one of the most well-known books on the subject, *Stalking the Wild Asparagus*, by Euell Gibbons (Brattleboro, Vermont: A.C. Hood & Co., 1988).

Amaranth

A common summer "weed," amaranth can be found growing near or in gardens or along roadsides. It is a wild beet (but without a bulbous root) and its leaves can be cooked and eaten like beet greens or spinach. Steam or sauté amaranth for a few minutes and use in place of spinach or beet greens.

Chickweed

Chickweed is a common garden weed, a hardy specimen available almost year-round except in very cold weather. It has a rather sweet, mild taste. Try chickweed stems and leaves raw in salads, ground in a pesto, or steamed. Naturalist Russell Cohen enjoys the succulent raw stems, which he says taste like raw corn, as a sprout substitute in sandwiches and salads.

Chicory

Close in appearance to dandelion, chicory is a wild variety of cultivated chicory. It tastes mild in early spring and fall, but grows bitter in warmer weather. Mild chicory can by used raw in salads; blanch the more assertive leaves.

Curled Dock

Another common plant found in the spring and fall, curled dock has a pleasingly sour flavor and can be used as a substitute for sorrel. Try it in a soup or simply sautéed in a skillet. "Sorrel is so expensive in the store, and curled dock is essentially the same thing or even superior," says Russell Cohen.

Dandelion

Easily the most recognizable of all wild plants, dandelion greens taste best picked in early spring before the flowers blossom, or in the fall from new shoots after the plant has been cut back. Eat young raw greens in mixed salads or blanch to use in pasta dishes, soups, or side dishes. Eating dandelion greens is a springtime ritual in many cultures. In traditional use, the dandelion's bitter greens have been used to cleanse the liver and kidneys. (See additional information in chapter on dandelion greens, page 129)

Lamb's Quarters

Lamb's quarters is another backyard weed, often found growing in or near gardens. Also called wild spinach, lamb's quarters has small, delicate leaves, and when cooked has a deliciously mild, soft taste. It is the mildest tasting of the wild greens, but one that is packed with nutrition. It surpasses spinach as a source of protein, iron, vitamin C, and vitamin A and contains more calcium than most commercial dark, leafy greens, including kale and collards. It can be steamed or sautéed and used in any recipe that calls for spinach.

Mustard Greens

There is a large family of wild mustard greens, but all are edible and recognized by the clusters of yellow flowers with 4 petals arranged in the shape of a cross (hence their botanical latin name: *Cruciferae*. Taste varies among the different types of wild mustard greens but is usually spicy and hot—like that of their cultivated cousin. The greens will be their mildest in early spring before hot weather arrives. Use in place of commercial mustard greens or mixed with other milder greens in sautés, stir-fry, or soups. The young leaves can also be added to a mixed green salad. Add the delicious wild mustard flowers, too!

Nettles

Nettles, or stinging nettles, is a common wild weed that must be harvested with gloves because of stinging hairs on the stalk and leaf undersides. You will be rewarded with a rich green taste, almost as mild as that of lamb's quarters, and great nutrition. "It's a super food," says Cambridge, Massachusetts, herbalist Ruth Dreier. "It's like blue-green algae, a complete food with vitamins, natural oils, and minerals." It is generally steamed or briefly blanched.

Pokeweed

Pokeweed, native to the United States, is probably best known in the South, where it is even sold in supermarkets. The only edible parts of the plant are the young shoots less than one foot high, which should be blanched in boiling water for 3 to 5 minutes, not eaten raw. The roots, mature stems, and berries of the plant are toxic.

Purslane

Purslane has thick, rounded leaves that resemble the leaves of a jade plant. Both leaves and stems can be eaten raw in salads—they offer a mild, but slightly tangy, juicy addition. It is not a pronounced flavor, which makes it good mixed with spicier salad greens. Purslane contains high amounts of vitamins C and A and iron.

Violet Leaves

Violet greens are easiest to recognize when the violets are in bloom. This is when they have the mildest flavor as well. The leaves can be served raw or cooked. The edible flowers make a stunning contribution to any salad.

Wild Tim's Soup

Cathy and her roommate, Tim, picked curled dock, a leafy green similar in taste to sorrel, along a bike path just 10 minutes from their Cambridge, Massachusetts, apartment. Once home, they cooked it up. Dock can turn a dark green color, so after puréeing the soup, snipped chives and purplish-blue edible wildflowers were added for garnish. It was gorgeous as well as delicious.

SERVES 4

2 TABLESPOONS BUTTER

2 MEDIUM ONIONS, CHOPPED

2½ CUPS CURLED DOCK, WASHED, WITH CENTER RIB REMOVED

4 SMALL POTATOES, PEELED AND SLICED ¼ INCH THICK

5 CUPS WATER OR STOCK

1 BAY LEAF

1 TEASPOON SALT

¼ TEASPOON FRESHLY GROUND BLACK PEPPER

¼ CUP LIGHT CREAM (OPTIONAL)

VIOLETS OR DAME'S ROCKET FLOWERS TO GARNISH

CHIVES TO GARNISH

1. In a heavy-bottomed soup pot, heat butter over medium heat. Add onions and sauté until soft, 5 to 10 minutes. Add dock and cook until wilted, about 5 minutes.

2. Add potatoes, water, bay leaf, salt, and pepper and bring to a boil. Reduce heat, cover, and simmer for approximately 30 minutes.

3. Discard bay leaf and purée soup in batches in a blender. Return to pot. Add light cream, if desired, and taste for seasonings.

4. Garnish each bowl with edible flowers and snipped chives.

Note: If you make the stock with water, the light cream will add richness and flavor. If you make it with stock, you can add the cream, if desired, or skip it altogether for a lower-fat version.

Ruthie's Wild Green Pesto

"For a mild, wonderful pesto, use any of the following wild greens: lamb's quarters, violet greens, or chickweed," says Ruth Dreier, a Cambridge, Massachusetts, herbalist. Use as a topping for hot or cold pasta.

MAKES ABOUT 1 1/3 CUPS

2 TO 3 CUPS WILD GREENS

3 GARLIC CLOVES

½ CUP PINE NUTS OR WALNUTS

¾ CUP GRATED PARMESAN CHEESE

¼ TEASPOON SALT

⅓ TO ½ CUP EXTRA VIRGIN OLIVE OIL

1. Remove leaves of the wild greens from stalks. Wash well in a bowl of cold water, letting any sand or dirt settle to the bottom. Lift greens out of water into a colander. Pat dry with a towel or dry in a salad spinner.

2. Place peeled garlic in the workbowl of a food processor. Process to chop. Add the wild greens and process to chop.

3. Add the nuts, grated cheese, salt, and ⅓ cup of olive oil. Process until ground into a fairly smooth paste. If the mixture seems too dry, add the rest of the olive oil.

Wild Greens Spanikopita

Russ Cohen has been leading edible wild plant walks and courses in the Boston area for more than twenty years. Each fall he hosts a harvest party with more than thirty dishes made from wild foods, including his popular spanikopita.

SERVES 6 TO 8

2 TABLESPOONS OLIVE OIL

1 CUP CHOPPED WILD ONION (IF UNAVAILABLE, SUBSTIUTE CULTIVATED)

3 CUPS WILD GREENS, WASHED WELL (LAMB'S QUARTERS, GALINSOGA, CHICKWEED, OR OTHER MILD GREEN; STRONGER GREENS SUCH AS FIELD MUSTARD CAN BE ADDED OR SUBSTITUTED FOR A STRONGER BITE, BUT YOU MAY WANT TO PARBOIL THEM FOR A FEW MINUTES FIRST)

1 CUP FETA CHEESE

2 EGGS, SLIGHTLY BEATEN

2 TABLESPOONS CHOPPED PARSLEY

2 TABLESPOONS CHOPPED WILD CHIVES (OR SUBSTITUTE CULTIVATED)

SALT AND PEPPER TO TASTE

12 PHYLLO (FILO) PASTRY LEAVES

4 TABLESPOONS BUTTER, MELTED

1. In a heavy-bottomed soup pot, heat olive oil over medium heat. Add onions and sauté until soft, 5 to 10 minutes. Add the greens. Cover and cook for 5 minutes, or until the greens are wilted and tender. Remove from heat.

2. Add cheese, eggs, parsley, wild chives, salt, and pepper. Mix in well, then cool slightly.

3. Cut phyllo leaves to make 24 sheets. Layer the first 12 sheets in a well-greased oblong baking dish (6 by 10-inch or equivalent), brushing each layer with the melted butter (a pastry brush is useful here).

4. Spoon the cooked greens/cheese mixture into the baking dish and spread evenly over the phyllo.

5. Cover with the remaining 12 sheets of phyllo, brushing each layer with butter as before.

6. Bake at 350°F for 1 hour, or until golden.

Index